TOUCH, PAUSE, ENGAGE!

*This book is dedicated
to the memory of my father,
Robin, a life-long lover of rugby.*

'Mr Ref',
lets have fun
to-gether!
R.W.C. 2015.

TOUCH,
PAUSE,
ENGAGE!

**EXPLORING THE HEART OF
SOUTH AFRICAN RUGBY**

Liz McGregor

Jonathan Ball Publishers

JOHANNESBURG & CAPE TOWN

© Liz McGregor, 2011
Published in trade paperback in 2011 by
JONATHAN BALL PUBLISHERS (PTY) LTD
PO Box 33977
Jeppestown
2043

ISBN 978-1-86842-309-5

Edited by Jan Schaafsma
Front cover photograph: Peter van As
Cover design by Marius Roux
Text design and typesetting by Triple M Design
Set in 10.75/15pt ITC Sabon Serif Std
Printed and bound by CTP Book Printers, Cape

CONTENTS

TOUCH

ONE

Driving up to Riebeek Kasteel, the trendy little olives-and-wine town in the Swartland, about an hour north of Cape Town by road, I pick up two hitchhikers: a bent, toothless woman who looks about seventy, but says she is the mother of the child with her, who is ten. He too is undersized and vacant-looking. Both have clearly been damaged by the fruit of the vine. The woman talks non-stop, but I can't understand a word because of her thick burr or 'bry'. As we approach the village, there is a signpost to Allesverloren. All is lost. I hope this is not a sign of things to come.

I drop mom and son off at Riebeek Kasteel and carry on through the next little village, Riebeek West, to the Alan Zondagh Rugby Performance Centre where the University of Cape Town (UCT) team has been training for the past week. When I arrive, they are gathered in the team room, taking turns to present their research on the various teams they will be taking on in the Varsity Cup, which kicks off in a few weeks. Genteel Bishops accents mingle with harsher Cape Flats vowels. It's my first dip into what will become a very familiar setting, and what strikes me first and most strongly is the extreme physicality of it. It's very, very hot – more than 30 degrees – and the smell is of sweat and testosterone, gamey but not unpleasant. There is an abundance of prime youthful flesh on show. The 40-odd boys are dressed minimally, in shorts and sleeveless 'wife-beater' vests, bare feet up on tables and spare chairs. Muscles bulge from exposed calves and arms. They are, I suppose, lounging, although that doesn't capture their arrested alertness, which is more like big cats biding their time under a shaded tree, anticipating their next kill.

The following morning sees their first big match of 2010,

a warm-up against a Stormers side, who have driven up from Cape Town. In the UCT team room, the boys are gathered. There is no lounging of any kind now. Adrenaline gives an edgy tang to yesterday's eau de testosterone. Murray Mexted, the driving force in many great All Blacks teams of the eighties, is handing out the jerseys. In his late fifties, he is tall, tanned and rangy. Well-exercised biceps emerge from a sleeveless vest. His grey hair is thick and well cut. There are copper bangles on his arms: surfer meets rugger bugger.

He has a practical message for the boys: 'Know yourself. If a player plays very well one week and badly the next, it is because he doesn't understand himself. There are two types in this room.' He picks up a marker pen and writes them down on the whiteboard:

LOW AROUSAL: quiet, calm, laid-back, low confidence.
HIGH AROUSAL: nervy, excitable, amped, angry.

'Usually the spread is around 50:50. The high-arousal guy is more likely to try to punch some guy. A fly half might drop the ball or throw a bad pass.

'So you have to understand your type and then know how to bring yourself down or ratchet yourself up. Once you know how to do that, rugby – and life – will be much easier.'

He does a kind of haka to show how you might hype yourself up. 'If you need to bring yourself down, sit quietly by yourself, try to focus on the key aspects of the game.'

Then it is time to hand over the jerseys. John Dobson, the UCT head coach, more commonly known as Dobbo, calls out the name of each cap, and the boys echo him with the corresponding nickname, clapping and cheering, so excited.

After all the jerseys have been handed over, Tim Noakes

solemnly says to them: 'We are on the verge of the greatest year the Ikey Tigers have ever had.'

Dobbo says: 'We love toppling giants. We are going out to compete!'

Privately, he says he hopes for four tries to one in favour of the Stormers: after all, the boys are playing a professional side.

The playing fields on which the duel will take place are basic, but the setting is magnificent: fringed by the brooding Swartruggens. Bakkies line the road – one would think every farmer within a 100-kilometre radius had arrived for the occasion. I sit on the grass verge, surrounded by barefoot children, coloured and white. They whisper excitedly to each other and I catch the name: Bryan Habana, who is not playing but is reported to have come up to support his new team. Another whisper goes up: 'There's Peter de Villiers!'

At half-time, I join the UCT huddle. Looking at each of them in turn, Dobbo says: 'Reach very deeply into yourselves. If you are fucked, say you're fucked. I'd take my hat off to you.' None of them admits to being fucked.

Afterwards, the score is 21–3, with only three tries conceded to the Stormers. In the full-time huddle, Dobbo says: 'It should have been 14–10, but I'm proud of you.'

That evening, there is a braai at the centre. Murray Mexted wanders around with a baby in his arms. Someone congratulates him on his bonny grandchild. 'It's my son,' he says, unfazed. Later his wife, all of 20-odd, joins him. They met at the luggage carousel at OR Tambo Airport. She is an ex-South African, a Kiwi now. They settle down over a bottle of champagne, affable and loquacious, the toddler playing at their feet. Two of the current UCT first team squad have trained at his rugby academy in New Zealand. That evening, a third is recruited: Pallo Manuel, 20-year-old son of Trevor Manuel. Pallo is six foot six, a talented lock. He plays for UCT Under-20 but is training with the first team squad.

After dinner – wors and potato and pasta and more pasta – it's chill time in a veritable Garden of Eden, otherwise known as the Farmers' Arms, a charming little pub down the road. The heat of the day has subsided into a glorious balminess and we take over several tables in the garden, beside a lily-strewn pond and a chorus of vociferous frogs.

It's my first fines evening, a ritual that's steeped in arcane code and deep history, so I'm a little slow on the uptake, particularly after several sips of the large glass of white wine which John le Roux has put into my hand. John le Roux is the elder statesman of the group. A tall, lanky man, he runs a financial services company but, like the rest of the UCT management team, he once played for the UCT first team – from 1966 to 1971 – and is volunteering his services for free, as is Paul Day, the forwards coach and another former UCT player. Paul's day job involves collecting iguana dung and flogging it as potent organic fertiliser. Hot shit.

The Ikey hooker, Dayne Jans, better known as Danger, is impresario for the evening, and he calls the boys up one by one to do a down-down, as punishment or approbation (the consequences seem to be same). Marcel Brache, the Man of the Match, is first up. He downs his beer as the boys sing: *'There's only one Marcel Brache. Walking along, singing his song. Walking in the Ikey wonderland.'*

I assume that I'll be left lurking in the shadows, quietly taking notes and sipping my wine, so I'm alarmed to hear my name called. Very aware of my female otherness and my outsider status, I am eager to please. In the end, the christening line is charming: something about welcoming me into the group and thanking me for taking an inter-est. Then I have to pour the entire glass of wine down my throat in front of 40 boys who are chanting 'Down! Down! Down!' This is a wholly unfamiliar experience.

Then the boys are split into groups of six, and each has to take on an identity. Somehow one group ends up with most of the guys who aren't white, including Pallo Manuel, Marcel Brache and Selo Sampson, a wing, so they call themselves the Number 28s. Another group is the Hippos, who then have to compete with the Croaking Toads. It's funnier than it sounds, everyone gets into the spirit and it is all great fun.

Still later, one of the boys walks past, carrying a tray of shot glasses filled with clear liquid. He sets the tray down on a table lined with boys on either side. They invite John Dobson and me to join them, and we end up playing a game which goes something like this ... we each put both hands palm-down flat on the table inside the hands of the guy on either side of us. We have to drum our fingers on the table, each in quick succession, echoing the number of beats of the hand alongside ours. One pat means keep the chain going; two pats means skip the next hand; three means reverse the chain. If the signals have not been interpreted properly, someone cries foul and the culprit has to down one of the shots, which could be water, cane, gin or vodka. Slightly befuddled from the large glass of wine I had recently downed, I soon miss a beat. Fortunately, my fine turns out to be water. The next time it's cane, and I toss it over my shoulder. A general booing ensues and I am forced to drink another ... and so it goes on until all the glasses are empty. I discover I am hugely enjoying myself. There is something exceptionally pleasant about this sultry, star-lit night, its silence broken only by the rhythmic drumming of fingers on wood and the manic croaking from the lily pond beside us. The pressure of flesh on either side of me is warm, brown arms and white interlinked.

Then Pallo and Selo start break-dancing, and they are still partying when I stagger back to my B&B, no longer feeling like an outsider.

When I get back to Cape Town, I head for Long Street, where I find a cute little blue-and-white hooped rugby jersey, especially tailored for the female form. From now on, I'm one of the team.

TWO

I first got to know Dobbo over a long and very pleasant lunch at the Vineyard Hotel towards the end of 2009. He had already begun training the UCT first team for the 2010 Varsity Cup which kicked off on 1 February. This was to be his last stint at coaching the team and he wanted to go out with a bang. In the two years since the inception of the Varsity Cup, UCT had been pipped to the post by the University of Stellenbosch. This year, Dobbo was determined that the Cup should be won by his alma mater.

In his early 40s, bald with bright blue eyes, I found him excellent company: clever and well read with an anarchic sense of humour. What drew me most was that beneath the apparent lightness ran a darkly fierce current. It seemed to be either chanelled into, or springing from, rugby. I was never quite sure which.

Over grilled fish and tangy sauvignon blanc in the Vineyard's glorious gardens, I asked Dobbo where it all began. Initially, at least, he says, it was with his father, Paul Dobson, legendary Latin and rugby master at Bishops. Paul Dobson was driven by two religions: Catholicism and rugby. It was the latter that took stronger root in his son.

Because he taught at Bishops, Paul Dobson could get free board and tuition for his son, so Dobbo – and I use his rugby nickname here – was a boarder there from Grade R to post-matric. The school, as much as anything, shaped him. Rugby is very important at Bishops.

'In my final report, the headmaster said: "John did very well. He won the history prize and the writing prize, but his greatest desire was to play rugby for the first team." He was absolutely right. I couldn't care less about academics or anything like that. At Bishops, you've got other competitive sports like cricket and hockey, but, you'd get 10 000 people at a first team rugby game. At a hockey game, you'd get 20 parents, an ice cream seller and a packet of raisins. And once you realise that, it's what defines you.

'School was clearly divided between the minority of boys who weren't interested at all, and the majority who supported the system. The first team captain – which I wasn't – was an absolute hero.'

Dobson understands the pain and failure of rejection. 'Dropping a guy is quite cruel, actually. It has a big effect on people. I know that. In my first year at senior rugby, I didn't make the first team, and I felt a deep sense of shame about that.'

Once you make the first team, however, everything changes. 'Everyone knows who you are. Everyone likes you and respects you. If you win the history prize, no one cares, so you feel insecure about yourself. I suppose rugby was the remedy. If you're in the first team, you can talk to girls afterwards. You can talk to a Herschel girl, which you can't do if you are playing in the fourth team. It's tragic, I know, but it's absolutely true. I did a post-matric in order to play another year of rugby for Bishops.'

The acme of any year is the biannual derby with Rondebosch Boys' High, traditionally Bishops' biggest rival. I went to one. The Rondebosch and Bishops boys each massed in their respective stands, in their school uniforms, singing their hearts out for their teams. It was, unusually, a nice Cape Town winter's day, and literally thousands of parents and old boys stood and sat in the sunshine, transfixed by the vision of these schoolboys at each others' throats. Bishops won by a good margin, and after the game was over, all the Bishops boys, followed by a few hundred old boys, swarmed onto the field, forming a huge circle around their conquering heroes.

This scene is played out every year all over the country:

massive derbies that usually boil down to duels between two ancient rivals: Michaelhouse vs Hilton; Affies vs Pretoria Boys' High; Gimmies vs Volkies in Potchestroom. Their followers – families, several generations of old boys, gangs of nubile girls from sister schools – gather faithfully each year. Chops and wors are braaied over huge fires. Moms sell tea and home-made cake while dads fuel up in the beer tents.

It's a fun-filled day in the sun for the whole family yet, despite the fact that it is officially a school event, there is an edge, a sexiness to it, due to the extreme physicality of the game and the passionate intensity of the competition between the rival schools. Schoolboy rugby is high-impact, cutting-edge entertainment. I know, from having spoken to many of them, that it is intoxicating for the players. I remark on this to Dobbo and he nods vigorously.

'You can imagine the pressure on that youngster. All you want to do is play in front of that crowd; to have that rush.'

The catch, he says, is its transience. 'The tragedy for the boys who have put their all into this throughout their school years is that it all disappears in a flash after that final derby, never to be repeated. The next year, there's nothing. It's absolutely gone. After the last game – in my case, Bishops vs Rondebosch – that's it. The next thing is you've got to report to a club and play in front of 20 people on a grim, windy afternoon somewhere out on the Cape Flats, so you can see why that last school game is, for some guys, their defining moment.

'I used to work with a guy who is now 68 and who was a very talented player. He played for his school, then for UCT and then for Western Province. He got used to playing in front of 40 000 people. Everybody knew him. There were lots of kudos, lots of drinks. He never moved on, however. He didn't finish his studies. He remains defined by being a

Western Province player. That was his crowning moment and nothing that has happened since has come close to matching it. I've got some friends who are still living in 1986, when we played our last game for Bishops.'

Nothing has changed, he says. If anything, schools rugby is even stronger.

By now our plates have been emptied. A waiter comes to remove them and refill our wine glasses. Dobbo asks: 'Is this okay?'

'It's great,' I say. 'Keep talking.'

'Well,' he says, 'at UCT now, I get a lot of students coming to me who are really good players and really good guys, but all they really want to do is recreate what they had at school. So many South Africans remain defined by that experience, even those who are overseas. If you meet a guy for the first time, he will ask: what school did you go to? When you name the school, he asks which team you played for. Your answer to that question defines whether you are in or out, because schools rugby is so strong, stronger than it's ever been. Everyone wants to be part of that.

'Every year, in the schools rugby season, we run a schools' Top 20 chart on *rugby365.com* (the website Dobson owns), and it gets the most hits of any story. It's all old boys. So, if you meet a bloke and he says he comes from Joburg and you say: 'The Lions are shit, hey,' he'll just say: 'Ja.' If he tells you he went to Wits and you say: 'Wits rugby is shit, hey,' he'll just say: 'Ja', but if he tells you he went to KES and you criticise KES rugby, your life could be in jeopardy. That is why two South African teams are the top in the world – because of the strength of schools rugby.'

He pauses, gazing up at the shadows slowly darkening the slopes of Table Mountain. 'The thing with rugby now is that it's at a crossroads: it's becoming like American football where you don't play unless you are professional. There are no guys playing social American football at club level. They play for their college and they get their home-coming queen and then they either stop or they sign up for Texas State or something. Rugby here is almost at that level. In the old days, you'd play right through. Now, because school is so hyped and club rugby is so poor, lots of guys stop after school. The logical thing would be for a guy who played at school to play for his province: play for Western Province against Griquas at Newlands. That's what they are driving towards and a lot of them end up being very disappointed.'

To his credit, Dobbo took the windy afternoon on the Cape Flats option after he finished post-matric, swapping the elegant and expansive playing fields at Bishops for the scruffy pitches of Elsies River. 'It was a bit of a change,' he said. 'I'd been used to climbing into someone's dad's BMW to get to away matches. At Elsies River, the guys would come straight off night shift to play. They came in taxis, on bicycles, on foot. Guys didn't have boots, or their boots were held together with tape. It was quite a sobering experience. The cliché is that all rugby men are the same. That's a fallacy. You can't be the same when you are playing under such different conditions. In Elsies River, you'd hear gunshots and police sirens while you were playing, but the effort those guys made to play rugby was quite humbling, especially if you had come from Bishops. They were so passionate about rugby. I could never have played straight after finishing a nightshift.

'Those guys were very good to me. This was before Mandela was released. All the clubs were racially-based – whites, coloureds, Muslims, Africans. I was the only white guy playing for Elsies River, and the reaction to me when we were playing mostly white clubs was a bit depressing. They'd have a go at me: who is this guy playing with the Hotnots? It was quite sweet because our guys used to protect me, especially the props.

'I played for them for a whole season and it was great fun. Truth be told, if I had really made a good fist of it, I would have stayed on, but I was quite keen to scuttle back to the ivory tower.'

From this and from subsequent conversations, I learnt that, after school, Dobbo enrolled for a BA LLB at UCT. As soon as he had finished his first-year exams, he headed off to Verona in Italy where he got a gig playing professionally. This he did each South African summer until he graduated, managing to eke four months out of the end-of-year holidays to play a season for Italy and later Portugal. This paid for his studies. He also learnt the languages of both countries. 'The rugby was pretty horrendous, but being immersed in different cultures was amazing.'

After he finished his LLB, Dobbo went on to do an MBA at UCT and an LLM through Unisa. He is currently writing the life of Eugene de Kok, the Vlakplaas killer, as part of an MA in creative writing at UCT. His day-job is as entrepreneur. With Nick Mallett and Richard Whittingdale, he started the *SA Rugby* magazine, and subsequently several other sport-oriented titles. In the late 1990s, just as the Internet began to take off, they took their product online with *rugby365.com*. He has since bought and sold it six times, most recently to Primedia.

Dobson's position is hooker – 'the guy in the middle, between the two props'. The 'rogue's position – all the dirtiest players are hookers: look at James Dalton and Uli Schmidt. You are so vulnerable, with both your arms pinned behind your neck. You've got to protect yourself.' It's one of the most physically taxing positions. 'Your body takes such strain, particularly your neck.' When a neurosurgeon warned him that he would end up in a wheelchair if he took one more knock to the neck, Dobbo stopped playing. 'That's why I started coaching. It's the closest you can get to playing. You still get to slay Goliath every week. You still get that rush, but it's agony watching.

'As a coach, you go through shit all the time. You go through all those miserable practices, all the admin; you've got all the politics to deal with. Not politics on a grand level, just petty politics. You lose games and you go home and cry yourself to sleep. But it's all done for that rush when you win, when people come to you and say "well done". That's why I coach, I don't referee. I don't sit at home or watch rugby in the pub. Coaching is as close as you can get to being part of a team without being a player. If you can't play, you've got to coach. I'm being honest, it's quite nice when people pat you on the back and say "well done" or "good luck for Saturday". You feel quite pleased with yourself. In my case it's definitely an ego rush. The flipside is that you go home some nights and you cry yourself to sleep when you lose. You feel like the world is going to end. Then you just live for the high of a win.

'I think coaches are lying if they tell you they do it only for the development of players, because that would make you a uniquely good individual. Rugby's changed. Ten years ago you never knew who the coach was. It was some bloke who came up to do a few drills a week. Now the coach is a dominant persona, and if the team is not performing, he gets fired. That's not part of the traditional rugby thing. It comes from soccer. Coaches do like the limelight. You can't pretend it's for development. If it were just for development, no coach would ever move up. You'd stay coaching Under 13s.

'I know from playing myself that the whole experience is very different for the players. The game passes in a flash, it's like you're asleep, whereas when you're a coach, you go through absolute agony. When the Ikey Tigers are playing, I always get a strong urge to get the dogs out of the car and walk up to Rhodes Memorial and wait for someone to SMS me with the score. The thing is you've got to be there at half-time to talk to the boys. They wouldn't think much of you if you just stayed away at half-time.'

His stint with the Ikey Tigers began in 2008 with the inauguration of the Varsity Cup. Together with former Springbok Robbie Fleck – now the Stormers' backline coach and another Bishops old boy – they decided to build a UCT team strong enough to have a decent crack at winning it. 'We had to do everything from scratch. We had to create the right culture, and to do that we had to get the right people. We had no money so we couldn't go out and buy players, but we were at a university so we had access to decent people: people who had a perspective on life; who were free thinkers. They weren't playing just for a contract but out of passion.

'We wanted to create a new brand of UCT rugby: running, expansive rugby. We realised that people aren't interested in rugby unless it is winning rugby – look at Fiji; they run all the time and no one takes any notice of them.'

They also had to build a culture around the team, historically known as the Ikey Tigers. Andy Schar composed a song for them called 'The Warrior Poet'.

'We couldn't stack up on all levels – on rugby, on money – but we could on people, on values and intellect.'

The Varsity Cup has racial quotas – there have to be at least five black players in every squad and three on the field but UCT have been lucky in this regard. 'We've always exceeded the quota without looking at skin colour. As soon as we select according to race we will destroy the team dynamic. Our job is to ensure that we have enough players so that this is just never an issue – and we do. In 2008, the forward of the tournament was Herbert Mayosi of UCT and the back of the tournament in 2009 was Therlow Pietersen of UCT.'

The UCT team has access to the rich facilities of the

Sports Science Institute but, unlike some of the other competing universities, it has no rugby academy. Dobbo believes this is not a bad thing. 'I'm very sceptical about academies because those chaps are defining their lives by rugby and contracts and that's all they are after. Our guys are studying, and rugby is just an outlet. I think that collectively you get more passion and more vibe than you would from guys who are playing for a contract, who are a bit more cynical. To us, it's fun; it's a laugh. You are playing for the love of the team, for the love of the guy next to you. There's something about team sport that brings out decent characters, and at varsity you are dealing with students, so they have got something else in their lives.'

By now, the mountain's shadow is beginning to fall across the gardens. The endlessly patient waiters are clearly wanting to start setting the tables for dinner. I am sufficiently intrigued to want to know more. I phone up Dobbo the next day and ask if I can follow the Ikey Tigers through their 2010 Varsity Cup campaign. 'Of course,' he says.

THREE

The Ikey Tigers' first game is to be played in Port Elizabeth, against the Shimlas, the team from the University of Bloemfontein. We are all to meet at Cape Town International Airport. As I park my car, I bump into Selo Sampson and Marcel Brache who insist on helping me with my luggage, picking up my suitcase as if it weighs nothing at all. Such gentlemen. They had trained for three hours the day before, they tell me. It was tough but Dobbo had said this was the last big push. Now they are amped for the game. In the departure hall, quiet on a Sunday morning, the UCT team are instantly recognisable because they are all wearing their blue-and-white hooped golf shirts, they are mostly huge, and there are so many of them. Twenty-three in the squad and another seven or eight in the management team: there's Dobbo, John le Roux, Paul Day, manager Lisa Brown, Kevin Foote, the assistant coach, a kicking coach, two biokineticists, a physiotherapist and a doctor. All are volunteers.

We arrive at our hotel in Port Elizabeth just in time for lunch. The Chapman is a small hotel on a hill overlooking the beachfront. I have a big corner room with sea views from every window. The team doubles up and Lisa walks around with lists of who is sharing with whom. Dobbo has masterminded this: roommates are constantly rotated to avoid the formation of cliques.

Lunch is lusty: hamburger patties on ciabatta bread, with chips and salad and fruit to follow. The boys, always hungry, tuck in. Danger, just recovered from a groin injury, has a new look: he has peroxided his hair a yellowy-white and shaved his facial hair into two furrows that line his mouth and jut back under his chin. He tells me he is reading Peter Harris's book, *In a Different Time*. 'It's hectic, hey.' He says he thought my publishers were smart to get a woman to write about rugby because boys would talk more easily to a woman. You would expect her to be sympathetic, whereas a guy might just try to humiliate you. 'Not here,' he adds hastily, 'this is a family.'

The sun is hot and bright, but the wind is pumping. Much of the talk at lunch is about the wind: how to use it; how not to let it be destructive.

At 14h30 we are on the bus, headed for the Captain's Run at the site of tomorrow's battle, the Nelson Mandela Metropolitan University. We drive along the seafront, past the strollers on the promenade. There are a few surfers way out: the wind is whipping up monstrous waves for them.

Nelson Mandela Metropolitan University is a capacious campus flanking the ocean. Low buildings are spread between expanses of open land. The stadium itself is infinitely grander than UCT's scruffy Green Mile. There are high, covered stands and an athletic track enclosing a well-kept pitch. The floodlights are powerful and plentiful, unlike UCT's ancient, blinking pair.

Dobbo urges the boys to walk around the pitch to get a feel of the wind. Afterwards, they warm up: lying on the grass, twisting their hips from side to side, lifting first one leg and then the other off the ground, inch by inch. The backs line up to practise passing, and the forwards crouch for a scrum. I am the only spectator, but the wind is a constant companion, whistling and howling through the tall gum trees that line the stadium.

Back at the hotel, we all gather in the team room – a large conference room with floor-to-ceiling windows overlooking the sea. Dobbo embarks on a Powerpoint presentation: The Wind: EMBRACE IT. It is our friend, says Dobbo, because we are used to it. The Shimlas come from Bloemfontein where there is no wind. We must play to it: suffocate them with the wind.

Afterwards, the management team leave and sports psychologist, Simon Wiseman, takes the boys through a mindfulness session. Afterwards, Simon is on a high. 'That was incredibly powerful,' he says. 'These guys are so committed to the team and each other. They would live and die for each other. We talked about the wind and boiled it down to ball possession and ball security. Then we did visualisation around this.

'Don't shout at them tomorrow,' he advises the coaches. 'They're on a slow burn. They are focused. Keep them there.'

That night the wind disappears, but when morning comes, the sea is coated with white ruffles. The palm trees are flapping wildly. The wind is back.

It is 09h00 and time for the one-on-ones, although it is more like the five-on-ones: Dobbo, John le Roux, Paul Day, Kevin Foote and Gareth Wright, the kicking coach, sit in a semi-circle, facing an empty chair. There is a knock on the door and Grant Kemp, a 124-kilogram prop from Wynberg Boys' High, enters and sits down, looking like a schoolboy coming into the headmaster's office for a dressing-down.

Dobbo: 'If we are going to get a card, it will be from the front row and we can't afford that, hey, Kempie. You are the most skilled tighthead in this fucking competition. Just remember that!' Kempie nods vigorously. He clearly falls into Murray Mexted's high-arousal category.

Next in is a lock, Martin Muller, a tall, good-looking boy with untidy blond hair. He has been with the team since 2008 but is also semi-professional, having played for the Stormers and Western Province in 2009.

Dobbo: 'You are playing for two teams, but this is where you come from. These are your mates. This is your team; who you are. We are very grateful to have you here today. The guys look up to you. You are a Super 14 lock forward. If you help lead that charge against the Shimlas today, the game will be over in 20 minutes. Be aggressive but controlled. Don't let Kempie blow his top.'

Then Marcel Brache, a centre from Rondebosch Boys' High, takes the chair.

Dobbo: 'We are absolutely thrilled you are here. You are a fantastic presence and not only on the field. You were our Man of the Match against the Stormers.'

Nick Fenton Wells is the captain and left flanker. A former Bishops boy, he is a member of the Mallett rugby dynasty. His mother is the sister of Nick Mallett, former Springbok captain and Dave Mallett, current director of rugby at Bishops.

Dobbo: 'We very pleased with you as captain. You have a tendency every now and again to get into a black rage, and that can't happen to a captain. The only way to lead is by example. Your inspiration in that physical charge is crucial. Playing into the wind, it's just ball security that counts.'

To shaggy-haired openside flank, Mike Morris: 'No one knows who you are now but at the end of the Varsity Cup, everyone will know who you are.'

Next up is JJ Gagiano, a loose forward, also from Bishops. He is a tall boy with dark curly hair and a moustache and sideburns, wearing a T-shirt with two faces exchanging tongues on his chest. JJ has been with the UCT team since 2008 and has just been selected to play for the American Eagles.

Then comes Yaya Hartzenberg, a Muslim and loose forward from Paarl Boys' High who has been in the Western Province system since he played in the Under 16 Grant Khomo Week in 2004. He is one of the few players at UCT not registered as a student and this is his first year in the team. His hair is shaved down to a centimetre and his arms bulge out of his blue wife-beater. Despite his menacing appearance, he comes across now as docile, almost shy.

Dobbo: 'A few weeks ago, we were like okes at a first dance – no one knew what to do. Now we all know you and we like you. You've got a real future. You're a big rig. You carry the ball well. We're really honoured to have you.'

Paul Cohen is the baby of the team, having just matriculated from Bishops and registered at UCT. He plays on the wing. Gareth says to him: 'It's no different to playing schoolboy rugby, but it will test your thinking and your capacity for work. Try to do one thing out of the box that could change your game – like chasing a kick.'

Blond Stu Commins, the scrum half, is also the vice-captain. Another former Bishops boy, he has played Western Province Under 19 and Under 21 and has been in the UCT team since 2008.

Dobbo: 'You are in prime shape. You have grown as a leader. Use your brain out there.'

Nic Groom is small and compact with ferocious sideburns. He is a scrum half and a Rondebosch old boy. This is his first year with UCT, but he played WP Under 21 the year before.

Dobbo: 'You are the sheepdog. It's blowing 10–15 kilometres harder than it was yesterday. Back your ability. Bring what you keep bringing to the party. You're a good, calm "kop".'

On his way out, Nic says: 'Shit, I'm so looking forward to it, hey.'

Matthew Rosslee is a slightly wild-eyed Willem Defoe lookalike, with fine features and cropped blond hair. A fly half from Rondebosch Boys, he has also been in the system since 2008, playing for both WP and UCT.

Dobbo: 'I'm thrilled that you are here. Sometimes we give you a hard time; but it's because we're desperate for this project to work. You are the best fly half in this competition. Just make sure you are in the right place at the right time.'

Doug Mallett is the son of Nick Mallett. This is his first year out of the Under 20s.

Dobbo: 'You are the best passer of a rugby ball in the club.'

John le Roux adds: 'Always use your brain. Think. Calculate.'

Selo Sampson is a left wing from Wynberg Boys High. He has played for WP since 2006 and UCT since 2008.

Dobbo: 'We're absolutely delighted with you. You are one of the most skilled rugby players I've seen. Raw talent.'

Tim Whitehead is a centre from Grey High in Port Elizabeth. He has been with UCT since 2008, but is also contracted to the Stormers. As with Martin Muller, the focus is on his potentially divided loyalties.

Dobbo: 'When I played in Italy, I played with all different nationalities in a professional team. It is not the same. These are my people. This is where I want to be. These are your people. Playing into the wind, you guys have literally got carte blanche. You and Selo have to work as a team – talk to each other. You have got to be physical.'

Next is Therlow Pietersen, fullback from Bellville Technical High School. Therlow is not a UCT student but this is his second year in the team. Last year, he was named best backline player of the Varsity Cup. Therlow has recently been laid low by loss. His stepfather, Tommy, died two weeks ago and he is still very cut up about it. Around his wrist is a bandage with RIP Tommy scrawled across it in black ink.

Dobbo: 'You are in a position to honour Tommy now. If you asked me to name two players who are crucial to this team, one would be you. You are integral. Just remember, if you are going into the wind, keep the ball secure.'

Last in is Pete Haw, and Dobbo has very bad news for him. Another ex-Bishops boy, Pete is a fly half, but Dobbo has decided to drop him for this game.

Dobbo: 'I'm really sorry, Pete, but you're not playing to-day. It's the wind and we need a stronger goal kicker. If it were the ordinary UCT wind, we'd have kept you, but in this wind, it's going to come down to territory. Gareth has just driven to the field and the wind is 15 kilometres stronger than it was yesterday. I'm really sorry. I've fucked you around unconscionably. You are fundamental to this team. You sum up everything we want: cerebral, teamwork. This will never happen again. I promise.'

Looking very upset, Pete says: 'Obviously I'm disap-pointed, but I understand.'

After he has left the room, Dobbo, looking equally upset, says: 'That wasn't nice at all, hey. I said at the beginning that one of them would have to sit out because there are 24, but he didn't think it would be him.'

After lunch, we all assemble in the team room for the final team talk. Coldplay's 'Viva La Vida' is blasting forth as the boys crowd in. They are all newly showered and in their formal clothes: club tie and long-sleeved pink cotton shirts tucked into neatly pressed jeans, their hair clean and combed. Finally all are seated. They are silent and inward-looking. Dobbo introduces Rob Louw who will hand out the jerseys. Rob is a former Springbok and champion surfer who has just undergone intensive treatment for cancer. He still looks pale and gaunt. He says: 'It's so important to be positive, to talk to each other on the field and support each other. To lift each other up.

'I've been through hell the last three months and when you are lying in bed seeing 18-year-olds with cancer, you realise life always has to be lived to the full. Make every game an adventure. Love the game and love life. Next thing you will be like us: old and past it and desperate to be on the field again.'

On the bus, UCT's haunting theme song, 'Warrior Poet', blasts into the silence:

Do you know how it feels?
When it's running through your veins?
When everything feels like fire,
And you fear no pain …
When the drum begins to beat,
And the crowd begins to sing.
And you see in the eye of the tiger
The fear in the enemy king.
Well, lift up your hearts to the night,
For they will be here at first light …
And as tears run down my warrior face,
I swear that I will come for you,
Through the windswept fields of this lonely place
I swear that I will make it through.
Do you know how it feels?
When the sky begins to fall,
When hurricanes of blue and white
Play out the art of war.
When you swear your allegiance,
To your brothers in arms,
Together on the Green Mile
With the sound of the enemy's alarm.
Well, lift up your hearts to the night.

While the boys are warming up on the field, I find Pete Haw sitting up in the stands, still dressed in his formal pink shirt and tie and looking forlorn. I sit beside him and ask how he's feeling. He bursts out: 'Everyone says: "You are taking it so well" but what else can I do? Anyone would be devastated. What makes it so difficult is that you put so much mentally and physically into this and you don't get a chance on match day to show what you're worth. It's very frustrating.'

He doesn't blame Dobbo at all, he says. 'This is my fourth year with him – I've been with him since Under 20s, so I know his ways and I have a very healthy relationship with him.'

Pete is studying mechanical engineering, presumably as a precursor to joining the family firm, Haw & Inglis, which is at that moment transforming the chaos of De Waal Drive at Hospital Bend into a streamlined motorists' delight.

Pete was a boarder at Bishops, where he played fly half for the first team. He now shares a house with two other students who like partying, but he has to be disciplined. 'The Varsity Cup only comes once, and it's a lot bigger than another party with your friends, so you are willing to make the sacrifice.' He has recently met a girl he likes but that too is on the back burner. 'I told her I can't get into anything serious because of this.

'These are my friends,' he says, gesturing towards the boys on the field. 'They are my family. Even though we come from different backgrounds, all the guys come from strong families so we feel the same warmth and respect we feel towards our brothers.'

You've got to work harder at it than at school, he says. 'The rivalry between schools is very big but at varsity, it's a different story. You make your own group, your own family on campus. It's the team against everyone else.'

There is another reason for his melancholy: 'Last night Simon Wiseman went around the circle, asking everyone to reveal something about themselves. The guys before me were quite light, but all I could think of was this time last year when we were in the same place, playing for the Monte Taljaard Cup, and I got all choked up. Then the next few guys did too. I had spent half an hour in that very room with Nick Fenton Wells the year before, bawling my eyes out.'

This was the first time I had heard about Monte Taljaard. An old boy of Grey High School, he had been captain of the UCT Under 20s when he was killed in a car accident in Main Road, Claremont, in 2008. In the most vicious of ironies, the driver of the other car was Danger's sister, Roxanne.

Down on the field, the boys are streaming back towards the changing room. The game is about to begin. Pete and I head down to join them. The players pull on their jerseys and get into the huddle. Simon tells them to breathe in deeply. Hold it. Breathe out.

Dobbo says: 'Remember, these are closed-minded fucks of the first order. They think we are the "sagte" Ikeys. Play in their half. Suffocate them with the wind. We are all brothers. We love each other. There is so much love in this room.' As he speaks, they slip their arms around each other and begin the UCT rallying cry: 'Varsity! Yes!' Finally, it's about to begin: everything they've been working for and striving towards for the past three months.

It does not go well. By half-time, we are down 14–6. The Shimlas had the wind at their backs and UCT tried to play with ball in hand, as kicking into the wind was not an option. Mike Morris breaks a rib and comes off, weeping with pain.

In the changing room at half-time, the mood is sombre. Dobbo warns them against conceding any more penalties. Simon gets them to focus on their breathing again.

In the second half, Therlow's leg starts cramping until he can't walk. Eventually, Gerald, the physiotherapist, picks him up and carries him bodily off the field. Therlow hasn't been training enough because of Tommy's death, and it is showing. Then JJ comes off, bleeding from a cut above his eye. The doc quickly stitches it up, without anaesthetic, reasoning that an injection would mean yet another prick. It only takes three stitches.

Martin Muller is slashed under his chin and it's deep. Just as it seems UCT is doomed to an ignominious loss in their first game, Selo Sampson scores a try. Then Doug Mallett kicks a last-minute penalty to bring the UCT score level with the Shimlas at 30–30.

The darkened bus on the way back is silent and heavy with disappointment. It wasn't meant to be this way.

Simon says to them: 'Remember this disappointment. Experience it so that you don't want to feel it after next Monday's match.'

There is a brief, alcohol-free awards ceremony around the pool at the hotel. Man of the Match is Selo for making one try and setting up another. There is no award for the best tackle because they were uniformly abysmal. The award for the best team member goes to Pete Haw, who instantly perks up.

I walk down the hill with the coaches to Primi Piatti for pizzas. The atmosphere is bleak as all hell. Every second of the game is replayed, with mounting gloom. John le Roux tries to look for the positives: this is the best we've ever done in a first match, he says. In 2008 and 2009 we lost the first games. At least with this one we take away two points. It doesn't help. He and Dobbo eat and go. They've had enough of today.

The forwards coach, Paul Day, and I decide to head off for the Boardwalk casino where the boys have been gambling away their misery. We find them in clumps at the blackjack tables. Some are actually winning. As midnight closes in, we retire to the SuperSport bar in an annexe off the main gambling hall. There is a giant TV on the wall and the curtain-raiser to our match – University of the Western Cape vs Fort Hare – is coming to an end and the UCT–Shimlas match is starting up. The boys spot prop Kempie on the screen and break into his totem song, which is in isiXhosa. A black man sitting with two women at a nearby table joins in, and then wants to know who they are, these white and coloured boys singing in isiXhosa. Big blond Ash Wells points to the TV and says: 'That's us – UCT! We've just played Bloem University – you know – where the Reitz Four are from!' I find it sweet, this eagerness to bond. We watch for a while, but it's not a game we want to dwell on.

FOUR

The second game is against the University of Potchef-stroom, to be played on UCT's Green Mile. On the Sunday before, preparation begins with a session of mindfulness at the Sports Science Institute. We sit on the floor in a circle: me, lovely Lisa and 24 large boys. Simon Wiseman, the sports psychologist, tells us all to lie down and close our eyes, which we dutifully do. He then takes us through each part of our bodies – clench, then relax; clench, then relax. After 15 minutes, one of the boys is so relaxed he goes to sleep. We know this because he is snoring.

Now that we are relaxed, we have to think about war. The over-riding weakness from the unmentionable match the week before was the failure to tackle; insufficient aggression was displayed. This is what must be remedied for the next match. We are told to breathe in very deeply, focus on whatever tumult is going on in our abdomens and then sharpen that into a weapon. Visualise flattening them, boys.

Next afternoon in the changing rooms at UCT, Dobbo is more forthright: 'Fucking crush them!' he bellows. They do. The difference from last week is extraordinary: they tackle like titans; pilot the ball half the length of the field into a prevailing wind with such strength and skill that it sails through the goalposts.

Eight minutes before half time, Marcel Brache scores a try. They're barely back on the field when Danger is hurtling across the tryline. Matt Rosslee converts it. Hooker Mark Goosen gives away a silly penalty, but we still win. The pretenders from Potch are defeated 18–11. Fucking crushed.

There are hardly any injuries, unlike last week. Pete Haw,

back on the field, tells me it is because they went in so hard. The tougher you tackle, the less likely you are to get hurt.

Perhaps they were emboldened by the support: Helen Zille handed out the jerseys, the first woman to do so. She spoke about her loyalty to UCT and how much their putting their bodies on the line for UCT meant to her. She stayed to watch, sitting beside the UCT vice-chancellor, Max Price, both of them cheering their hearts out. Afterwards, they join the post-match huddle on the field with the boys and coaching and support staff, joining in the cry, head down: 'Varsity! Yes!' Dobbo congratulates the boys – 'Except Goose, who did a fucking stupid thing. Sorry, Goose, but you did.' Goose looks suitably chastened.

It is exhilaration all round, the polar opposite of the previous week's despair. In the changing room, the boys can barely hide their grins. We all link arms again and sing the haunting rhythms of 'Warrior Poet': *Do you know how it feels? When it's running through your veins? When everything feels like fire and you fear no pain ...'*

Then it's drinks with family and supporters in the UCT Rugby Club bar. John le Roux introduces me to some of them: Therlow Pietersen's mom, Pauline, there with a friend and her pretty daughter. Pete Haw's dad, Rick. Therlow arrives and immediately sinks into an animated conversation with the friend's daughter, who is clearly in love with him.

'If I had a son, I'd never let him play rugby. I'd be so scared he'd get hurt,' says the friend, 'but Pauline is so unselfish.'

'I couldn't hold him back,' says Pauline.

John le Roux recalls his first meeting with the Pietersens. 'I was walking up and down the tryline during a match and Tommy, Therlow's stepdad, called me over and offered me a glass of wine from their box.' Pauline nods sadly. She says the loss of Tommy feels particularly painful at Therlow's games because Tommy enjoyed them so much.

Rick Haw tells me that six generations of his family have played rugby for Bishops. Both Pete's brothers and his grandmother were also at the game. Another strong family.

Then it's on to Forries and a beautiful night for it, it is too – still and balmy and all lit up with our delight. UCT rugby, from its elder statesmen to the players, are still in their formal uniform of pale pink long-sleeved shirts and blue jeans. In most cases, however, the tie has been abandoned; the sleeves are rolled up; shirt-tails trail. Much beer is drunk and pizzas wolfed down. Pink blurs dot the dusk of Forries' garden long into the night.

FIVE

The spirit of Monte Taljaard hung heavy over the third game. It was an away game against the Nelson Mandela Metropolitan University in Port Elizabeth, Monte's home town. A Monte Taljaard Cup had been inaugurated in his name, and Lisa carried it up on the plane, wrapped in a pink tablecloth.

Port Elizabeth, of course, was windy. I was wearing a dress and regretted it as the wind whipped it up the moment I got off the plane. At the Chapman I got the same big corner room as last time, with the same beautiful view of the ocean. In the dining room, we were given the same three long tables and the same lunch: gravy-laden beef patties with chips and salad.

After lunch, in the team room, John le Roux did a SWOT analysis with the boys, first explaining what a SWOT assessment was: Strengths, Weaknesses, Opportunities, Threats. One of the Weaknesses was the line-outs. The jumpers weren't jumping high enough. The ball wasn't being thrown accurately.

Prominent among the Threats and doubling as a Weakness was Complacency. NMMU was one of the weakest sides in the contest: Stellenbosch had beaten them 68–20 in their opening game. We need a win and at least four tries to stay at the top of the log. We'd have to work hard for it.

At the Captain's Run at the NMMU rugby field, line-outs are practised, over and over again.

There are two PE boys in the management team: Geoff Huber, the doctor, and Gerald Muller, the physiotherapist. Both went to Grey PE and both are now based at Bishops. Gerald's dad, who was a Currie Cup referee and is now a ref administrator, has invited us all for dinner. Frans is his name and he comes to fetch us: a small, bespectacled man in a large Mercedes.

Frans and his wife, Stephanie, live in a double-storey house with a glorious view over the city. Just below wink the lights of the new FIFA World Cup stadium. It looks hugely impressive. Beautiful even. This is where the Southern Kings, the great hope of Eastern Cape rugby, will be based.

We are directed down the stairs to Frans's bar. The walls are lined with the jerseys of various teams and eras, displayed in glass cases. Pictures of Frans with virtually every rugby personality of the past 30 years are dotted on every available surface. One of the seats is an elephant's foot. He gets us drinks and starts piling charcoal onto the outside braai. Dinner, it seems, is going to be a while. Better pace the drinks.

Stephanie shows us the garden, which boasts a few cycads and succulents and not much else. The drought has been terrible, she says. They aren't allowed to water their gardens. As ever, the bloody wind is blowing, but we sit outside anyway, under the stars and a glowing crescent moon.

A few bottles of wine later, Frans starts talking local rugby politics and it is clear that passions run deep and dark. He doesn't like the head coach of NMMU rugby and wants us to thrash the team – remember they will come at you with great ferocity; their physicality will be intense because brute strength is all they've got. They haven't got technique or skill. I can see Dobbo filing that away.

A quiet plea is made on behalf of a player who is often dropped from the squad: André Goosen. I don't recall having met him, but Frans reveals that his girlfriend's family goes to the same church as he and Stephanie. Ah, the great handshake power of religion in rugby. Not that it is likely to work in this particular team. Eventually, Frans lifts two perfectly cooked sirloins from the braai. Stephanie emerges with shrimp and potato salads and garlic bread. We are about to fall on the food, starving now, when Frans stops us. We have to pray first.

Afterwards, we drink more and then go up to the TV room to watch a Rugby Sevens game. Kenya is playing England and we're all rooting for Kenya. Frans brings port and small crystal glasses, urging us to drink. It's almost midnight when we leave.

The next morning, the day lies heavy in front of us. The wind is stronger even than the day before and it is hot and muggy. The game is only at 18h30 that evening and somehow the boys have to occupy themselves until then. The one-on-ones are conducted from 10h30 until 12h00: as usual, Dobbo leads them, but Gareth Wright is there for the backs; Paul Day for the forwards; Kevin Foote offers his penny's worth, as does John le Roux. Captain Nick Fenton Wells is also present, for the first time. Chief amongst the advice given, especially to the forwards, is the inside information gleaned last night from Frans Muller: they will be very physical – it's all they've got. We have to match might with might. The old mantra is marked big on the whiteboard: EMBRACE THE WIND.

Then it's another carbo-loaded lunch and an attempt at a nap.

I find Therlow and ask him how he's doing. Therlow was born in Belhar into a working-class family, and educated at Bellville Technical High School. He is small with a powerful upper body, his head topped by a mullet with the central bit swept up into a cockscomb. He exudes a truculent grief. He misses Tommy terribly, he says, a swamp of loss which deepens around every game. Tommy was the only father he had ever known – he only met his real father when he was in Standard Seven and it was Tommy he called dad.

Tommy had always been there for him. He took him to and from games. 'He was my spy – he'd stand where no one else was and then phone me afterwards to tell me what had been happening.' Tommy's voice has always been in Therlow's head: loving, supportive, protective. Now he is in the ground and Therlow feels very alone.

When we gather again in the team room at around 15h00, the sky outside is black and heavy. Spray-fringed waves bash the shoreline. It's not looking good.

Sydney Taljaard, Monte's dad, has been chosen to hand out the jerseys. The reasoning is that deep and potentially corrosive emotions are inevitably going to be stirred up; better to try to harness them than bury them. The Monte Taljaard trophy, an elegant Carrol Boyes affair with four players lifting the giant cup aloft, stands on a white cotton-covered table in the front of the room.

Sydney, a tall, bespectacled man with a moustache and a sandy-coloured fringe cut abruptly across his forehead, quotes his son on the subject of the day, namely the Dangers of Complacency. He speaks briefly and hesitantly, either from shyness or because he is afraid he won't be able to control his emotions. The boys are dead silent, not even a shuffle is heard.

Afterwards, one of the boys who had been closest to Monte – lock Mike Ledwidge – gets up and urges them to play for their lives in memory of Monte. If he was looking down on them from somewhere up above, it was what he would have wanted. Dobbo rounds it off, urging the boys not to let their grief become debilitating. Focus instead on bringing the Cup home, for Monte's sake.

As we set off for the grounds, it starts raining. The wind is still pumping. I ask someone if that's good for us or bad. Bad, is the tense reply. A ball that's slippery with rain or moves erratically in the wind undermines our technical advantage. So much for all that embracing of the wind. It's just trying to make the best of a bad situation.

Big, boisterous Yaya says he likes the rain. He can run all day in the rain. The sun makes him tired. As 18h30 approaches, the rain stops and the wind drops. A beautiful muted light bathes the NMMU stadium. We all stand for a rousing rendition of the national anthem. There's a moment's silence for Monte and then the boys go at each other.

The Nelson Mandela Metropolitan University, once the very conservative University of Port Elizabeth, is a strange place. It clearly had large amounts of money pumped into it at some stage of its history. The rugby stadium is sumptuous: the product, presumably, of apartheid-era budget priorities. Apartheid seems to linger here. All the cheerleaders are white, eight of them blonde. They prance and preen on the track in their little navy-and-white skirts and frilly red pom-poms. They are pallid by comparison with what is going on in the stands, where hundreds of black students are dancing, beating drums, blowing vuvuzelas and belting out the muscular songs of the anti-apartheid struggle. Despite all the positive energy being beamed down on them from the stands, the NMMU team, the Madibaz, quail before the superior skills of our lads. Yaya, running like a Trojan in the cool evening air, scores four tries. All in all, we score nine tries and the score is a very decisive 65–9. That means we are still unbeaten and second on the log. I rush down to the field, convinced our guys will be jubilant. But no, clearly I have understood nothing. Paul Day is furious: 'There were fourteen scrums, which means our guys made fourteen mistakes!'

Poor Pete Haw's nose is hugely swollen and pushed to one side. Ten minutes before half-time, he and Yaya tackled the same guy from each side and Pete's nose collided with Yaya's forehead. Yaya briefly lost consciousness but nevertheless continued to play. He is named Man of the Match.

Pete's nose was broken and dripping blood. He had to leave the field. 'I'm so disappointed,' he says, 'to have had so little game time.' The doc says hopefully he might avoid an operation and only be off for two weeks, but there's no guarantee.

Sydney Taljaard comes down to the pitch to award the Monte Taljaard trophy to Stu Commins, and then we all repair to the reception room for drinks and supper.

I seek out Sydney and his wife, Michelle.

It is clear at once that, although Sydney and Michelle are very close, she is the stronger of the two. He is warm and friendly but it is she who decides whether to engage with me, and to what extent. A small, dark-haired woman, her face is carefully made up, mask-like, I assume to protect what is really going on. Monte Taljaard, she tells me, died on 14 September 2008. He was coming home from a party when his car collided with that of 18-year-old Roxanne Jans at the junction of Main and Protea Road, Claremont.

Michelle Taljaard recalls that night. 'When we first heard the news, we did not want to move. We didn't want to go anywhere. Then I said to Sydney: "We've got to go and get Bev" (their daughter). She was studying at Stellenbosch. We drove down and I'm so glad we did because the whole way we were getting phone calls and SMSs. By the time we got to Cape Town, we had realised how special he was to so many people.

'It was such an eye-opener for us. Parents always think their children are special. You've been pushing your kids all their lives to be a certain way. You think: this is my child and you love him, warts and all. For us, it's very precious that he had such a special place in all their hearts.'

Monte Taljaard packed an enormous amount of living into his short life. Born in Port Elizabeth in 1987, he was a talented boy. He learnt wrestling as a young child, but also excelled at tennis and cricket. He got his Eastern Province colours for swimming and played the trumpet in the school orchestra. Rugby was his first love, however. He went to that excellent rugby school, Grey PE, where he 'captained every age group side, from Under 13 on'. A natural leader, he was also a prefect and head of house.

He was determined to go to UCT. 'He contacted the UCT director of rugby to apply for a rugby scholarship. He said to him: "I'm coming to Cape Town to play at the SACS rugby festival. Come and watch me." He filled in all those countless application forms himself, and in 2006 he registered for a BSc in Property Studies at UCT.' He also arranged free board as a 'stooge' or unpaid housemaster at Bishops, courtesy of the rugby connection.

From the start, he made an impact on UCT rugby as captain of the Under 20 side. 'Dobbo coached them and they were unbeaten in the League. They beat Stellenbosch twice that year.' Ten of the current first team squad played with Monte in the Under 20 team. Dobbo had told me there was no doubt Monte would have captained the current side.

In Monte's second year at UCT, he organised a rugby tour of the Eastern Cape, setting up everything himself: meals, accommodation, fixtures. Perhaps unsurprisingly, his studies took a dive and he dropped out. Again rugby connections came to the rescue: Neil MacDonald, another of the Ikey Tigers' godfathers – a UCT alumnus who managed the club's finances – gave him a job in his property company. 'I couldn't believe it: at the age of 20, Neil was flying him to Durban to negotiate with businessmen! He was very excited about that job.'

Although living in Cape Town, Monte remained close to his parents, still in Port Elizabeth. It was his mother who had to ring him at 04h30 on the days he flew to Durban to ensure he was up in time.

After his death, a memorial service was held at the Bishops chapel. It can accommodate 750 people, but so many people came, they were flowing out of the doors.

'We were overwhelmed,' says Michelle. 'And we are still overwhelmed.'

I say to her that one thing that has struck me about these boys is how intensely they live: that each time they run onto that field, they are risking their bodies, their health, not to mention their egos, because defeat is so crushing. She eagerly agrees. Also the trust they have in each other, she says. 'I think that to win, they have to trust each other.'

Because she has lost her son's future, she is trying to mine his past: going through the family computer, she says, she keeps finding things he has written, like 'ten things I want to tell my children one day'. I find this absolutely heartbreaking. I'm not sure how she copes. How does she feel about Roxanne?

'I just feel sorry for her,' she says. 'She was so young.'

The Taljaards sounded a bit like the Mullers: close-knit and loving, with their lives centred around their children and their church. Monte and Sydney went hunting and fishing together. The boy was also very close to his sister, Bev, a year and half younger than him. Sydney is financial director of a local company. Michelle is a primary school teacher. She says her Christian faith has helped her come to terms with her tragedy. 'I feel consoled by God.

'There is so much to be grateful for: that he died instantly. Because I was in Port Elizabeth, I couldn't have been with him. Also that he was alone in the car. That only one life was lost.'

As we part, I say to her: 'I think you are so brave.'

She says: 'We still cry a lot, and we miss him so much.'

I think of the deaths that have seeped into the UCT team: Monte, and Therlow's stepfather – and wonder if the fact that we, as a nation, have to deal with death very often infuses our rugby: whether our greater awareness of our mortality gives rise to a greater physicality, a greater capacity for risk.

Later that evening, I catch up with the coaches. Dobbo is quietly pleased with his lads' performance. They have done Monte proud. 'It wasn't about the result,' he says. 'It was something much more fundamental.'

S I X

I realise that I'm becoming addicted. It's something to do with the huge anticipation before each game: the combination of heady hope, edged by fear of failure. Week after week, there is this rolling build-up, with all its preparation and rituals, and then the wham-bam, all-or-nothing blow-out of the game itself. Afterwards it's either elation or despair – nothing in between – and the following week it all begins again.

I deliberately skip the fourth game, played at the Green Mile against the Tshwane University of Technology, in order to get a break from the intensity of it all. I need to focus on the rest of my life, which has been shoved into the background over the past few weeks. All afternoon, the Ikey Tigers are on my mind, however. I wait a decent interval after I know the game will be over and SMS Dobbo to find out the result. 'Awful. 25–19,' comes the reply. We lost?!? Surely not, not against TUT. 'To us?' I type back. 'Yes. But we were dreadful.' At least we won.

Ash Wells, the prop from Wynberg Boys' High, is in his final year in the UCT media studies department and, practising for life after university, he writes up game reports for the university news website. This was UCT's 'worst performance of the year', he wrote, quoting Dobbo's verdict: 'Diabolical!' Played in strong south-easterly winds, it was 'an error-ridden encounter', which nevertheless allowed UCT to maintain their unbeaten record with 15 points on the log, still lagging the Maties.

I was glad I wasn't with them, knowing how deep the gloom is after a game in which the boys don't perform.

A braai had been planned for the Wednesday evening on the beach at Noordhoek for the boys and their families. It was summarily cancelled. No one was in the mood. They had played so badly, said John le Roux, that they didn't deserve a treat. Over the week, I found my thoughts constantly returning to the lads: I knew how, with each practice, the momentum would again begin to build towards the next game and another chance at redemption in rugby's endlessly forgiving cycle.

The fifth game was an away game against the University of Johannesburg.

I arrived in Joburg a few days before the match and sent an SMS to Dobbo: 'No wind!' It would be the first game I'd been part of where we wouldn't be battered and buffeted by the wind. On the other hand, it did rain. Joburg was having a wet summer, with torrential downpours for a few hours every day, mostly in the evening, interspersed with sodden humidity. Monsoon weather. All the rain meant abundant fertility, and every now and again, in those days leading up to the game, I'd have to stop my car, gobsmacked at the beauty of purple and crimson against vast, shimmering fans of green.

After the languid rhythms of Cape Town, Joburg is big and brutal and raw. Gaping dongas line the roads where the Bus Rapid Transit System or the Gautrain or some other completely random project will eventually spring up; red earth deepened to ochre by all the water.

The second of March, the day of the match, was also a big day in the FIFA 2010 Football World Cup lexicon: 100 days to go. Banners fly from lampposts and trees to announce this milestone. At midday, radio stations everywhere sing out the national anthem. Slowly, we are all beginning to sing the same tune.

Mid-afternoon, I set off to meet up with the team. They are staying in Auckland Park, at a guesthouse a few blocks away from the University of Johannesburg campus. The roads around here are a nightmare: en route to Soweto, they are dense with traffic, squeezed into single lanes by endless roadworks. Hardly any traffic lights are working, so each intersection entails a kamikaze race across oncoming traffic in hopes that the other guy will give way.

By the time I arrive, sweating, the boys are all gathered around the long table in the dining room, and the atmosphere is tense. As always, I'm slightly thrown by the sheer physicality of it: the size and muscle of this group. Lots of taut bare flesh and something in the air that's not fresh but not off either: that combination of testosterone and adrenaline.

The coaches are giving their last-minute pep talks, now focusing on the positive, trying to motivate the boys and not criticise them, but at the same time keep them on their toes. It's a delicate balance. Dobbo is first: 'Play with a smile on your face,' he urges, 'love that ball.' For the first time in the competition, they will be free of the wind, but what nature will throw at them instead is oxygen-hogging high altitude. Another challenge. 'Tackler, leave the ball. The next man on the ball! Attack their food and water: their scrums and line-outs.' The goal is: 'We must go to the Danie Craven Stadium next week unconquered. That is our goal for today.'

Dobbo fires up his laptop and the screen fills with the words of 'Invictus' – unconquered – by the English poet William Ernest Henley. It might have become famous through the eponymous film, but remember, he tells them, it was Nelson Mandela who first read that poem to François Pienaar before the 1995 World Cup, which South Africa won. He reads it aloud to them, ending with the ringing words: 'I am the master of my fate. I am the captain of my soul.' There is dead silence in the room.

Neil MacDonald, the UCT Rugby Club's financial guru, comes in to hand out the jerseys. It was to have been John Robbie but he couldn't make it and Neil was fortuitously in

Joburg anyway, having arranged a business trip to coincide with the game. Neil tells the boys he comes from Joburg and, even though he now lives in Cape Town, he retains a strong loyalty to the city of his birth. 'There is a serious energy here. It is tangible.' He picks up on the 100-day celebrations: the team should feed off all the positivity in the air, he says. 'In Joburg, you have to be street smart to survive. There is a real can-do attitude in this city, and I can feel the same thing in this team.'

John le Roux stands up and says in his stately way that he had been talking to Stu Commins, captain for the day, about the fact that the team had an unfortunate tendency to 'go to sleep in the second half'. To counter this, they had come up with a new call: 'Killer!', specifically for use in somnolent moments during the second half.

The finale is a specially made film. To the evocative strains of 'Warrior Poet', the boys are shown on the steps of Jameson Hall in their blue-and-white hooped jerseys. There follows a commentary on the proud history of the Ikey Tigers: the third oldest rugby club in the country and the progenitor of 50 Springboks. Then cut to the team performing at their finest: pouncing on their opponents with all the speed and fearlessness of a cheetah at the kill; tearing down the field to score ecstatic tries; pounding scrums. The boys love this and request a second showing.

Afterwards, each member of the team is given a length of blue wool to tie onto the wrist of his next number. This was to be done when they were alone, accompanied by a few words which would have special meaning for the recipient. John le Roux ties one around my right wrist, saying how much they appreciate my support. I'm touched. It's still there, long after the tournament has come to an end.

Outside, I find the boys hanging around on the deserted road, waiting for the bus to take them to the University of Johannesburg stadium. Selo, who has become one of my

favourites, is sitting on the pavement. 'How are you feeling about the game?' I ask. 'Okay,' he says. 'Psyched.' The
coaches had been very hard on them earlier in the week
but 'they realised the guys are nervous and there are new
caps here and they had eased up on us.'

Like all the boys, he is superbly fit and muscled. He has
shaved off all his hair and on his bulging upper right arm is
a tattoo – Japanese characters; blue ink against brown skin.
'It says kamikaze,' he explains. 'It's how I want to live my
life. Always going at it 100 per cent.'

Pete Haw is throwing a ball around. The last time I saw
him he had a black eye and a swollen, crooked nose. His
face looks normal now but he tells me he's gone through
a lot of pain in the last few weeks and is nervous about exposing his tender appendage to the brutalities of the field.
In the past week, a doctor has broken his nose again to
straighten it, buffered only by local anaesthetic. I like the
fact that he can talk about being in pain, his fear of pain
and yet not have a shadow of doubt about re-entering the
fray. To me, that's courage.

The changing room at UJ has that familiar clammy,
sweat-laden feel. I am struck again by how unselfcon-
sciously physical these boys are: even with me and Lisa
wandering in and out. In the row of toilets leading to the
changing room, one of the boys is shaking himself dry after a wee. JJ is vomiting into another toilet. There is none
of the shame or coyness – or fear – of their bodies you
would get with girls of the same age.

All dressed in their UCT jerseys now, they quieten down,
and a mood of solemn, almost religious intensity takes over
in the cramped little changing room. One can see them entering a different zone; preparing to transcend their bodies,
their fears, their everyday, hived-off selves.

It's minutes now before they have to run out and they
get into their huddle, arms around each other. Dobbo says:

'Fucking get out there and win every collision. Not every-one gets this chance to go out there every week and put yourselves on the line for those you love. I'm jealous of you. All the coaches are jealous of you. Reach deep inside yourselves, guys, like you didn't do last week!'

He moves out of the circle, and acting captain Stu Com-mins – Nick Fenton Wells is injured – takes over for the last word, which is a prayer. It surprises me, this. These boys don't usually pray. Some of them drop to their knees; bow their heads.

Then I quickly move out of the doorway because I know that, focused as they now are, nothing and no-one must get in their way. They head out of the door and down the concrete path in single file: heads down, eyes trained on the heels of the guy in front, oblivious to everything but the battle ahead. The only sound is the rhythmic tap-tap of their studs on the hard surface, like the prelude to some ancient shamanistic ritual.

The rain has held off and it's a beautiful, still evening. The UJ community is out in full force and ready to party. Their stadium is magnificent, with floodlights and steep covered stands. Like NMMU, what used to be the Rand Afrikaans University benefited from the old regime's love affair with rugby. Yet, how far we have come. The lower stands are full of black girl students – and the odd white one – all dressed in the orange and black UJ colours and singing their hearts out for their team. The drum major-ettes come in all colours and are actually very good, leap-ing and twirling and gyrating around the athletics track circling the pitch, in sync with each other and the music. I sit in a stand full of little boys in orange shirts, with their large, Afrikaans-speaking parents. It feels much more in-tegrated, much more in tune with the times than NMMU did.

On the field, our boys play their hearts out but it is nerve-wrackingly close from start to finish. We are up 17–13 at half-time. As the boys run on for the second half, I watch the lanky form of John le Roux striding up and down the far perimeter of the match and imagine him shouting: 'Killer! Killer!'

If he does, the boys hear him – or at least Selo does. With seven minutes to go, he streaks down the field to score a brilliant try, unerringly converted by Doug Mallett. It ends 30–23 to us.

Afterwards, the relief morphs into exhilaration. The boys stream off the field and there are lots of sweaty hugs. We all clasp arms in a circle and sing 'Warrior Poet'.

'I'm fucking proud of you,' says Dobbo.

Back at the guesthouse we gather round the pool with a few cases of beers. Danger leads the down-downs. Therlow has one as Man of the Match; Samkelisiwe Peter, a UCT business science student and Dale College old boy, has one, as does Selo, try-scorer supreme. Marcel Brache, that very day appointed to the Springbok sevens team, is another. They burst into his song: *'There's only one Marcel Brache. There's only one Marcel Brache. Walking along, singing his song. Walking in the Ikey wonderland.'*

They surprise John le Roux with a new song, which goes something like this:

'John le Roux, he's taller than me and you. He'll fuck you up black and blue, John le Roux le Roux.' John gamely swallows a can-ful.

This time, I don't get away with sitting on the sidelines either, but they are gentle with me. Danger says: 'We love your team shirt and we love having you with us.' I have to stand in the front and down a can of beer, which I normally loathe. But with that sort of enticement, who could resist?

Then we're off to jol – at Stones, a place in Melville I've never heard of but which is pumping, even though it's close to midnight. It's very noisy and quite shabby but full of life. Young people of all colours are dancing in the disco, playing pool or hanging around the bar, which features a large TV screen on which the Varsity Cup matches of the day are being replayed.

We drink and dance and watch the replay. Some of the boys are great movers. Some find girls, but mostly they seem to hang with each other, still bonded by the battle of the day. We leave around 02h00. In the deserted street outside, Marcel Brache and Sam Peter are chanting up at the crowd spilling onto the balcony outside Stones: 'Give us a U! Give us a C! Give us a T! Give us a UCT!'

The next game is the big one, the first of the season against ancient rivals, the Maties. John le Roux captained the UCT side from 1966 to 1971 and he remembers the annual Inter-Varsity between UCT and the University of Stellenbosch as the big match of the time. Apart from the one in 1968, which they drew, UCT lost every game. Dobbo came to it much later: 'The whole university came and we had 14 000 people watching. It was us against the forces of darkness, the forces of evil, the rock-spiders. We could hear the UCT crowds shouting: "Voetsak, hairyback! Voetsak, hairyback!"'

Of course, that's all completely different at Stellenbosch now, particularly under its new black vice chancellor. It is very much part of the new South Africa. What has remained the same, however, is the intense rivalry between the two teams on the rugby field.

The Maties are still the Ikeys' *bête noir*. For the past two years, they have repeatedly narrowly beaten the Ikeys, except for one exhilarating pool game in 2008. As ever, the Maties bestride the log, six points clear of UCT, who are second.

Over in the Cape Town camp, tension has been mounting. It does not help that the match is to be played at the Maties' home ground, the Danie Craven Stadium. Once again the weather is a force to be reckoned with. This time it is neither wind nor altitude nor rain, but heat. It is incredibly hot – well over 30 degrees all day and, at 20h30, when the match kicks off, it is expected to be 28 degrees. Lisa has spent all day collecting ice and has managed to round up 300 kilograms, enough for a bucketful for each boy.

The team talk starts at 18h30 in a large, air-conditioned

room at the Protea Hotel in Stellenbosch. It's high up on a hill, overlooking vineyards. Assistant coach Kevin Foote begins with the theme of the day: gratitude. 'Boys, you tell me people keep telling you how lucky you are to be in the UCT first team. Well, we coaches feel grateful that we are coaching you. We all feel grateful to each other. Gratitude is the right attitude.'

John le Roux says: 'Show them our physicality. No lapses in the second half. We have the Killer!'

Dobbo adds: 'We are coming up for a slug-fest. Defeat is unlikely, but also inconsequential. It's not crucial that we win.'

He hits a button on his laptop and 'Invictus' comes up on the screen above a photograph of the team in their blue-and-white hooped jerseys lined up on the steps of the majestic Jameson Hall. 'I am the master of my fate. I am the captain of my soul.'

The next slide shows a caption across the same picture: 'Our time has come. The tide has turned.'

Then comes that sacred moment: the handing out of the jerseys. Former Bishops boy, former Springbok and current Stormers backline coach, Robbie Fleck, has been chosen for the task.

He tells them: 'It's the biggest game of the year. The Maties are the team against whom you have the biggest rivalry; the most tradition. There is a huge difference from two years ago: you are more mature, more confident. You have a great team spirit. You are like brothers. I sense a calmness and confidence here. You take from the Maoris and the All Blacks. You play attractive rugby and draw the crowds to UCT. It used to be David against Goliath, but now it's Goliath against Goliath. The reason you will beat them is because of your unconventional approach. You run at them and they will get tired. They are no longer the big brother bullies.'

He ends with the wistful: 'As great as being a Stormers coach is, I would love to be here because of the great vibe you've got.'

And then it's onto the bus, with 'Warrior Poet' ringing in our ears. There's a nervousness, a wariness I haven't felt before as we climb off the bus and head through the sea of maroon to the changing room. The boys are quiet and stick together – they are already in enemy territory.

It's another huge, beautiful stadium, another legacy of an apartheid-era obsession with rugby. The stands are already packed with girls and boys wearing maroon Maties wife-beaters and maroon face paint. The UCT team change quickly out of their formal pink shirts and head out onto the field to warm up. When they come back 15 minutes before the game starts, they are already sweaty and flushed with the heat.

The changing room is the usual cramped, claustrophobic concrete box ringed by a wooden bench, but a space has been designated for each boy with his name neatly written in pink, a pink rosette and a handful of jelly beans. In the centre of the room is a toddlers' plastic swimming pool filled with ice. The boys grab handfuls of it and rub it into their faces and shove it down their shirts. Selo is sitting on the bench by himself, his face in his hands. I wonder what he's thinking.

They all form a circle and sports psychologist Simon Wiseman starts a meditation: 'Shoulder to shoulder, boys. Breathe in, breathe out. Breathe in centredness, breathe out tension. Breathe out the individual. Breathe in the team.'

Dobbo says: 'This is a very special opportunity. I'd give anything to be in your position. Remember to ignore all the booing. Focus only on what happens within those four white lines. Cling on with every sinew. And enjoy it, boys! Belief, belief in the blue and white tribe!'

Then the adults leave and the boys get into their most

intimate space. Stu Commins, again captain for the day, says: 'Look into the guy's eyes opposite you. See into his soul.' Then it's the final rallying cry: 'Varsity! Yes! Varsity! Yes!' And they raise their heads and there is that glazed look in their eyes as they make for the door. I scuttle out of the way as the tap-tap-tap of their boots gets louder and steadier and the procession of blue-and-white hooped muscle and sinew and single-minded focus streams slowly past.

The SuperSport floor manager is standing in the corridor shouting with increasing urgency: 'UCT! Two minutes! UCT Now! Now! Now!'

On the pitch, war cries are coming from the massed maroon stands. The floodlights are glaring down at us. The Maties come running on and the stands erupt in ecstasy. UCT has been allowed only 2 000 spectators and they are crowded into a far corner. Inhospitable though it is, I can't help feeling what a glorious theatre this is. The pitch is surrounded by stands and ringed by mountains. The temperature is perfect, like silk on the skin. I stand with the boys on the bench and the medics, opposite our team. We put our hands on our hearts and sing the national anthem.

Then battle commences.

The Maties have come up with a nasty bastardisation of the UCT cry: 'A U, a U, a useless team!' It's cruel and recurrent.

One image I have is of Matt Rosslee standing, tensed, to pounce on a Maties wing streaking toward the tryline. Matt's teeth are bared; his arms and legs taut and outstretched, ready to leap, but he fails to down his opponent.

The stands explode as the Maties score their first try. Then the Ikeys score and the loudspeaker belts out the song: 'In the Eye of the Tiger'. Danger is injured so badly he can't walk and has to be taken off on a little quad bike. Then Therlow goes down and a new song comes thumping out: 'Another one bites the dust!' It's hardly sportsmanlike, I think crossly.

Half-time and we are 16–5 down. Poor Matt Rosslee at fly half has missed every penalty and conversion. The boys are sweaty and anxious, shoving ice down their fronts and backs.

Danger, having gone into the game with a strapped shoulder, comes out limping on crutches, his knee heavily bandaged.

The final score is 23–17. With the Maties celebrating wildly behind us, we gather in a circle. The boys are universally downcast. Dobbo tries to cheer them up. 'You were great in the second half, guys. Keep your heads up. Don't think tonight is the night for a piss-up. Start preparing for next week.'

JJ Gagiano says with passion: 'What we have to focus on now is Tukkies next week. That must be a big game!' Everyone cheers. UCT Vice Chancellor Max Price joins us and we do the last 'Varsity! Yes!'

In the corridor, I bump into Danger, hobbling around on his crutches, and I ask him what he thought of the game. He said the guys were a bit overwhelmed. 'The whole build-up; being in the papers; the stadium sold out with 30 000 people out there. Some guys have never seen that. Suddenly you look up and see it's 13–0 and think: Shit! It's started! Stu said: Don't worry guys. Smile. You're on the field. Do something. Before you know it, it's over. That's rugby.

'I'm unhappy we lost but we know we ran them ragged. You have a long phase of play and you get exhausted but because we're so fit, we recover quickly when we have a break, when they bring on the water.'

In another part of the long, concrete corridor under the stands the coaches, smart again in their light pink cotton shirts and pale grey ties, are in a depressed huddle. Matt Rosslee is always terrible against the Maties, says Gareth

Wright fretfully. 'He seems to have a mental block. He is intimidated.'

The post-match function is in a long, narrow, high-ceilinged room, reeking of money and tradition and very good wine. We sit down at long tables covered in white linen and eat a quick dinner. Man of the Match, Andrew Prior, an Englishman playing for the Maties, gives a gracious speech: 'It was very tight. We haven't been stretched before in this tournament but you really pushed us.'

Then the funkiest Matie team member, Cameron Peverett, a very dark-skinned guy with a dramatic Mohican flanked by cornrows, gets up to say grace. He keeps it to the 'thanks, Lord, for a wonderful day and a wonderful game' variety rather than 'thanks, Lord, for ensuring we beat the shit out of them', which is surely what he was really thinking.

After dinner, we head off to the Coetzenburg pub; a big room dominated by a large oil painting of Danie Craven. The walls are covered with photographs of every Maties team since records began. The wine is good and eventually – it's after 01h00 now – we begin to fraternise with the enemy.

Chean Roux, the Maties head coach, is a tall, good-looking man: blond hair, getting a bit thin; blue eyes. I'm still wearing my faux UCT rugby jersey, courtesy of Long Street, so there is no point in trying to hide my true colours and come across as the objective journalist. 'What's the trick?' I ask him.

'It's all psychology,' he says. 'You've got to beat a close team and then you get that invincible self-belief. Luck, too. The reason the All Blacks lost the World Cup was because the coach believed he should rest the Super 14 team.'

He says he coaches to the last 30 seconds. 'You've got to be able to bring in the points in the last 30 seconds. The coach can only control 60 per cent: the rest is luck, the players, the weather, the bounce of the ball.'

Afterwards we head into town for more partying. A bunch of Dobbo's former team mates from his UCT playing days are in town for the game and happy to make a night of it. As we walk, a light rain falls, but it's still gloriously balmy. A passing security car gives us a lift to the only club still open: the Springbok. There's a queue to get in which we somehow manage to jump. Inside, we head for the bar. A sign above the door says 'The Rhodesian Bar'. Indeed, most of the young things are white. Black people struggle through the merry mob with crates of beers and glasses. One of our guys comes back from the bar with a glass and a bottle of white wine which he hands to me: it only cost R20 for the whole bottle, he says. I hope it's alright.

Despite Dobbo's imprecation to the lads earlier, several of the team become evident through the strobe lights and pulsating crowds: there's Levi Odendaal and Sam Peter; Wes Chetty, Marcel Brache and Doug Mallett.

It is 04h30 by the time I get to bed. We may have lost, but we had fun. Isn't that the point of it all?

EIGHT

One of the many reasons I find this competition so compelling is that everything goes into the game every week. We've barely finished one; absorbed the pain or the pleasure; analysed the mistakes to death; celebrated the moments of brilliance; drowned our sorrows; bonded and re-bonded; celebrated our love for each other ... than it is time for the next duel.

On 15 March on the Green Mile, we are champing at the bit to take on Tukkies. No longer unconquered, our new mission is to secure a home semi-final for the following week. To do that, we have to beat them. The game is played late: at 18h30, without TV. It's been a beautiful, hot day, 29 degrees and virtually windless, but at 18h00 the wind rouses itself and begins roaring across the Green Mile.

The clock strikes 18h15 and we cram into the changing room, festooned with pink rosettes and pink towels. Wizened, bent Judge Tebbutt is the first to address the boys: 'In the second half of last week's game against the Maties, every Ikey in the land watching you on television was proud of you. Play like that every minute this week and you will make every Ikey in the country proud of you.'

Then Dobbo comes on and it's all ratcheted up several notches: 'We are going to win this game and secure a semi-final. I want that more than anything else in my fucking life. Patience, discipline – win every collision. Go out there and fuck them up, guys. Fucking stamp on them! We're coming back here next week!'

The coaches file out of the room and the boys get into their own huddle: all I can hear is: 'Come, buggers! Come, buggers!' And then the rousing cries of 'Varsity! Yes! Varsity! Yes!' and they are breaking into their hypnotic trot out onto the field.

It doesn't go well. They fumble passes, tackle without conviction and struggle to control their own ball in the scrum. Prop Grant Kemp crashes over for a try, converted by Doug Mallett. Then the wind snatches up a ridiculously long pass and a Tukkies player scores an easy try. At half-time, the score is 20–12 to us, but we haven't exactly ex-celled ourselves. I see Dobbo striding towards the changing room, his face set, and I gather up my notebook and follow. The boys array themselves on the benches, the smooth, clean-cut appearance of 40 minutes ago gone. They are red-faced, shiny with sweat, with dirt browning the white pants and white hoops of their jerseys.

I've never heard Dobbo speak to them like this. His voice is breaking with anger and despair: 'I've given my fucking life for this and this is what you do in return. You are a fucking embarrassment.' He turns to Selo, rubbing his bald head tenderly: 'This kid has made more tackles on his own than all of you put together. It's fucking unacceptable!' He turns on his heel and storms out.

There's a moment of shocked silence. Some of the boys look as if they're going to cry.

Kevin Foote hastily steps in to calm things down: 'Okay boys, take what Dobbo says on board because you know he wears his heart on his sleeve. Just get back out there now and make us proud.'

The boys get into their own huddle and it feels as if they are holding each other together, those big muscular arms wrapped around each other for comfort rather than the usual solidarity. Stu Commins says: 'Take the criticism, boys. Look at the guy next to you. He is your brother. You love each other.'

Then, grim-faced, they are charging back onto the field and they are dynamite right from the start. Within the first few minute of the second half, JJ Gagiano hurtles across the tryline and Doug Mallett kicks a long and beautiful conversion. It's 27–12. It's rapidly followed by another try by Stu Commins.

Then, more drama. A player is down across in the far left corner. The medics run on, followed by the man with the stretcher. The other boys retreat into their teams, huddle together. It looks increasingly alarming. The coaches head across and I'm wondering whether someone has died or is paralysed. For ten minutes, we watch, helpless, as the crowd of officials around the prone figure gets bigger and bigger. It's almost dark now; the pitch barely lit by UCT's pathetic attempt at floodlights. The wind is howling. It feels very cold. Then an ambulance drives down the steep embankment behind the clubhouse and reverses onto the field. The stretcher is loaded into the back and the ambulance drives off. Someone comes to tell us that it's okay. It's UCT scrum half, Jean-Paul Robert, just on from the bench, his first game. He has responded well to the initial tests. In other words, he is alive and not paralysed. Later I learn he was deeply unconscious – snoring, said Doc Huber – and was convulsing.

The boys come out of their huddle and the game goes on, finishing 38–24 to us. Dobbo walks onto the field and, subtle general as ever, leads them to the far corner, to acknowledge the group of black students who have been singing their hearts out throughout the game, much the most vocal and passionate supporters.

Afterwards, in the changing room, the mood is transformed from that at half-time. Dobbo is smiling at his boys: 'We've got our home semi! That was a very good comeback. I'm very proud of you and very grateful to you. We've got our home semi!'

Selo, shy and proud, is Man of the Match.

The boys start stripping off, relieved now and happy,

aglow with a mission well accomplished. They're singing in the showers – a large communal room separated from the rest of the room by just two low walls. They wander up and down, naked or almost naked; singing their club songs, celebrating each other and the team. From the showers I hear snatches of Matt Rosslee's song:

> *I saw my mate*
> *The other day*
> *He said to me*
> *I have seen magic*
> *I've seen the white*
> *The white Pelé*
> *His name is Matt*
> *Matthew Rosslee*
> *Matthew Rosslee.*

With the coaches, I head off through the packed bar, loud with song and celebration, to the formal reception, which is held in a room at one end of it. The rugby dignitaries are there: the Tukkies management in their blazers and the UCT brass. We all have a couple of drinks and head off to the Hussar Grill in Rosebank. Stu Commins and several of the players have gone straight off to the Vincent Pallotti Hospital to visit their fallen mate.

Don Armand and JJ Gagiano come with us. I ask Don how he felt about Dobbo shouting at them. The only thing he and the others feel is how they have let Dobbo and the other coaches down, he replies. They give so much and this is how they, the team, repay them. They feel ashamed. Nice boy. He points at JJ Gagiano, sitting further down the table, and says: 'He gave back last week's Man of the Match award.' Why? I ask JJ. Because it wasn't just me who won, he says. It was the whole team.

At midnight we part, the coaches back home to watch

replays of that day's matches, plotting their next moves.

Before midday the next day, the next week's schedule appears in my inbox.

Training week 16 March

Excludes:
- Gym
- Sherylle Calder individual work
- Video projects
- Simon Wiseman

Tuesday 16 March
18h15 brief chat in SSISA foyer
16h30 – swim session

Wednesday 17 March
13h00 HIMMS – UCT
17h00 OFF

Thursday 18 March
24 km/h south-easterly, 25 degrees

08h30 Specific One-on-Ones
12h00 Sherylle Calder session UCT
13h00 Kickers
17h00 Training UCT. Warm-up fun game (15 min) and stretch. D (20 min) and 10 min contact vs U 20s. Set-pieces – line-outs then scrums from 18h00 on.

Possible team-building theatre sports
Mark reports handed out and individual DVDs and Shimlas video projects

Friday 19 March
OFF

On 16 March, the day after the game, there is an e-mail from Doc Huber:

> *JP spent a comfortable night at Vincent Pallotti.*
> *CT brain scan = normal*
> *He is just waiting to be seen/discharged by consultant neurologist but is in good spirits.*
> *Kind regards,*
> *Geoff*
> *PS Before any coaches ask: NO he is NOT fit for the semis!!!!*

09h00 Specific One-on-Ones

Saturday 20 March
25 km/h south-easter, 22 degrees

08h30 am: Shimlas video
08h50 am: line-outs & kick-offs – SBM backs strike run throughs/kickers/catchers
09h20: Breakdown D touch 7 stretch
09h35: D
09h45: Maps
10h05: ICE, Forwards scrum

Sunday 14 March
23 km/h south-easter, 25 degrees

16h30: Captain's run

Monday 15 March
27 km/h south-easter, 25 degrees

UCT vs SHIMLAS

NINE

22 March: the semi-final against the Shimlas on the Green Mile.

The ante-room resembles a casualty station on a battlefield. When the Varsity Cup began, only a few of the boys were strapped, mostly to protect ancient injuries. Now, after six big games on the trot, the numbers have multiplied. Half-naked boys lie around on the stretchers as the medics wrap long white strips of bandages around a thigh here, a shoulder there.

Cricketer Graeme Smith hands out the jerseys. For him, he says, it all began in a changing room at school. 'There is no better feeling than being part of such an occasion. I can feel the buzz here, and being part of it brings back memories.

'It's a big moment. You are well trained, very well prepared. What I always do is to visualise the guy I am up against. Stay calm; follow the game plan. Have the patience to achieve what you want. Sport offers so many rewards – money, fame, cars – but what I remember are the moments when every one of our team gave of our best. When you can run a bit harder when your team mate needs you to; when you can hit that ruck when your mate needs you to. Play to your game plan and give each other your best. It's amazing what you can achieve when the individual is taken out; what you can achieve as a team.'

One by one, Dobbo calls out the names of those playing. The boys echo each name with the corresponding nickname as they walk proudly up to fetch their jerseys. Graeme Smith shakes each hand. I'm struck, as always, by the solemnity to these occasions. It's as if, with the handing out of the jerseys, they are being inducted into some sacred order. The jersey – and the strapping that precedes it – resembles a coat of armour that will somehow render them impregnable.

Graeme Smith leaves to go and sit in the VIP stands. Nick Fenton Wells, recovered from injury and reinstated as captain, turns to Stu Commins and silently they hug each other. It's a poignant moment: one gets the sense of much that has gone before this hug and beyond it.

Simon Wiseman gets them into a circle and tells them to stand with their shoulders jammed into each other, arms dropped to their sides. 'Shoulder to shoulder; feel the connection; feel the warmth; feel how your mates on either side are holding you up, making sure you don't fall.' There is silence apart from Simon's quiet, steady voice, deliberately monotone.

Kevin Foote: 'Boys, ask for passion, a fire in your belly. This will be the last time you run out onto this field as a family.'

Dobbo: 'There comes a moment in every athlete's life – a seminal moment – which defines who we are. TODAY will define who we are. We are well prepared; now you just have to remember the fundamentals. Remember, it cannot be physical enough.'

The coaches leave and the boys get into that final, intimate huddle – arms round each other, staring intently into each other's eyes. Nick Fenton Wells says: 'There is nothing more special than running onto that field with you guys. Boys, go out and play like fucking champions!'

They do. With a howling, freezing gale at their backs, they play like fucking champs. At half-time, back in the changing room, they are sweaty and grubby but glowing.

Dobbo is pleased: 'No penalties. No offloads. Bodies on the line. You played perfectly today. Just keep that up for the next half!'

Kevin Foote: 'Frustrate them! Frustrate them! Guys, we love this wind now!'

In the huddle, Stu Commins says: 'Just keep up the same fucking intensity for the next forty minutes.'

After the game, everyone is on a high. It was a brilliant match. Best they've ever played.

Dobbo says: 'An outstanding rugby performance, chaps. Nobody opted out; everybody put their bodies on the line.'

John le Roux starts talking, but they can no longer contain themselves, and burst into song: *'John le Roux le Roux; he's taller than me and you; he'll fuck you up black and blue; John le Roux le Roux!'*

John fetches a crate of beers from the bar and hands them round. The boys start drifting into the communal showers at the end of the changing rooms; singing the fines songs. The party continues in the bar next door for a while, but not for too long. The Big Game now looms. In the final in a week's time, they take on once again the only team they have not yet been able to beat when it counts: Stellenbosch.

Midweek, there is an agonised selection meeting in the boardroom of the Sports Science Institute. Just the coaches, Lisa, John le Roux and me with my notebook.

First up for discussion is prop Chris Heidberg. Chris has badly injured his knee and needs an operation. He is refusing to have it until after the final. He shouldn't really play but they are running out of options. 'Chris has a fantastic work rate. We will be in the shit without him.' It's decided to wait till Saturday to make a decision.

Next is whether to start with Nic Groome or Kyle Wickins at scrum half. It is Kyle's third year with UCT but only Nic's first. It would be great for his confidence to start him in the final and he is a generous player. 'Groomie always thinks: what's in it for others?' remarks Dobbo.

The most anguished discussion is around the fly half: will Matt Rosslee, another consummate team player with a startling work rate, let Coetzenburg blunt his boot again?

In the end, consensus falls on Doug Mallett to start. For Dobbo, in particular, this is done with a heavy heart.

31 February: Coetzenburg Stadium, Stellenbosch. The Final.

In the changing room, Dobbo has his final word: 'I want to thank all of you for a very special time in my life. Be as physical as never before; remember composure; remember set pieces.'

The boys are tense, inward-looking, quietly hugging each other.

In the huddle, Stu Commins says: 'We are so fucking well prepared for this.'

'Varsity! Yes! Varsity! Yes!'

They head down the corridor, tap-tap-tapping till they burst out onto the field where 28 000 hostile maroon-clad Maties are waiting.

In my blue-and-white hooped jersey, I stand on the field alongside Danger on his crutches with the medic and the boys on the bench. The teams line up opposite us, we belt out the national anthem, led by Kurt Darren with the entire stadium singing lustily along. Stellenbosch and UCT, singing the same tune, the tune of a democratic South Africa.

It's such a glorious setting: it's a warm, still evening. The stadium is cradled by mountains, with a luminous full moon peeping out from behind. I feel a pang of impending loss. This is the last game; the last time I will stand on the sidelines as my team takes the field.

Stellenbosch unashamedly uses every weapon in its arsenal. Every time we have the ball in hand, the music is cranked up distractingly loud. The booing and jeering are 28 000-strong. The couple of thousand UCT students who managed to get seats can't compete.

We make a good start, with Doug Mallett converting a

penalty, giving us the early lead. Almost immediately the Maties wing Tythan Adams scores a try, successfully converted, followed by another try from the Maties centre, Charl Weideman. Then Marcel Brache kicks over a long-range penalty. By half-time, we are down 12–6.

In the second half, Doug Mallett misses a penalty and then the Maties centre Danie Poolman crashes over for their third try. Mallett misses another penalty but then our Sam Peter scores a magnificent try. It is not enough. The full-time score is 17–14. It's close and the boys have played their hearts out, but we have lost another final – by just three points.

We gather in the final huddle. Several of the boys are sobbing. Maroon-clad students gather round, taunting: 'A U, a U, a useless team!' Eventually security guards arrive and form a protective ring around us.

The changing room is a scene of devastation: the boys sit around, hunched, openly weeping, too stunned to move.

Dobbo comes in, looking shaken. Matt Rosslee makes a brave attempt to cap the occasion off with some style. 'Dobbo, you've changed us over the last three years. We've become better people.'

John le Roux calls for a formal vote of thanks to Dobbo: normally this would have instantly inspired a burst of his song, but not tonight.

Nick Fenton Wells says: 'It's unbelievably gut-wrenching to have come this far and lost. Still, we played for each other and we have made some unbelievable friendships. Coaches, you have created this insane vibe; we can't stop now just because they've won.'

But they just sit there, inconsolable. I look at these big, tear-stained boys and think what nonsense the stereotype of brutish, insensitive rugby players is. These boys' world has come to an end and their despair is there for anyone to see.

Allesverloren. All is lost.

PAUSE

ONE

In the winter of 2010, I made a trip to the Eastern Cape, spurred by a conversation with a friend, Peter Church. He had recently accompanied his son, a pupil at Bishops Prep, on an Under 13s rugby tour. Dale, he said, had beaten Bishops 54–0. Given the huge discrepancies in resources between wealthy, independent Bishops and state-run Dale, this was a remarkable result. The question was: what happens with these boys? Ex-Bishops boys can be found at every level of professional rugby, but there are only one or two ex-Daleans. The vast majority just don't make it beyond school. Given their obvious talent, why not? I thought it was particularly intriguing in light of the fact that Dale is in the Eastern Cape, the heartland of black rugby, the one province where rugby is more popular than football. It is also the province from which the Bulls and the Sharks recruit many of their black players.

King William's Town, home to Dale Junior and its big brother, Dale College, is a former garrison town established by the British as a base for their wars against the amaXhosa. During the apartheid era, it was part of the Ciskei homeland. In 1980, there were 30 000 white residents, now there are 4 500. It is a pretty, well-laid out town, with wide avenues and elegant villas lapped by sprawling succulent gardens. Once in the white part of town, many of these villas are now owned by black people and it is their sons – as well as the sons of residents of nearby Bisho and Mthata and the villages dotted in between – who attend Dale.

The acting principal of Dale Junior is a young white woman, Pat Thatcher. Dale Junior is 50 years old, she says, and outwardly it has changed little in that time. The honey-coloured Herbert Baker-designed buildings with their curved arches and broad, stone-flagged corridors are well maintained. The military traditions of the school are also upheld, although largely ceremonially now, with regular celebrations of First and Second World War heroes. The school song is the same. However, the colour of the boys has changed since the arrival of democracy in 1994: it is now 90 per cent black. There are 500 of them, and almost all of them play rugby.

Two thirds of these boys come from single-parent homes. Each of the ten male teachers doubles as coach and male mentor. Each is responsible for two teams. They coach for four hours a week and there are matches twice a week. The kids put in two hours' practice each day.

'It's not now and then, it's all the time.

'Because a lot of the kids here are brought up by their moms, their coach is like a father. The men are looked up to. There is a lot of responsibility for the male staff because the boys look to them as role models for everything, every male quality. Their bond with their coaches is amazing.'

She finds it a useful tool for instilling discipline. 'If we have any disciplinary problems, the most effective threat is to say: "We will tell your rugby coach." Parents do it as well: "We will take away your rugby."'

Luyanda Mpande is head of sports at Dale Junior. An ex-Dalean, he played eighth man for the Dale College first team. He matriculated in 2002 and has since then coached rugby at two other Eastern Cape schools, namely Port Rex and Hudson Park. He has come back to Dale to complete the cycle.

'Most of our boys go on to Dale College,' he says. 'Hopefully they will one day have a successful first team side. That is why we put in the hours at the bottom here so that they will go on to be better rugby players and better men.'

He echoes Pat: 'Any child this age can become aggressive, and the perfect time to go off is on the field. You have to be disciplined, however. It's a good kind of aggression: a fearlessness. They are forced to learn to control their aggression. If one guy steps out of line, the whole team suffers. We make them all do 500-metre sprints. We don't allow swallow dives or high fives. We instil team spirit, and always tell the boys there is no I in the team. If you can't control your aggression, you can't play rugby because you will get a yellow card. Be aggressive, but within the laws of the game.'

Everything went right for us for the game against Bishops, he says.

'The ball bounced properly. We were clinical. The guys just stuck to their guns and the game plan and everything worked for us. Our Under 13s are the smallest, size-wise, in the province, but they play with big hearts.'

My visit happens to coincide with the public service strike of 2010 which included Sadtu, the teachers' union. Pat asks the male teachers to stand at the gate, to protect the women and children from any aggressive picketers. As I leave, I look back at this muscular phalanx of young men and think: I wouldn't like to mess with them.

Further up the hill is another grand-looking school. Dale College is 150 years old and looks like an English public school with its elegant buildings and expansive, if slightly unkempt, grounds. The boys, all dressed in the same red-and-black ties and blazers that Daleans have worn for decades, greet me with the same sort of courtesy I get at Bishops or St Johns: 'Morning, Ma'am.' There is a rush to volunteer to guide me through the endless corridors to the principal's quarters.

Mike Eddy has taught at Dale College since 1992, rising through the ranks until he got to occupy this spacious corner office. The school is still run on English public school lines, he says. 'We have houses. We try to inculcate good manners. Be proud of your uniform.'

Their matric pass rate is 98 per cent, but he is determined that it will be 100 per cent this year. Some 90 per cent of the 516 boys currently enrolled are black.

Their biggest challenge, he says, is collecting school fees. Even though the fees are only R3 500 a term, many parents struggle to pay. 'Most of our children live with single mothers, so it is very difficult for them to support their sons. Only around 40 per cent go home to two parents.'

The fact that racial transformation of the school was so rapid and recent has also had its financial impact. The old boys, who have now reached the age where they are earning decent salaries, are mostly white and do not send their sons to Dale or identify with its rugby teams, nor do many of them contribute to its coffers. This sets Dale at a huge disadvantage against the English-speaking private schools like Bishops or St Johns where old boys – particularly those who played rugby – remain loyal and generous, or the Afrikaans state schools like Affies, Paul Roos or Paarl Gim. Afrikaans people tend to keep their kids in state schools, which means far less of an outlay for fees, so wealthy Afrikaners can afford to pump money into school activities in which they feel personally invested, like rugby. This means these schools can afford good staff and state-of-the-art facilities. They have entire departments devoted to rugby: ranks of specialist coaches as well as biokineticists and physiotherapists; large budgets for national and international tours, as well as for buying in talent from poorer schools to boost their own teams.

All Dale has – in abundance – is great natural rugby talent and passion. After an initial chat, Mike invited his two rugby coaches in to meet me: Grant Griffith, head coach, and Vince Gelderbloem, who doubles as Under 15s coach and head of accounting. Both are white ex-Daleans.

I put my question to the three of them: if Dale Under 13s are good enough to beat Bishops 54–nil, why don't they go on to dominate rugby like Bishops or Paarl Boys' High or Affies do?

Simple, they said: *They don't get enough to eat.*

'Their daily diet is bread, three times a day,' said Grant. 'Their families are poor and they basically just eat starch: bread and some samp and beans.' They get hardly any of the protein needed to build muscle, particularly at this crucial adolescent growth phase.

'When we play the Afrikaans teams, the guys are ten kilograms heavier, which is big in rugby.

'The boys do an hour of gym and then two hours of rugby and then they go home to a supper of starch, so it doesn't assist their growth. We have great talent and flair, but to be successful, you've got to be ranked in the top 20 schools every year. If we had nutritional support for our boys, we could do that.'

No funds also means no touring, which means they miss out on competitive rugby. They don't get to pit themselves against stronger teams, with the concomitant gains in confidence and skill, and a sense of community.

The collapse of their provincial union, Border, had hit schools and clubs in the area hard, said Grant. They now get no institutional support at all.

I ask about Steyn Swart's academy (about which more later) and they say that it really hasn't taken off. The boys' only real hope is to get noticed by the Bulls or the Sharks and land a contract with them. That is every boy's dream, but only one or two a year are chosen.

'We try to get basic supplements for the boys,' they said. This means tapping the few old boys still interested, so it is an uphill task, which is massively frustrating for them. What they would really like to do is to get all their promising players into the hostel because there they are fed a balanced diet, but that means an additional R14 000 each a year. The boys love the hostel because they are with their mates and there is none of the hustling for taxi money to get to school and back for practice and matches.

I am moved by the dedication of these guys, Vince and Grant. Against all the odds, they keep at it. 'We love these kids,' says Vince. 'You couldn't ask for a better bunch of boys. They are so polite, so humble, so hard-working.'

Their reach extends beyond Dale: they run a Border zonal Under 15s day, which means they scout all the local village schools as well. 'To get those boys to Dale, we would have to raise at least R28 000 each a year for fees and boarding because we would be taking them on wholesale. They have nothing but talent. There is absolutely no money for uniforms or books or transport, never mind fees. We give them lifts when we can and we drop them off at a tin shack. The kids walk eight kilometres to get water.'

A couple of years before, I had travelled to East London to see the Border Rugby Union. I interviewed one chap whose first words to me were: 'We've got a lot of talent in this province, you know. Unfortunately, it's mostly non-white.'

I remember thinking at the time: 'This racist pygmy is supposed to be developing rugby in this province!'

I've no doubt the black Border Rugby Union officials were equally small-minded, otherwise it wouldn't be such a mess, but now that this pathetic excuse for a provincial union has finally collapsed, why is no one else stepping into the breach? There is so much talk about developing the black talent that everyone knows is abundant in the Eastern Cape and they can't even get it together to make sure these boys get enough to eat! All those crucial, elusive elements are in place at Dale: talent, passion, infrastructure. All they need is food, which takes a bit of organisation, perhaps corporate sponsorship or development funding. So simple and so fundamental.

All the time I was at Dale, I felt mounting fury at the waste of it all, because the contrast with the promise was so stark.

21 August 2010 marks Dale's last match of the year and it's the big one: against their historic rival, Queens College from Queenstown. Queens beat Dale in the first game of the season. Now it's payback time. All the boys from each school are massed on two adjacent stands: the red-and-black of Dale on the left and the yellow-and-black of Queens on the other. It's a day-long derby, starting with the Under 14s, but it is only in the afternoon, when the first teams square up, that the crowds start to form. There is the usual parade of nubile young female flesh, mostly from the neighbouring girls' high school. Two hundred or so parents mass on the touchlines and in the visitors' stands. At the clubhouse, near the entrance to the fields, the pub does steady business.

A tractor appears from in between the Dale and Queen's stands. Behind it is a trailer with a full drum set and a couple of black boys in top hats and tails. The tractor does a lap around the field, to the accompaniment of an impressive and progressively louder drumbeat. The boys alight from the tractor and I see that one is wearing a little yellow velvet skull cap with black tassels. He wears dark glasses and twiddles a black cane. In his long black gown, he looks ever so camp. Behind him emerges the other boy, similarly dressed, but in the Dale red and black. The guy in yellow stalks up to the Queens' stand, where he is greeted with delight. Twirling his cane to great theatrical effect, he has the boys on their feet and belting out the school song which, from what I can make out, is mostly Latin and English. Queen's, like Dale, is mostly black.

The Dale cheerleader does a similar number with his lads, only with the help of the drums, now offloaded at the foot of their stands. The Under 15s advance on the stand and perform a pretty impressive haka to wild applause from the massed ranks of their classmates. Then the game begins.

Both sides sing throughout the game – beautiful songs, increasingly in isiXhosa. Boys get down from the stands and dance around the drums. A bevy of pretty girls gathers a few metres away. Pretending not to look at the boys gyrating around the drums, the girls start a rival dance-off. A few of the braver boys approach the girls on the edge of the group, but then Dale scores a try and they rush back, all on their feet, mad with delight.

At full-time, Dale has won 21–8 and everyone swarms onto the field while the drummer performs a final triumphant lap around the field.

The hero of the hour is the captain, Andile Jho, otherwise known as Ace. This is his last game for Dale. In January, he starts his career as a professional rugby player with the Bulls. Excited as he is, there is also a sense of loss. Richer schools have tried to poach him over the years but he stayed loyal to Dale because it is like family to him. He's been at Dale since he was seven years old and has been taught by the same coach throughout – Grant Griffith, who has moved up from the junior to the senior school with him. Grant was the only non-Xhosa that Ace invited to share that intimate rite of passage, his initiation ceremony.

Ace tells me that although the songs sung at the beginning of the game are traditional school songs, they switch to isiXhosa as the game progresses. They have this tradition, he says, that when hostel guys go home, they tap the elders for ancient war songs and apartheid-era struggle songs. When they return to school, they teach them to the other boys, and have thus built up a repertoire. Particularly after half-time, once the drums start, the songs get increasingly intense and they can feel this on the field and it spurs them on. I'm fascinated by this – that rugby can play this subtle role in reviving and enriching culture – and think again about how we lucky we are in this country to have this wealth of history and culture: and how much more we could do with it.

Ace is looking forward to the Bulls because, he says, it's a good place for a player to develop. 'They are like a family and, at Dale, that is what I am used to.'

He says the Bulls have arranged for him to study business management. He knows it will be very hard work, but says: 'Life is about working hard, so if I put all of myself into it and work very hard, I will succeed. I really want to make it in rugby. I want to be a Springbok.'

His hero, he says, is Mils Muliaina, the captain of the Chiefs, the Kiwi Super Rugby team, 'because he plays the same position as I do and has the same build'. I wonder if it's also because he is of a similar colour. It must make aspiration easier if you can see yourself in your hero.

Then I let him go, because all his mates and a particularly pretty girl are waiting for him. As I leave, I see Vince and his girlfriend coming towards me, carrying Spar bags bursting with fresh meat. His boys want a celebratory braai and he is going to make sure they get one, even if it means paying for it himself.

TWO

I'm going to take you back a bit now, to much earlier in my journey through South African rugby. I'm at Loftus Versveld, home of the Bulls. It's 2008 and a glorious Highveld winter's morning: the sun is intense enough to warm your bones but not hot enough to make you sweat. On the field before me, all 124 kilograms of Bakkies Botha is being hoist into the air to catch the ball hurled at him in the line-out. Suspended in mid-air, Bakkies appears weightless, his body open, his arms outstretched. Seen in isolation like this, on the still, empty field, the movement has a peculiar grace, like a ballerina being held aloft by her partner, all apparent effortlessness. They do this again and again: stocky hooker Derek Kuun standing with the ball held above his head, listening intently to the arcane calls before hurling it decisively toward the front or the back. At the other end of the field, Bryan Habana and Akona Ndungane, dreads flying, are passing the ball along the backline. Again, there is this appearance of seamlessness; of the ball as a hot thing that must leave the hands before barely touching them; passed along to the next man and then the next in one fluid, flowing movement. I think to myself: what a glorious way to spend a winter's morning, basking in the sun, with a front-row seat at such a performance. Superb young sportsmen in their prime, all tightly honed speed and strength. There is a relaxed air to these training sessions that you don't see in matches: a sense of camaraderie and fun. The Currie Cup is soon to begin, and then things will get serious.

As must I. A short walk away, on the B training field, the next generation of Blue Bulls hopefuls are going through the same manoeuvres, albeit at a slightly reduced pace. These are the Under 19s, the Bulls' newest full-time recruits.

A young black guy is making a bunch of them practise tackling: 'Drop to your knee. Keep your head straight. Aim your head at his chest. Aim your front leg between his legs. Grab his right thigh between both your hands and tip him over. Thaaat's it!'

I ask one of the boys to direct me to Paul Anthony, and he points to a smallish, erect figure in blue with a whistle around his neck, which he frequently lifts to his mouth for a piercing blast.

I'd already heard a lot about Paul Anthony: that he was a brilliant fly half in his day, only just pipped to the post by his then Northern Transvaal contemporary, Naas Botha. That he was one of the best schools coaches in the country, serving as English teacher and rugby coach at Pretoria Boys' High for 16 years before being lured across the road by the Bulls to nurture their emerging talent.

It seems to me that to get a good insight into the state of South African rugby after the World Cup win of 2007, it would make sense to follow two teams in particular, Western Province and the Blue Bulls. One inland, one coastal; each anchored in a strong and very different culture; each at the top of their game.

Western Province, I imagine, will be easy because they come from a similar culture to my own: liberal, eclectic, mostly English-speaking. The Bulls I view with some trepidation: I assume sexism, racism, general boorishness. I remember asking a Cape-based rugby journalist only partly in jest how he thought I should present myself: would the girly, fluttery approach work best or should I go for the androgynous professional look? He thought the former. 'Wear pink,' he said. 'They'll understand that.'

So here I am, all togged out in my pinkest dress, waiting for Paul to take a break so I can introduce myself. When he does, he is charming.

He leads me across to Trademarx, the café near the

main training field where the first team is also packing up, sauntering in ones and two across to the gym beside Trademarx. Over a cappuccino, I learn that Paul was born and bred in Pretoria, and is deeply rooted in its rugby culture. Now 50, he still has the muscular physique of a player and the perpetual tan of his Lebanese heritage. He is warm, intelligent and entertaining. He is also highly knowledgeable and generous with that knowledge. He confirms what I have already heard from John Dobson. Schoolboy rugby is the bedrock upon which South African rugby rests.

'Overseas, it comes from clubs. Here the support is so fanatical and the sport so competitive at school that the boys' careers are launched there. There is huge competition for talented players because there is a perception, particularly among the big boys' schools, that a school is only as good as its first team.

'At the end of the day, a school is seen as being successful if its rugby teams are doing well. It's crazy. If you say a school is going downhill, it will be because the rugby team isn't performing, not because of their academic record.

'Some schools grant scholarships. They will deny it, but they offer a package: free schooling, boarding, uniform and books. They want to recruit the best and they want to bring them into the school at a young age. Unfortunately the parents are very into it because of the prestige, so you can have a multi-millionaire playing two schools off against each other.

'You have these great rugby schools like Grey College in Bloemfontein and Grey High in Port Elizabeth, or Afrikaanse Hoër Seunskool and Pretoria Boys' High across the road. Pretoria Boys' High – my old school – has produced two Springbok captains: John Smit and Chiliboy Ralepelle, who was the first black captain of a South African team, the Springbok Under 21s.

'After school, first prize for a player is to be recruited by one of the big unions – the Bulls, Western Province, the Lions, the Sharks. Not many players make it through, however.

'Given the budgets, a big union can realistically contract 15 players a year. If you offer a boy a full contract, you have to give him full board and lodging and, depending on the status of the player, you also have to give him pocket money which can be anything from R24 000 to R100 000 a year. This would apply to someone who makes it to South Africa's Under 21 team for example. So, even if you are only contracting 15 players, that could be a budget of almost a million – and you contract him for two years.'

He is interrupted by the persistent ringing of his phone. 'Sorry, babes, do you mind if I take this?' Being with Paul, I was soon to find, involved incessant interruptions. This call was from a journalist, quickly but politely dispatched.

Ten minutes later his wife, Laura, arrives, thinking they were to share their morning tea break but resigned and gracious when she discovers me there. 'She hates rugby!' says Paul with a laugh. Laura nods. A slim, blonde woman in her forties, Laura teaches English at Pretoria Girls' High. Their three children are at school at Girls' High and Boys' High.

Paul, I discover, has another life, as a rock 'n' roll singer and guitarist. He has a weekly gig – which happens to fall on that very evening – at a local café called Rhapsodies, and he is trying to persuade Laura to come along.

'Bring a friend,' he urges. 'I'll buy you both a fillet!' She looks sceptical. I suspect that Laura has spent much of her life as a spectator to Paul's passions. The lot of the rugby wife.

Barely has she left to return to school when Paul's phone rings again. It's Chiliboy Ralepelle, whom Paul has mentored since Chili's school days at Pretoria Boys' High. Chiliboy is also invited to Rhapsodies. He too is offered a free fillet. 'Fudge's [Mabeta] dad is coming. He's bringing a birthday party group of 20!'

Chiliboy has other things on his mind, however. I overhear snatches of the conversation from Paul's end. 'Good man. You must always be open.'

Afterwards, he explains: 'He's very upset, and he's very outspoken, hey. They told him he's playing and now he's not playing. He's been off with an injury. The coach said he would play off the bench on Saturday and he was so excited, now he's been told he won't play. There is a players' committee and they say he must practise first, which is fair enough, but unfortunately the coach had told him he would play. He's very upset. If you tell him something, he expects you to honour it. He told the coach he's upset with him. He's very straightforward and that's what I like about him.

'As a player, you've got to look after yourself. No one will look after you, I can tell you. You get bashed around. Chili is only 21; 22 in September. They have to grow up quickly, but at the same time they are still kids, so they need a mentor: it should be a father, but if you don't have a father, you need someone you can really trust to look out for you.

'In this game, you can't trust anybody. It's a hard, hard game. Agents put their interests first – to make money. To them, the player is a commodity. They don't have time to be a mentor. You can't talk to them about your problems with your girlfriend or why you aren't making a team.'

Paul's other famous protégé is John Smit. He spotted the talent in the chubby schoolboy soon after Smit arrived at Pretoria Boys' High from his Polokwane junior school. It was Paul upon whom Smit conferred the honour of handing out the jerseys before the Springbok captain's emotional 100th cap at the 2010 Tri-Nations test against the All Blacks in Soweto.

In the winter of 2008, it was Chiliboy who was still young and needy. Chiliboy and his struggles were to be a constant theme of my time with Paul. He seemed to be forever on the phone to the young black hooker, offering advice and encouragement, more like an engaged father than a coach.

But back to schools rugby. Paul says he strongly disapproves of players being 'purchased' after Grade 10 because of the effect it has on the host school's ecosystem. 'Some English and Afrikaans schools purchase quite a few players who get injected into their system – sometimes even in matric – because of their rugby ability. What happens then is that you have player X who has played for the school for four years. In Grade 11, his ambition is to play for the first team. That's a big thing for a youngster – to get his first team colours. So he gets to matric and suddenly they have imported another guy and he has lost his position. How do you expect that boy – or his parent – to react positively to that?

'I believe that purchased players should come earlier – up to Grade 10 is fair. To purchase players after that is insanity. If I were a kid or a parent who had been loyal to the school and given everything and suddenly find myself replaced, I would be devastated. A lot of schools do that, and also bring post-matrics in – just for rugby. It shows how powerful rugby is. It has a huge influence on the marketing of the school. It's massive. Massive.'

It's another lovely day on the Highveld, or, more precisely, on the B training field at Loftus. It's also a fairly tense one. The first game of the Currie Cup – that crucial domestic tournament for the blooding of young talent – is that Saturday. Paul needs to cut the current squad down to 22. He is going to have to tell eight of his charges that they won't make it, and it pains him to do so.

Later, over a cappuccino at Trademarx with him and

Steve Plummer, the Under 19s conditioning coach, Paul explains: 'It depends on how well you contract, but if you are laying out money on 15 guys, you want them to make it. These guys are really really good. We see them as the future Super 14 players, the future Victor Matfields. Yet you are looking at an intake of 15 guys each year with a two-year contract. So, over two years, you've got thirty guys in the squad, and you can also draw in others – players who are at the university over the road, for example – and you bring them into your squad. That would be the same at all the unions.

'For the Currie Cup, in particular, you need a big pool of players. It's so short and intense – eight games on the trot – that if you have injuries, you can find yourself short of quality players.

'That's why the Currie Cup is so aggressive and such a tough competition. These schoolboys are brought in and they are made pros immediately, and they are hoping to make it a career. We encourage them to study – we're doing that heavily now – and we give them life skills, that type of thing. We're trying to get away from that stereotype of "the stupid guy plays rugby". The more intelligent a guy is, the better a rugby player he is, without a doubt. You've got to be able to think on your feet. You've got to question. You've got to be able to balance your life. You've got to understand that your career might end at any time because of injury or because you just didn't make the cut. You have to understand there is more to life. The average rugby player is finished playing rugby at 28 to 30, and you are still a young man at 30. You might go and play in France for two years but then you are cannon fodder for the rest of your life. Any intelligent boy should realise that that is how it will go.

'If you go back to schools: what often happens is that a lot of boys who are good sportsmen also excel academically.

They realise there is more to sport than training and eating supplements. On the other hand we also have boys from very disadvantaged backgrounds, and all they have is rugby. We've got to manage them very carefully because they've got ten years to set up the next fifty. Unfortunately a lot of those boys who come in have been badly managed. They're illiterate. They suffer from dyslexia and that type of thing. They can be exploited. I'm talking about top players.

'In Chili's case, I mentor him. His lawyer does his legal transactions.

'We also have to teach the players that you can be everything today and be gone tomorrow. At the Bulls we therefore strongly emphasise that players must study, even if it's limited study, but they must get into the groove. Some of the Under 19s take a year off and only then start to study. They call it a sort of army year – the year after they've settled in. That's fine. They're just 20.'

I know that the Bulls are particularly good at development. It begins with school-level recruitment, but the crucial next stage is their first year of professional rugby in the Under 19 team. It occurs to me that it would be interesting to follow some of them over an extended period to see who makes it through to the senior team and who falls by the wayside – and why. I know that one of the Bulls' biggest battles is to recruit and retain quality players of colour, even though such recruitment brings with it great challenges in regard to integration. Most of these players of colour are from the Eastern Cape. Andile Jho – still at Dale College and as yet undiscovered by the Bulls – is a good example.

Over the next couple of years, I will spend many hours at Loftus, trying to understand their struggle to transform while at the same time trying to retain a world-beating excellence. It has turned out to be a fascinating journey, and one that continually confounds my expectations.

I ask Paul if I can talk to his charges and, helpful as ever, he sends them in batches to the table at Trademarx where I have set up an unofficial office. Face to face, they are surprisingly shy and very respectful. The Afrikaans boys call me 'Tannie', which I find a bit disconcerting, evoking as it does childhood images of large, motherly ladies in flowing floral flocks. I resolve to ditch the pink, but later realise it's less to do with me and more to do with how these boys are trained.

It's a hierarchy thing: superior age and status require a title. Paul is only ever Coach Paul or 'Coachie'. Even Dave Mukari, the assistant coach, and Steve Plummer, the conditioning coach, who are not much older than the boys, are 'Coach Steve' and 'Coach Dave'.

The first boy I talk to is Simphiwe Mtimkulu, an inside centre. I introduce myself as Liz. He says: 'Pleased to meet you, Ma'am.' Simphiwe tells me he is from a township outside Knysna where his dad, now dead, had a spaza and taxi business. Simphiwe was at Knysna High School when he was spotted by the Bulls at an Under 16 Grant Khomo Week. They arranged a scholarship for him to attend the Afrikaanse Hoër Seunskool aka Affies. It's a superb rugby school, but a massive culture shift for this Xhosa lad from the Cape. 'Everything was in Afrikaans. It was tough.' So, clearly, was he, and he survived the transition and is now enjoying the rewards.

Next up is dark-haired wing, Gerhard van der Heever, another Affies star, and very soon to shine at the Bulls too. Again I say hello, I'm Liz, and explain a bit about my book. He says: 'Yes, Tannie.' Gerhard also went to Affies but, for him, it was home from home. He is from the Afrikaans professional middle classes – his dad a medical specialist, his mom a teacher. Competitive rugby is in his DNA: his grandfather played for Natal; his dad made Free State Craven Week. Gerhard has been contracted to the Bulls since Grade 11.

The leader of the group, off the field as well as on, is hooker and captain, Zane Botha. A stocky, blond boy with a pleasant open face, he tells me that, at the beginning of the year, he took out disability cover and started savings and retirement plans, which seemed astonishingly responsible for a 19-year-old. All the others said they planned to do the same, but hadn't quite got round to it. Zane and Tom Seabela, a Pretoria Boys' High old boy whose dad was a manager at BMW, plan to study law together next year.

When Zane tells me his history, his caution makes more sense. He is steeped in rugby but he has suffered more than his fair share of injury, possibly because of the position he plays. His dad played for the University of the Free State and province before joining the police. He now sells agricultural equipment in Zambia. Zane started playing rugby at kindergarten and was playing first team for Grey College Bloemfontein from Grade 11, but was injured mid-year. The following year, he tore a ligament in his foot and was flat on his back for two months. He missed Craven Week through injury but made the St Johns Easter Festival and was picked up by the Bulls there.

These boys live and breathe Bulls. They stay in a hostel just off the training field called 'the Bros' – all expenses paid – and they get between R1 000 and R5 000 a month pocket money. There is no curfew: the only rule is that no girls are allowed. The training regime is so tough and the competition so intense, however, that anyone who parties too hard will fall through the cracks.

Only last week, two boys were sent home. This was 'very sad', they tell me, because, living as intimately as they do, they had become close.

The variety of home languages doesn't seem to be an issue: amaXhosa boys speak to each other in isiXhosa; the Afrikaans boys in Afrikaans. English is the common language, even although it is a first language for none of them.

A few of the black boys tell me they are learning Afrikaans. None of the Afrikaans boys are learning black languages. One boy speaks only Afrikaans, so the black kids speak to him in English and he replies in Afrikaans. They seem to understand each other perfectly well, this multi-lingual, multi-cultural bunch. I guess where it counts, there is but one language.

The coaches speak to them in alternate bursts of English and Afrikaans, translating one into the other where necessary.

Some weeks later, I made it to Rhapsodies and I discovered a different side to Paul. I arrived after supper, found a seat at the bar and looked around for familiar faces, but it appeared that neither Laura nor any of the Bulls had succumbed to the lure of the free fillet. I thought Paul was extremely good: his singing was full of strength and passion, lyrical and evocative. The man has soul and imagination as well as a rugby brain. No wonder the boys warm to him. For the first hour or so, I am on my own with my glass of white wine, and then another two glasses mysteriously appear alongside it. The waiter points with some amusement at a couple of moustachioed gentlemen waving hopefully from the other side of the restaurant. Rhapsody, it seems, is a bit of a pick-up joint. Fortunately, Steve Plummer appears at that point and we proceed to have a pleasantly mellow evening. Paul doesn't leave the stage till late, when he and Steve, both of them stone-cold sober and models of exemplary Bulls behaviour, walk me to my car.

I asked Paul over one of our many cappuccinos at the Trademarx (Steve has told him one a day is good for speeding up metabolism) whether he missed his days as school coach. One thing he definitely did not miss, he said, was the parents.

'Parents are shockers,' he says. 'A lot of parents want their sons to succeed where maybe they didn't. Their son is their trophy, and that is a problem.'

Not only do they push their own sons relentlessly, they also attempt to bully coaches and undermine rival players.

'The best way is to keep them away from the fields. Stick them in the grandstands. I went to Jeppe the other day, and there parents used to be on the touchline. Now they have moved them so that they can't get to each other and can't influence the boys. Their comments go up in the air.

'At Pretoria Boys' High, we lost one massive game because my fly half was being abused from the field. I only found out why he had done so badly two years later when he opened up to me, and he told me who the parent was. If I'd known at the time, I would have gone and flattened the guy.

'Some parents, because their son is not in the first team, will go out of their way to build up a little group of agenda-seekers against a certain player or against a certain coach. It's incredibly sad.'

It is crucial that coaches stand up to parents, he says. 'Too many coaches fall into that trap. Parents used to hound me for a drink after a game. I never went. I never spoke to any parents after a game because I'm not prepared to discuss their boys with them. Parents should never have a say.'

To his credit, Paul plays by his own rules. His son now plays rugby for Pretoria Boys' High. 'I know my son is playing in the wrong position but I would never tell his coach that. It's his decision and that is the bottom line. A coach has his ideas and you must allow him that freedom of thought.'

One parent tried to bribe him to put his son in the first team. 'He phoned me regularly, begging me to give his son a shot in the team. He hinted that he would "give me something". I said to him: "Excuse me. The fact that I am talking to you is a miracle. Your son knows where he stands with me and it's got nothing to do with you. It's between me and the player."'

The boys have just conceded defeat to the Sharks and Paul is angry with them. One of the lowest points in the game was when the eighth man socked a Sharks player in front of the ref and was yellow-carded. Without their eighth man in the last ten minutes of the game, the scrum fell apart.

Paul writes on the whiteboard:

DISCIPLINE! TEAM SPIRIT! TEAM UNITY!

'Discipline is everything on and off the field. If two guys oversleep, I won't only blame them, I will blame all of you. If a team isn't united in everything, it goes under. I don't want players acting like prima donnas.'

Paul breaks off here to explain what a prima donna is. He alternates between English and Afrikaans. The boys look on dumbly, clearly chastened.

Later he tells me that he had assumed the boy's lapse had to do with girlfriend troubles, but this turned out not to be the case. It was an emotional issue off the field that had affected him. This time, a girl wasn't to blame.

I ask the boys about girlfriends. Zane is the babe magnet, the boys tell me. He is now unattached, having recently broken up with his girlfriend in Bloemfontein because he didn't want a long-distance relationship. All the others claimed not to be in relationships, or if they were, the girl was safely tucked away in a remote part of the country.

It all feels quite monastic, a celibate, clean-living, all-male existence; all earthly pleasures sublimated for the higher purpose of rugby. One would have thought that, with all the testosterone around, combined with the pulling power any successful rugby player commands, these guys would have girls queuing up, and that they would have been taking full advantage. Not so.

'They are too young to have girlfriends,' Paul explained when I tackled him on the subject. 'They are only 19.'

Was this just a subtle attempt to get them to channel their sexual and emotional energy into their rugby? I asked. No, said Paul. It is, as ever, about focus. 'Girls will distract them and make them unhappy. They shouldn't be "vas" (going steady) with a girl at that age. They have to choose between relationships and a career.'

The boys showed me round 'The Bros', a neat single-storey building a few metres from the training fields. It has a large lounge with a TV set and a kitchen which lead into a long corridor, off which are small, bare rooms, each with two beds.

Is there any racial tension? I ask. All assure me vehemently there isn't.

'We are a band of brothers,' says Tom, and I believe him. 'These are the guys we struggle with and practise with.' They love rugby because it is a team sport. 'I used to do athletics but it is too individualistic,' adds Tom.

The appeal of rugby is its physicality. Zane says: 'It is one on one. If you scrum, you scrum against one oke. You against him.'

They all share a common burning goal: to play for the Blue Bulls first team and, ultimately, to be a Springbok. They are very aware of how competitive it is and are prepared to make the necessary sacrifices. 'We must train hard. We must focus.' They tell me that, at most, they drink a cider a month. 'We are so fit that we get drunk on any more than that,' said Zane. None of them smokes.

Cornell Hess, a lock from Oudtshoorn High School, who was recruited at the Under 16 Grant Khomo Week and given a scholarship to Affies, says Pierre Spies is his role model. The others nod their heads in enthusiastic agreement. 'He is a Christian. He is not shy to tell everyone he believes. He is playing for Jesus, not for money. If God takes rugby away, he will understand.'

Oswin Mentoos says his role model is Hilton Lobberts. 'He could have been a gangster. Instead he has made something of his life.' Oswin, a flank, was plucked from Kylemoor High School in Stellenbosch at the age of 17 after being spotted at the Under 16 Grant Khomo Week. The Bulls organised a scholarship to Menlyn Park. 'When I first came here, I cried because I was so homesick,' he confessed.

Once a week, a Bible meeting is held at the Bros. I asked if I could attend and they said: yes, of course. It was held in the sitting room and six or seven boys, black and white, sat in a circle on easy chairs and sofas. It was led by a thirtyish white guy called Peter who explained how he had been through a major crisis and, coming out of it, had been reborn as a Christian. As he spoke, the boys looked into their Bibles without speaking. Steve was there, and was marginally more vocal.

I have to say that I found just about everything that was said at this Bros Bible study incomprehensible. I experienced it as a series of non-sequiturs; exhortations without backing. I thought the boys staring resolutely into their Bibles did so because they were afraid their lack of comprehension might be revealed were they to engage. They weren't the only ones at sea. At one point, Peter unexpectedly addressed a question to me. 'What do you think, Liz?' Given that I had absolutely no idea of what he had been talking about, I fumbled my way to an answer, hoping I wouldn't be thrown out of class for not paying attention. It brought back all too strongly the claustrophobic catechism classes of my Catholic childhood – not an experience I particularly wanted to repeat.

Across from the training field is another academy, which

houses the also-rans. These are the boys who pay to come to the Bulls. In 2008, it cost around R35 000 a year for classes, coaching, board and lodging.

'The boys at the academy are the pretenders to the throne,' explains Paul. 'They want to get into the elite group. That's the hope those boys have.

'Realistically, out of fifty boys in the academy, one or two might make it. To get there, they've got to knock out a contracted player. They might study as well, but their big desire is to play professional rugby and this is their gap year to make it.'

The guys here at the Bros are the real thing, however. They are the boys with every chance of making it over to the A field, where the big boys play.

THREE

Paul told me the Under 18 Craven Week is an important recruiting ground. The next one is in East London, and I go along in the hope that I can hang around with him and see how it works at first hand.

He explains to me that, of the 400-odd boys chosen to play, around 70 will be offered professional contracts. Among them are the Springboks of the future, and the weight of it is evident in the line-up of rugby heavies who have made their way here. National coach Peter de Villiers; André Watson, head of referees; Eric Sauls, Under 21s national coach; and Ian McIntosh, national selector. Every major union has taken a box, where their scouts lurk, checking out the talent.

SuperSport TV is here, its cameramen perched on specially constructed scaffolding, lending glamour and an increased sense of import to the occasion. This reinforces the notion that the events unfolding on this tatty, windblown field may also go way beyond it.

Pubescent girls, both black and white, minimally dressed despite the cold, saunter up and down the edge of the field. Little boys throw balls to each other.

There are squads of parents who have followed their sons and are staying in hotels and B&Bs in East London and up and down its beautiful adjacent coastline. During the day they can be found in packs in the stands or in the cave of a bar with its shabby chairs, blaring TV and choking air which is constantly recharged by the ubiquitous cigarette smokers.

Mostly I hang out with Paul at the Blue Bulls box. Ian Schwartz, the Bulls' high-performance manager, is also there, as is a scout from Tukkies. Ian is accompanied by his wife, Alma, because their son is playing – for the Bulls, of course. Ian says they have a database, gradually accrued, of all available schoolboy talent and they have already signed 15 new players to bring into their system for next year. There is still money for more, however, and the point of coming to Craven Week is to see if there is anyone they have missed. 'We are looking for the three or four players we still need.'

The players who are to join their Under 19s the following year are already at Pretoria Boys' High School, Affies, Grey Bloem, St Albans, Menlo Park and Middelburg Hoërskool, in many cases having been transferred by the Bulls on full scholarships to these centres of rugby excellence from lesser schools.

The Bulls box is not large. There is just enough room for four or five bar stools pressed up against the window. On the opposite side is a basin and a bar fridge filled with bottled water, Coke and fruit juices. There is a kettle and an array of teas and jars of coffee. A succession of hefty men pop in for visits: each is introduced to me as some of sort of historic rugby great. None rings any bells. Each is offered tea, coffee, a cool drink. The warm hospitality is not unexpected, but what surprises me in this very masculine space is how house-proud the Bulls boys are. Mugs and spoons are washed straight after use. Not a drop remains on the pristine surfaces, which are constantly wiped down.

When the rain stops, we sit in the seats below the box, watching game after game. After a while, it becomes hypnotic. As the final hooter brings each match to an end, the competing teams shake hands with each other and then form a tunnel and clap in the next two teams. There is something about this elaborate courtesy, interspersed with the hand-to-hand combat in between, that is hugely compelling. As close to the field as we are, one can hear the boys calling to each other, and the thwack of flesh on flesh as they collide. Every so often a boy is downed. Sometimes they don't get up. Medics rush on with stretchers; a neck brace, huge and stiff as a cage, is fixed to the boy's head and he is carried off to one of the first aid tents at either end of the field. I hold my breath; can't relax until a report comes back – is this another catastrophic, life-altering injury? No one else seems particularly bothered. I would expect the game to stop, parents to get up and rush to the first aid tent, the outcome announced over the public address system. But no. The game goes on.

Most of these boys are in Grade 11 or matric. They weigh anything up to 120 kilograms, but they still have the fresh, unformed, slightly vulnerable look of adolescence. There are hugely varying levels of skill but what they all share is hope: that they will catch the eye of a scout with money in his pocket.

It's not a perfect system. Brilliant though many of these boys are, there are others just as talented who have fallen through the cracks. 'I think there are massive numbers of boys who are being lost,' says Paul. 'Most of the players brought into the professional system are scouted at the major festivals, but you can only bring 26 players each. How many are being left behind? François Hougaard, for instance: he's played Super 14 but he didn't make either a Craven Week side or an Academy Week side. It's not Western Province's fault. They select their Craven Week side from Paul Roos, Paarl Gim, Paarl Boys' High, Boland Landbou, Wynberg Boys' High, Bishops, SACS, Rondebosch. You pick 35 to 45 guys out of all these schools and the rest get lost to Craven Week and Academy Week. That's not even counting the coloured schools.'

One of The Chosen, a 17-year-old who has already won his place among the coveted ranks of the Blue Bulls elite squad, is Abednego Mamushi. He comes and sits with us in the Bulls box for a while and I get a chance to glean his history. It's an interesting one. He comes from a township near Secunda called Emhalenhle. Only soccer was played there and although he loved that game, he didn't see much of a future for himself in it because the competition was so intense. Rugby wasn't nearly as popular and he got a place in the Under 13 team attached to the township youth club. Sasol is the big employer in the region, and it was no coincidence that they sponsored the club. At the age of 13 he was spotted by a scout from Hoërskool Middelburg and offered a bursary. At first it was very hard, he says. He missed his family badly. His home language is Southern Sotho and although he was taught in one of only three English classes at the school, most of the kids spoke Afrikaans. However, his prowess on the rugby field helped to get him accepted and he got used to it.

Abednego was also wooed by the Sharks, who invited him to an Under 17 camp, but he decided on the Bulls 'because it is much nearer to home and I am very close to my family'. A wing, he also prefers the type of game they play, as it is 'more attacking and less defending'. His manner is wary, but confident. He comes across as quite self-possessed. The Bulls will provide food, accommodation and training and they have organised a bursary for him from Tukkies. He plans to study engineering. 'I know I will have to work hard,' he says, 'and I will have to study in between training, but I will just do it over an extended period.'

I thought if anyone could do it, he could. These kids have to grow up quickly; wrested from their home environments and under intense pressure to perform.

While I am talking to him, another pair of visitors comes into the box. An Afrikaans couple, heavyset. They want to meet Paul because their son, a tighthead prop at Middelburg Tech, is coming to study at Pretoria University and they are hoping he will find a place with the Blue Bulls. He is 1,92 metres tall and weighs 120 kilograms.

Paul is affable and welcoming. They leave smiling.

He explains that a tighthead prop has rarity value: you've got to have the right frame. It is a very technical position which anchors the scrum. It was John Smit's position.

'The kid is coming to Tukkies anyway, so they are doing me a favour. He can work with us, use our medical and physio facilities. He can train as if he is in the elite squad, but we won't contract him. We won't give him any money – yet.'

He is called down to the bar to meet another set of parents and I go with him, hang around while he talks to them. They look like every other parent here: overweight with badly cut hair and bulky, unflattering clothes. Many have cigarettes dangling from their mouths and a beer in one hand, even though it is still mid-morning. They look, in short, the very antithesis of their sleek, toned sons.

I remark on this to Paul and he responds: 'The sad thing is that these boys will look exactly like their parents when they are their age.'

Walking around with him is like being with a film star. He is constantly and respectfully accosted by hopeful parents. He is always extremely polite, switching effortlessly into Afrikaans as this is usually the language required. As soon as they are out of hearing, though, his real feelings emerge. 'I hate these flipping parents. This is just prostitution – parents pimping their young sons.'

Later, darkly, at another stolid back weaving unsteadily away from us: 'He says he is a farmer, but what sort of farmer is he? He probably sits on a plot somewhere and drinks his brandy and Coke.'

Much of his job is about managing expectations: of the boys, of their parents. The latter are by far the biggest headache. For some of the parents, he says, it is about money. They think their sons can earn big money which, presumably, can then be channelled back to the parents.

Anyway, there is an unspoken code of ethics among the recruiters at Craven Week. Boys should not be approached during the week itself. Any interested union should merely give their card to the parent, or the teacher who is mentoring the boy, and then contact them after a week or so and fly them up to the union concerned and pitch their sell and then let them decide in their own time.

The unions, of course, are also watching each other, afraid a rival will seize a future Springbok from under their nose. Furthermore the boys – or their parents – play the unions off against each other. All the hottest players here will have been wooed by more than one union.

Another regular visitor is the legendary Heyneke Meyer. Knowing about the seminal work he had done with the Bulls, I ask if we can chat. He readily agrees and we settle down in the stands late one afternoon. A chilly wind is blowing and the sky is fast blackening. The games are over for the day and the emptied fields look forlorn. I find Meyer edgy and restless. He is good-looking; taut and lean with well-cut grey hair, but he comes across as brittle, unlike most rugby men I have met. Possibly this is just a reflection of his current rootlessness.

'When I started at the Bulls, there was a bad culture,' he tells me. 'There was no work ethic. They had bad habits. It was a team that was at the bottom. We lost all our games in the first year, but I had the bigger picture in mind.

'I started with a young team and instilled a work ethic. I talked about life, not about rugby. I wanted to instil a specific culture: to respect each other and to play for each other, to be proud of what you do. The culture I put in is that you pick the person ahead of the player. You look for unselfishness: the team is bigger than the player. I pick guys who have character and can perform under pressure; persons of character and dignity. Keep them humble. It is a privilege to play rugby, not a right. I'm always straight and honest. I don't care if they like me. I want them to respect me.

'I've nurtured most of the current team since they were eighteen or nineteen. I think selection is my strength. I also know how to get the best out of people. The team is only an extension of the coach's personality. I know what it takes to turn a union around. It takes a lot of emotion.'

He speaks rapidly and with intensity. It feels as if he is talking about the present, rather than the past. One can understand why the past is still so alive to him. Under Meyer, the Bulls fought their way up from the bottom of the Super 12 and later Super 14 log to fourth, then third. In 2007, they won the Cup. Armed with this record, Meyer resigned from the Bulls and threw his hat into the ring for the job as Springbok coach. The national team had just won the World Cup and coach Jake White was on his way out. Meyer believed he had a very good chance of succeeding White. Incorrectly, as it turned out. Now Meyer is in the wilderness. He has recently had to give up his coaching job at the top British club, the Leicester Tigers, because his parents-in-law were seriously ill and he and his wife had to return to South Africa to care for them. Now he has a company called SportsMax, which does a bit of coaching, a bit of sports marketing, a bit of managing of individual players. He has a rugby column in the *Sunday Times*, but he is a coach without a team.

The next morning, I wander up to the Sharks' box, the only union occupying the south stand. There is a row of very fit-looking men standing in front of the long bar, about four times the size of the Bulls' cosy little box. I recognise one as an agent who pops into the Bulls box every now and again and is not particularly welcome. Pushy parents might be a nightmare, but at least their concern is not solely focused on making money out of a kid, as is an agent's. At this age, argue the unions, the boys need a mentor – a parent, a coach or a teacher – not someone whose only motive is financial gain.

Heyneke happens to be visiting and he greets me warmly. Also there is Rudolf Straueli, infamously of Kamp Staaldraad, now trying to stay below the media radar as the Sharks' high-performance manager. I've met him before and he shakes my hand but quickly passes me on to Hans Scriba, head of the Sharks Academy.

Hans leads me to a table and we settle down for a chat. How is the Sharks' foraging going? I ask. He says they are looking to contract 10 to 12 players this year, fewer than the Bulls, their chief rival.

The unions all say they have agreed on a code of honour between themselves, namely that no boys should be approached at Craven Week. 'We pick up Grade 11 guys who are outstanding, but we are honourable. We don't pull them out of their existing school at such a crucial juncture. Instead, we pay their school fees, give them bursaries. A case in point is Terror Mthembu, an eighth man. We pay his fees at Dale College, and next year he is coming to us. We buy a bit of honour and favour with the schools because we want them to keep feeding us for many years.'

The perennial robbing of the Eastern Cape's cradle of black rugby talent has given rise to a promising new initiative. The South African Rugby Legends, a league of former rugby greats who are now ploughing their skills and experience back into developing the game, have started an academy in East London. There was some drama around its birth: the Sharks had initially wanted to do it, and had secured funding for the first year from SuperSport. Rudolf Straueli had been earmarked to get it going, but the SA Legends got there first.

Hans Scriba is still a bit miffed about it. 'The Eastern Cape has the best black talent, but is managed the worst. We felt that, rather than pulling the best talent out of Border, we should keep it here. We were a bit disappointed that the SA Legends hijacked it, but the concept of setting up an academy to keep talent here is a good one. If they make it work, good for them.'

The man who is now charged with fostering – and keeping – rugby talent in the Eastern Cape is Steyn Swart, an extremely tall man whose body speaks to his long history of playing rugby. One of his ears sticks out at right angles to his head like a flag at full mast. Almost every finger is bent and buckled, jutting out at odd angles, from ancient breaks compounded, he says, by the fact that he is double-jointed. We find a seat in an empty beer tent and I ask him about his plans for the academy.

A devout Christian, Steyn sees it as a way to do good, which is why it is better the SA Legends got to run it, rather than the Sharks.

'At the end of the day, the Sharks are a private company. We are a non-profit organisation. Everything goes back into rugby. So we think that, for the region, the SA Legends is the best bet.'

Steyn has played for Eastern Province and coached its Under 19s and Under 21s.

'One of the province's assets is that we have got great schools. Queens, Selborne and Dale identify talent at a very young age and bring them into these great schools. The problem comes when they finish school. We complain that the other unions steal our players, but they steal only a few. What happens to the rest?

'Craven Week is a bit of a lottery. Whether you get to play here depends on whether your teacher likes you or doesn't, whether you are from a prominent rugby school or not. A lot of talent slips through the cracks and those are the guys we want.'

Even here at Craven Week, the playing field is not even. The boys playing in teams from the rural Eastern Province, for instance, are clearly smaller than those in the Bulls' side.

This is not an original observation: SA Rugby keeps saying it; anyone who knows anything about rugby keeps saying it, but the fact that rugby has not been able to exploit and develop the talent available in this province is absurd.

I keep thinking of something referee André Watson once told me: that South African rugby now draws on only a few million players, when it could draw on millions more. What a powerhouse it would be then! The Eastern Cape would be such an obvious place to start broadening the base of rugby.

Steyn puts the Eastern Cape mess down to politics. 'The reason the other unions are successful is that they are run by former rugby players who have only rugby at heart. They are not run by politicians.

'At the moment, Dale, Queens and Selborne poach from the local schools. Then Hilton, Kearsney and Grey Bloem come and poach from Dale, Queens and Selborne. We need to get all this talent back into a big Border team. That is why we need an academy here. Slowly but surely we will build a great team.'

Steyn spends every weekend at schools watching rugby, trying to recruit for the academy. He finds local sponsors for the kids who can't pay. SA Rugby Legends help with the funding, and their members, which include the likes of Bob Skinstad, Breyton Paulse and Robbie Fleck, come and coach at clinics.

The boys are also taught life skills, such as financial planning and public speaking, and take courses through Damelin in marketing and sports science to prepare them for life after rugby. It sounds like such a good thing that I hope it prospers.

Before the end of Craven Week, the Eastern Cape yields up another of its potential stars. It is here that Andile Jho, number 12 from Dale College, is spotted by Ian Schwartz and is shortly to enter into a contract with the Blue Bulls that will instantly see him R100 000 a year richer. Now in Grade 11, he will stay at Dale until he finishes his matric. Andile's dad is a teacher in a village school near King William's Town. He has somehow managed to find the funds to pay his son's school and boarding fees until now, but the extra cash will come in useful. In the short term at the very least, his son has a career as a professional rugby player mapped out for him. In 2011, Andile will move to Pretoria to join Paul Anthony's Under 19s. He then has a serious stab at eventually joining the Blue Bulls Super 15 team and, who knows, perhaps representing his country. But he will be lost to his home province.

Back at Loftus, I was sitting high up in the stands one afternoon, watching the Under 19s playing. It was around 16h00 and there weren't many spectators. They would start arriving in their numbers later on, when the senior team played. For now, I was the only person in my row and there was just one person in the rows behind me. I became aware of him because he was very vocal, continually shouting instructions and admonishments to the boys on the field. Then one of the black players dropped the ball and I heard him exclaim with particular viciousness, almost to himself. At first, I thought it was 'fucker!' and then, within a split second, I realised it was actually 'kaffir!' I hadn't heard the word uttered in so long – not since apartheid times – that I didn't immediately recognise it.

Up until now, I had tried to ignore the man, but now I swung round. He was middle-aged, balding, dressed in a blue wind-cheater. He looked like a salesman or an electrician. Perfectly ordinary, in other words. I was very uncomfortable now; just waiting for him to start again, and in fact I left soon afterwards.

I mentioned this incident some time later to a Bulls official. He said I should have taken a picture of the man with my cell phone and they could have put it up at the gates and denied him entry in future. This seemed to me unhelpful. Firstly, it would have put me at risk – the man was clearly deeply unpleasant. I was alone with him high up in the stands. If I had tried to take a picture of him, he might well have turned on me. Secondly, unless I had recorded his racist rants as well, it would simply have been my word against his.

Vata Ngobeni, the *Pretoria News* rugby writer, went to

Queens College, that centre of excellence in the heartland
of black rugby, the Eastern Cape. He is as passionate and
knowledgeable about the game as any of the Bulls insiders,
and close to several of their black players. As correspond-
ent for Pretoria's main English-speaking newspaper, he is
in a powerful position as the Bulls' conduit to a substantial
section of their fan base. He, too, has been the victim of a
racist attack. The perpetrator was one of the Bulls players.
'He muttered the word "houtkop". I was the only black
person within ten metres. He then shoved me as he walked
past.'

Vata went to the police and laid a charge of assault.
Eventually, the player was forced to come into the Pretoria
News offices to make a formal apology.

Vata sees black exclusion as a live and anguished issue
within rugby. He says that even though the Bulls excel in
bringing black youngsters into the system, life remains
particularly tough for them. 'No matter how good black
players are, they are still made to feel they are there only
because of the politicians. Any dissident voices get put
out to pasture. The coach talks to his guys in Afrikaans. I
understand that most of the team are Afrikaans, but in a
country like ours, one needs to be aware.'

Vata explained to me why the use of Afrikaans makes life
so difficult for black people. 'When, say, at a press conference, they speak in Afrikaans, I have to translate in a split
second from Afrikaans to English to Xhosa because I was
taught Afrikaans from English, not from Xhosa.'

His journalist colleague, Simnikiwe Xabanisa, is more
forthright. He wrote in the *Sunday Times* on 15 March
2009: '... after 17 years of "unity", one has to concede that
in rugby, nation-building has been one way traffic. It's a
place where black people and anyone who doesn't speak
Afrikaans have been made to feel like second-class citizens.
In most provinces, team talks are conducted in Afrikaans;

PAUSE ■ Liz McGregor

on-field calls are made in Afrikaans; the music is Afrikaans. I have no problem with the language but it is emerging as a tool for excluding those who don't speak it and for keeping things the same in rugby.

'The stadiums have become places where people can be as "Afrikaans" as they like which, unfortunately in some cases, has been interpreted to mean as racist as they like. What has emboldened these attitudes is the sense of protection that comes from the South African Rugby Union's lack of action over various racist incidents at the stadiums. Nothing has been done about a black photographer being attacked at Loftus last year. There wasn't a word of protest from Saru last year when the Pumas decided to play Gert van Schalkwyk, who had been convicted of a racially motivated murder. The response to the racial attack on Ziningi Shibambo, a fan attending the Australia game at Ellis Park last year, was a R10 000 reward and a feeble "No to Racism" campaign. It is unacceptable that I feel duty-bound to warn any black people who want to attend a rugby game to go in numbers in case they are attacked.'

I am reminded of a brief 2008 conversation I had with Gerrit-Jan van Velze, one of the up-and-coming bullocks. He was then captain of the Under 21s, a tall, blond boy. He said that, until he joined the Bulls, he had refused to speak anything but Afrikaans, even to waiters – it was up to them to learn his language if they expected to work in a restaurant where he was prepared to eat, he said. However, the Bulls had taught him that learning English was essential to professional success. He appeared to me to be at ease with the language. I have to say that the Bulls all spoke to me in English, with varying levels of fluency, but without any hesitation.

The pain of exclusion – albeit in a very different context – had been brought sharply home to me early on in my journey. Through a mutual friend, I had met Shayne

Richardson and her husband, Mike Bayly, at the beginning of 2008. Just over a year before that, Mike had lost his job as Bulls backline coach where he had worked alongside Heyneke Meyer for six years. Shayne was still furious about the treatment meted out to her husband. I arranged to meet her again to talk about it, and she designated a coffee shop in Hout Bay. It was one of those light, bright, lifestyle cafés. Fronting onto the water, you could drink good coffee and eat delicious home-made cake and afterwards browse through their collection of shell-encrusted mirrors and floaty linen dresses. Shayne and I settled down at a table in the corner and this intelligent, articulate woman proceeded to open her heart about her experience of being a Bulls wife, and the trauma of being expelled.

She said she had met Mike in 1997. He was head coach at Boland and she was running a company which supplied off-field clothing to rugby teams, including the Springboks.

From the start of their relationship, she understood that she would always come second to rugby. 'His life was rugby and I met him as a rugby coach, so my life also became rugby,' said Shayne. 'Mike had retired as captain and player/assistant coach of Boland under Nick Mallett due to injury and age. I sadly never saw him play for Western Province or Boland but, by all accounts, he was a gutsy player and a brave 12 and 15. It was an exciting time, as it was also when I learned to love the game. Besides, I was an endurance athlete and understood the commitment required to succeed in sport. However, I soon learnt that rugby is not a sport in South Africa. It is a religion.

'When Mike was head coach at Boland, he was away every second weekend in the season, and busy every other weekend. That was how I first knew him and that is how it has always been.'

Marriage and children didn't change anything. 'We planned our wedding around rugby. It was quite a feat to get his rugby mates, his best man, Nick Mallett, and our families and friends together for a free weekend in July.' In 1999, Mike missed the arrival of his daughter due to a game near Rome. 'He was coaching Rovigo at the time and we were living in Italy. Things took an unexpected turn and I had a Monty Pythonesque natural birth in an Italian general ward with a translator who fainted while I cursed in Afrikaans. I sent Mike an SMS saying he had a daughter called Alessandra. He and the team traipsed into the hospital to see her 24 hours later. She watched her first game at a week old in a tiny Rovigo rugby jersey knitted for her by a spectator.

'In 2002, we planned the birth of our son, Francis, between Bulls games so that Mike would miss neither the birth nor a game. The delivery was an elective Caesarean planned with military precision by Mike and our rugby-loving gynaecologist. From the day our children were discharged from the hospital, I took them along to games.

'This is how my kids grew up – in a rugby environment every single weekend. The Bulls used to have a pleasant family atmosphere and the wives, kids and girlfriends were allowed into the inner sanctum after home games. There was sort of an outer area, part of the changing room, where we used to go after a game. There would be bodyguards on the outside so no spectators could get in. It was probably the one place where everybody could just be who they were: win or lose, we would sit there and celebrate. There is a bar in there and snacks were available. If it'd been a good night we would have a bit of a celebration. The kids would be asleep on the tackle bags, exhausted after playing with Morné (Steyn) or Bryan (Habana) or one of the younger guys. Alessandra and Francis still talk about it and ask why we don't go there any more.

'If it was a loss we'd sit there and commiserate a bit and all go home early, avoiding the spectators. When the Bulls were the Super 12 wooden spoonists a few years ago, the union had to put one-way glass on the coaching box and had bodyguards to accompany the coaches and players to the press conferences. The fans could be really mean and angry. The girls feel it as much as the men, especially the older women, especially the wives. Some of the younger girls were just happy to be with the celebrities, win or lose. Frankly, the players take heat but mostly it falls on the coaches. It's management that takes the heat, the coaches who take the heat. The coaches do what they can off the field, but those eighty minutes are up to the guys and if the guys can't hold it together it's still the coaches who take the knock afterwards – from the press, from management.

'For me it's a contradiction – how much you can love and hate the game. Being involved in rugby in this country also involves absolute highs and lows. If you talk to some of the New Zealand, Australian or British coaches, it's not such a life-and-death scenario.

'At the Bulls, after a match, I would wake up the next morning and in that split second it would descend on me – that feeling – it's either euphoria or it's this horrible sinking feeling that they lost. If they lost, the gloom persists the rest of the weekend and the rest of the week until they have a chance to redeem themselves at the next game. You don't go out in public. It is the way people react to a loss that is the worst. The failure is so public. It's all-encompassing. Everyone wants to talk rugby. Everyone wants to know the inside story and it takes its toll on the entire family. That is how you live.

'It governs everything and yet you love it. You go back for those eighty minutes every week, and for those eighty minutes you just watch these gladiators, win or lose, and you love it. You bite your nails, shout at the TV and behave like a maniac, but you just love it.'

It's lunchtime now and the café is filling up. Busy conversations are going on all around us. I push my tape recorder closer to Shayne, afraid her voice will be lost in the hubbub. Helpfully, she raises it a little.

'I'm a very independent woman with very strong views and I sometimes surprise myself how, without question, I put the rugby teams – and the Bulls especially – ahead of everything … I put Michael's career and Michael's commitment to the team first. I would never have asked him to put me or the kids first. That includes things like planning the births of children, or birthday parties or family gatherings or holidays or anything. It's always within the rugby calendar, which runs from January through to December.

'I had a very responsible job in Johannesburg as marketing manager of one of the largest safari companies in Africa, and I suppose I could have said to him: "Look, we are in this fifty-fifty; we are earning fifty-fifty. I've got to go to London, so you've got to be here. Something's got to give."

'I would never have expected that of him, however. If he were a lawyer or a banker, it would have been different, but as a member of the Bulls, I would never have expected that of him. There were times when he'd be in Georgia or Argentina and I'd be in London or the United States and I would have to make sure that our kids were sorted or I would never have been able to go on a business trip. I would never have thought of saying to him that he can't go or that he should go a day later or a day earlier, or should fly home.

'I would never ever do that because the team came first. It always came first. If I think about it now: was I indoctrinated? Did they show us the same kind of loyalty? Without question, we always put the Bulls first. No discussion or complaint. That's just the way it was. Perhaps that's what it takes to be as successful as the Bulls are.'

It was not even as if coaches' wives were accorded a special status, she says, or that their sacrifices were recognised. 'Of course, we weren't in it for that: we simply supported our husbands and the team. As the wife, you are expected to be there in the wings, part of the back-up. Obviously you meet some decent wives and girlfriends who are in the same situation and equally passionate about the game. You instinctively form your own little team because they feel as anxious as you do. Certainly we were not there for the kudos or the limelight, unlike some of the younger girls who come and go, hanging out with this or that Springbok or about-to-be-Springbok. For us, it was our lives, our livelihood.

'As a coach's wife, you can't really say what you feel. You have to mind your Ps and Qs. You also take the strain. I mean, coaches and players put everything into a game, and when the team loses, there's nothing you can do to help because there's no silver lining in a loss. All you can do is hope and pray that they win again. On the other hand, a win is not a celebration. It's just relief that they didn't lose, so you certainly don't throw a huge party.

'You just have a low-key celebration with the team afterwards and you get up the next day, feeling good. I could watch the game again because I'd missed so much of it out of emotion and having my head down between my knees or my back turned or hiding in the corridor, biting my nails. I often missed half the game because I was in such a state.

'If you'd won, you can sit on your couch with your cup of coffee the next day and actually watch the edited Super-Sport highlights of all the games and really appreciate all the matches, not just who won, who lost and where the Bulls were on the log. If you've lost, you don't watch TV the next day or week, especially not "Boots 'n' All".'

She pauses for a minute, lost in the memory.

'I think it's impossible as a wife not be caught up in it, absolutely impossible. The kids as well – and I have particularly un-rugby children. They weren't given a choice, however – this was their life. I suppose I could have decided to avoid the rugby games, but then I would have seen Michael even less given that he was away every second weekend and that he was on the road for six weeks during the Super 14 and generally on an overseas tour somewhere else during the year.

'So if I didn't go to the home games or make an effort to go to Australia every now and again or travel to some of the domestic games, like in Cape Town or Durban, I just wouldn't see him and he wouldn't see his children. I would have been on the outside, looking in on his passion and not understanding his commitment to the game and the Bulls. During the week he used to leave at seven in the morning and often come home after dark. He would get one day off a week but the kids would be at school so he wouldn't have seen his children.'

Even on extensive overseas tours, wives would not be invited to accompany players and coaches. 'Rugby is different to cricket in that the cricketers are often on the road for seven months. I mean it would be utterly unfair for them not to invite the wives. With our guys, the rugby guys, the game is so fast – only eighty minutes – so they are travelling as fast. Once a game is over, they pack up and move to the next training and game venue.

'I don't know if it's just the Bulls, but certainly the wives were not invited. A couple of times I invited myself over to Australia for a few days and they never said no. Once when the Bulls were playing the away leg in Australasia, their first game was in Perth and their last game was in Brisbane. They had three New Zealand games in between so I went over to Perth with the kids, watched that game, hired a camper van, drove across Australia while they were in New Zealand, and met up with them in Brisbane. We did stay in their hotels. Mostly I would be the only wife there and it certainly wasn't something that was done. I used to feel guilty and Michael would always ask: "Is it okay? Can Shayne share my room?" They were always very sweet and very accommodating, but it was because I'd asked, not because we were invited.

'I suppose they can't because it's so tense, they can't have a bunch of women and kids dragging along. It would just get too hectic. You have to be quite independent. I could make no demands on Michael. I wouldn't even expect to have breakfast with him. I would simply share his room as a base so that I could save money and didn't have to pay for a room elsewhere. I would simply fit in where I was allowed to. I would never ask for him to come and do this with us or go shopping or whatever. I knew that if he had spare time he'd be with us, but I never expected it because virtually every second of every day there's an itinerary, so there isn't really time for wives.'

In return for this extraordinary level of commitment from himself and his family, Mike Bayly got to do a job he loved with one of the world's top rugby teams. It was not about the money: the pay wasn't fantastic. There wasn't a lot of job security either. It was life on the edge, for Mike as well as his family. He was paid 'an average market-related corporate salary', said Shayne. 'There's no ways we could have afforded to be a one-salary family. If you live in Joburg and you want to send kids to a private school – which you pretty much have to do – and live on a safe estate and have a reasonable standard of living, you could not do that on a support coach's salary. I think the head coach gets a very good deal and, of course, the top players do, but not everyone else does. There was no way that Michael could have put anything away. We lived from month to month, which is fine; it's how most people live. If you want to go on holiday and you want private school education, however, your wife has to work and when it's over, it's over and there's nothing for a rainy day.

'Coaches are employed as consultants on a contract basis. Support coaches, as Michael was, do not have a glamorous job. Their job is to back the game plan of the head
coach. It is a special job for singular men without egos who
are able to put their personal agendas aside. They are not
permanent employees, so there are no first, second and
third warnings. Labour law does not apply. They are on
contract at the behest of the head coach and even the best
contract is weighted in favour of the Union rather than
the coach. It can be terminated at any stage and they don't
have to pay you out.'

Nevertheless, this insecurity appeared to be theoretical.
Their lives were so enmeshed with the Bulls, and the Bulls
were doing so well, that it didn't cross their minds that it
all might end prematurely. Then, in August 2006, a friend
mentioned having seen a story in *Rapport*, the Afrikaans
Sunday paper, about the Bulls planning to hire a backline
and attack coach from Australia.

'Michael's position was backline and attack coach ... and
I remember this friend saying to Michael: "Oh, we read
this in *Rapport*." I looked at Michael and he said: "Ag, you
know the media, they've always got to find an angle to
sell the paper." So you end up with a knot in your stom-
ach, but you think well, Michael's been part of this team
for six years. He's been with Heyneke Meyer from the very
beginning. The Bulls came from nowhere. They came last
in the Super 12. In a few years, they've won four Currie
Cups; they've made two Super 14 semi-finals. Other than
not winning a Super 14, what have they done wrong? How
can they do this to Michael? It has to be a lie.

'Then it was the *Sunday Times*; it was a long weekend
in September 2006. The *Sunday Times* ran the story with
a picture of the guy. His name was Todd Louden. He'd announced to the press in Sydney that he'd been to the Bulls
for interviews and he'd been employed as the backline and

attack coach for the Bulls. Again a neighbour brought it to us because we seldom read the newspapers. We just hated reading the newspapers because there was always something ugly in the newspaper, so we just never read them.

'And there it was … a half-page story about this new guy who had been employed, and our world fell apart.'

The intensity of the shock is visible on her face. Through the window, I watch the midday sun cast a translucent blue sheen across the sea. I wait for Shayne to recover.

'That was it, it was all over. It was six years of hard graft for Michael, and he was axed. The Aussie coach stayed a few months and went home. Then the Bulls won the Super 14, and Michael was sitting at home watching it on TV with friends. That was probably the lowest point in my rugby involvement, yet when I felt most proud of Michael. My husband was sitting at home watching the Bulls winning the Super 14 and holding up that magnificent trophy, and then he called up Heyneke and the team to congratulate them. After six years of hard work, he'd read in the newspaper that he was no longer required, lost his income overnight and yet he has never said a bad word about anyone at the Bulls.

'I've thought about it a lot since. In a team, it's a really, really close-knit environment. Take Michael. Michael has always been an incredible team player. He was captain of just about every rugby team and every cricket team he ever played in, from school through university to the army and club and professional rugby. Then he went straight into coaching at Currie Cup level. He spent more time with those squads than he did with his family: his own family, his married family.

'I mean, that's where he spent his life. He probably shared a room as many days in a year with whomever his room-mate was as he did with me. Suddenly he's axed and it's not like just being fired from a corporate entity. It's a highly publicised "failure" that the press feeds on. It's the same when a player gets dropped; there's no debriefing session or weaning off it or even a warning. It's just over. In a split second it's finished and you lose your livelihood and "family", while the powers-that-be simply move on.

'I have always thought that the unions and the sports agents are missing a trick. The rugby players are essentially boys who have shot to stardom and into money without being equipped to handle it. They are seldom tutored along the way, and then are often dropped with no support system. It is no wonder many go off the rails and end up in a mess, with their stories trumpeted in the newspapers. Hero to zero is often a tragic ride. They need coaching in life skills, not just rugby coaching.

'Men are defined by what they do, and that's why a player who is unexpectedly dropped, or a coach who is unfairly dismissed, suddenly loses that team environment. It is horrible to watch. It was terrible to experience it with Michael. You don't easily bounce back from something like that. Michael was stunned, like a buck caught in the headlights. There was nothing he could do, nothing he could say. His record meant nothing. The contract was worthless and he was out in the cold.

'Rugby is brutal. It is vicious on the field ... because they are gladiators ... they put their lives on the line. As a player Michael certainly did. He is physically broken. Then, as a coach, they put everything else on the line. It is absolutely brutal: emotionally and physically. It's impossible as a wife and as a family not to be affected.

'When it happened, I just shut down all my activities and I turned all my attention to working with Michael because Michael is not like me, Michael's not confrontational. He is one of God's gentlemen. He is devoid of ego and all he wants to do is be a great rugby coach. All he wants to do is get the best out of the players. He is in coaching for the right reasons: he wants to get the best out of the players and be an extraordinary contributor to the team – and, of course, win. He doesn't have that kind of peripheral vision or mindset for off-field politics. He just concentrates on the job at hand, which he is passionate about and great at.

'He was just devastated. He literally went into shock, so I put everything aside and concentrated on him. I was very angry. I know I didn't handle it that well. Maybe it's a girl thing, a wife's duty, a protective instinct, but I also know that the downside of rugby taught me valuable life lessons.'

I left the café feeling drained by the intensity of the emotions – loss, anger, bewilderment – that I had absorbed in my hour and a half with Shayne. I can only imagine what it must have been like to go through it all at first hand.

Three years later, I caught up with her again and found the family happily settled in Llandudno, Cape Town. The children surf and, says Shayne, have watched only two live games since 2006, both of them the Bulls at Newlands.

'Our blood is still a little blue,' she says with a smile. Mike is now a highly regarded rugby consultant. He is director of rugby and cricket at Reddam School in Constantia and he consults to Paarl Boys' High School and Villagers' Rugby club. The Richardson-Baylys have successfully moved on but, they say, they miss the adrenaline and elation of the professional game. Shayne says she is sure that, one day, Michael will coach at top level again. 'He loves it too much and is too good at it not to give it a second chance.'

It took me a while to feel comfortable at Loftus. First I had my initial prejudices – reinforced by my encounters with Shayne and the racist in the stands – but the more time I spent there the more it grew on me. The fact that my point of entry was Paul, who seemed to me to be all about a boundless humanity, helped. Usually I'd time my arrival with the Under 19s morning practice session, heading straight up to the B field where Paul would be blowing his whistle and shouting instructions at his lads, completely immersed in it all. When I appeared at his side, his tanned face would crease into a huge grin and he'd say: 'Hello, babes.' I'd find somewhere to sit and watch, basking in the dual warmth of his welcome and the crisp winter sunshine. Afterwards, Paul, Steve Plummer and I would head across to Trademarx for cappuccino and conversation.

Wandering around the vast Loftus complex, I'd frequently bump into his boys and they always greeted me with friendly courtesy: 'Môre, Tannie' (I never did get them to use my first name) or 'Morning, Ma'am.' They seemed to move around in batches of three or four, backwards and forwards from the Bros, the physio, the team meeting room: large, muscular, eager.

I asked Paul if I could attend one of their mentoring sessions and the answer was, as ever: you're welcome. The session I found myself in was for potential mentors, held in one of the seminar rooms in the concrete catacombs under the stadium. There were around 20 Bulls staff members there. I recognised some of the assistant coaches. The man conducting the workshop had the slightly frenzied gleam of a preacher in an evangelical church. This impression was reinforced by the fact that he ended every sentence with a resounding 'Amen!' The session passed, for me, in a haze of repetitive injunctions. It was all highly interactive. Everyone else there seemed very familiar with the format and responded at all the right times and in all the right places. I realised that at some point the finger would point at me. Fortunately, by the time it did, I had gleaned enough to be able to give what passed for a satisfactory answer: 'Control the controllables!' I cried. 'Amen!' echoed the facilitator.

These sessions are run according to something called the PALM programme, which was devised and is taught by a man called Jannie Putter, a sports psychologist. It describes itself thus: 'The PALM programme is the result of the cry from our youth for strong leadership and guidance in this day and age. The quantity of input, the pressures of life, the expectations and trends amongst peers and the demand for excellence to be able to excel in life has opened up a gap where teenagers are lurking around in the dark, looking for a guiding hand to show them the way.

'The PALM programme has the intent of empowering those amongst us who has the call to guide our youth whether it be as parents, coaches, teachers or simply being a friend to be better equipped and more accurate in giving your hand and showing the way ...'

The hyperbole and questionable grammar notwithstanding, a lot of what the PALM programme offers seems to make sense. I took the literature away with me for a thorough read. For a start, there was no obvious religious bias. Faith and religion were 'within the domain of the family; however this is an area of great concern/hunger for many young people ... It might be difficult to address this area unless you yourself have undergone true spiritual change and enlightenment', presumably becoming a born-again Christian in the process.

Basically, what the mentor is supposed to provide is a

steady, supportive adult role model. He/she should guide the young sportsman/sportswoman through whatever lifestyle change is required. There are a set of rules: one-on-one time amounting to some four to six hours is required. The mentor is supervised by a mentor co-ordinator. The parents or guardian of the young participants must have given permission.

Although I found the evangelical fervour of the workshop quite alien, I thought that at least the Bulls were making an effort to provide some sort of emotional and spiritual guidance to these boys, who might be brilliant sportsmen, but who were still children, many of them far from home.

Paul's Under 19s who make it through the first two years end up with Nico Serfontein, who is in charge of the Under 21s. Nico is also involved with PALM. He has been working with Jannie Putter to try to perfect the mentoring programme, partly in an attempt to stem the haemorrhaging of players of colour between the junior and senior levels. I make an appointment to see Nico, and when I arrive at his small office under the stadium, he comes to the door and holds out his hand, bright-eyed and welcoming. He ushers me to a chair on the other side of his desk and I ask him to explain what PALM does.

The junior coaches go through the PALM programme so that they can mentor the players in their charge, he tells me: 'We train the mentor to assist new young players to find the right rhythm and comfort in the training structures and the culture. We have looked at what stops certain young bright sparks from making it at a senior level and we have identified certain major challenges to a youngster's progress: instant fame, money, exposure; the sudden competition with other superstars.

'From Under 16 to 21, we use a five-point plan to train the whole person:

1. Develop the personality.
2. Develop the body: make him stronger, bigger, faster.
3. Enhance his technical ability: in scrumming, kicking, passing, tackling.
4. Tactical – his understanding of the game; his ability to read and assess tactics on the field under pressure.
5. His exposure: expose him to a higher level of fitness and of competition.

'We have also found that, given all this training, for an Under 21 to make it to international level, he needs to be willing to work harder than others; to fight back and get over disappointments; and he needs intelligence and the ability to handle pressure. Suddenly you are out there in front of 40 000 people: can you still kick the ball over the cross-bar?

'You start testing him as soon as you can: how hard can he train? Ask him to be here at five in the morning – will he set his alarm or will he lie in?

'In the end it is your personality that gets you there.'

Is it about helping kids from poor and remote homes to adapt? I ask.

No, he says, because it is not only kids from poor backgrounds who struggle.

'You get middle-class kids who have played for their father or their coach their whole lives. They have never found it in themselves to be self-driven, and as soon as they are on their own, they find there is not enough in the tank.'

With poorer kids, the challenges are different. They might not have had the benefit of going to a top rugby school where they would have been properly trained, fed and exposed to the intense pressure of high-level competition.

'I've had players here who earn R3 000 a month and they send R2 500 back home to their family for food. This kid doesn't have the money to buy himself vitamins and proper nutrition. When he goes on holiday, there is a drop in his protein intake and that puts pressure on him.'

Alternatively, at home, he is the glamour boy and has to live up to expectations by buying a flash car. Then all this income is swallowed up in payments.

'When it comes to personal development, a player must ask for guidance. We are all trained for the one-on-ones; if a topic is broached by a player, we are trained in how to deal with it.

'At Under 21, they suddenly see they are not going to be offered a contract, and they think: What am I going to do now? I have lost years of studying.'

As I am leaving, Nico remarks enigmatically that another of the Bulls' challenges is to hang onto their junior coaches such as Paul and himself. They have developed unique skills in developing players, but once you've been at it for nearly a decade as he has, one needs a change. The significance of this only strikes me later when I hear that Nico has been poached by the Lions, who have everything to learn about development.

Fudge Mabeta has been through Nico's Under 21s and through the PALM programme. He said the latter helped him to believe in himself, but he found the religious element too prescriptive. He is a Christian and he prays, but in his own way. The seniors, he said, had refused to take part, finding it too didactic.

I thought, looking at this tall, elegant 23-year-old lock with his coffee-coloured skin and shoulder-length dreads, that if anyone demonstrates the diversity of Bulls players, it is him. He was born in the United States where his dad, an ANC activist, was living in exile. His mother is a white American. In 1991, after Nelson Mandela was released, the family returned to South Africa. Fudge's dad, Masio Mabeta, is from the Eastern Cape, and that is where he settled his family upon his return. Fudge attended Queen's Primary School with Vata Ngobeni, but moved to Grey

High in Port Elizabeth for his secondary schooling.

Meanwhile Masio Mabeta was working for the South African Department of Foreign Affairs and transferred to Pretoria. In 2004, when he was 17 and about begin Grade 11, Fudge moved to Pretoria Boys' High. It was at an introductory lunch for new boys that Fudge met Paul Anthony, then still head coach at the school.

'Paul asked if I played any sport. I said I had played fifth team rugby at Grey High. He invited me to the first team trials and even though I didn't make it into the first team that year, Paul helped me get my mind right. He made me believe I could make Craven Week. He helped my game enormously. I had always dreamt of playing professional rugby and he made that dream tangible. I worked very hard and I made Craven Week and from Craven Week, I made it to SA Schools. When I finished matric, the Bulls signed me up.'

In his final year with the Under 21s, his team won the Currie Cup. 'As a result, a lot of the guys from my year got signed up, if not here, then somewhere else. My greatest fear was that I would have to play for a smaller union like the Falcons because if you don't perform there, no one else will look at you again.

'This is the best place in the world to play rugby because they are a very talented union when it comes to developing young players through rugby. At the junior levels, you learn a lot and that is why juniors burst through. They just excel.'

Fudge has just signed up for another two years with the Bulls. Only three others from his initial Under 19s intake have made it this far, however, and he is suddenly finding himself a little lonely.

'I used to have a lot of friends here, but now I don't go to people's homes. I used to at junior level, but I don't have much in common with those who are left.

'We play for the same team. We bleed for each other: if you have to lift me in the line-out, you lift as high as you can because in the end, it helps us both. The camaraderie is fantastic. You feel as if you are part of something and I love that.'

Off the field, he feels like an outsider. 'They are very polite and very kind but you feel you're not really part of the family.'

Why not? I ask. Language and culture, he replies.

'It's old-fashioned. Straight and narrow, which is cool but I don't have much in common with it. Even some Afrikaans guys who didn't grow up on a farm and didn't go to Grey Bloem don't really fit in, but they have a language in common and if you have a language in common, you already have a huge amount in common. My home language is isiXhosa and I have met a lot of Xhosa guys here. I find myself drawn to them because if you have a language in common, it pushes you to get to know guys well. If you don't speak the same language, that is when it gets tricky.'

We were talking over coffee in Trademarx, surrounded by Bulls staff and Bulls fans. The fact that Fudge felt able to talk freely about his dissatisfactions there struck me as an indication of Bulls' openness.

He is clearly a very bright young man and from a solid middle-class family. He is one of four boys – the next in line is a medical student at UCT, the third is also in the Bulls family in the Under 21s and the baby still at Pretoria Boys' High. His first language might be isiXhosa, but he speaks English as if he were born to it. His understanding of race relations is sophisticated, presumably thanks to his bi-racial, cosmopolitan family.

He worries that the fraught issue of selection might sometimes come to this: no matter how fair-minded and professional a coach is, when it comes down to the wire – having to choose between two equally talented, skilled and committed players – your subconscious will tilt you towards the one with whom you share the most in terms of language, culture, appearance.

Not Frans Ludeke, he hastens to add. 'Frans is very professional and very fair. He doesn't want to know about you. He just wants to know whether your attitude is good. If you play hard and train hard, he will give you the chances. He has done that for me.

'I'm talking about, say a forwards coach, a good guy with solid morals – it is just easier if you know more about a player and his family. If you find it easier to communicate with one player rather than with another, it becomes easier to trust him. A decision which should have been 50-50 then becomes 51-49, weighted towards the one you know better.'

I asked Paul Anthony about this later and he said: 'Absolutely not! If there is any choice to be made between a white player and a player of colour, it will come down in favour of the latter because of the pressure from politicians.'

Yet Fudge's point about birds of a feather flocking together certainly makes sense to me in the light of what I see everywhere else: clubs and teams in business and pleasure form on the basis of a hand-up for those perceived to be of their tribe, whether it's language, race, a common university or school.

South Africa is a young country when it comes to racial integration, says Fudge. Most people are still more comfortable with those who look like them and speak the same language. One can't argue with that, much as we may not want it to be the case.

Rugby is not like athletics, say – where there is absolutely no doubt who wins the race. Here merit is, in the end, subjectively determined. One can see how this can lead to perceptions of bias, on whatever grounds. You only have to read rugby blog sites to see how fervently the armchair critics dispute any team selection.

Presumably the intensely competitive nature of professional rugby exacerbates the situation. 'Everyone's good, but the more opportunities you get, the better you will get. The crucial determinating factor in sport is who gets opportunity.'

While Fudge was talking, my mind was wandering to a conversation I'd had a few months earlier with John Smit. He was a fellow panellist at an Aids conference in Durban and I had seized the opportunity to ask him what he thought about this vexed issue of inclusion and exclusion. As with just about everyone else I spoke to, he thought the quota system had been hugely problematic. 'The real victims were black players. Rugby excellence hinges strongly on self-belief, and if you believe you are there only because of your skin colour – or if anyone else tries to tell you that you are – it's hugely destructive.

'I've been here [at the Sharks] for twelve years. In the early days, a lot of guys just didn't cut it. They were under huge pressure and when there was a fuss [about quotas], they began to doubt themselves. Now they start in Grade 8 and we have a whole wave of players from nineteen to thirty of all colours who have had the same experience.

'As Springbok captain, I am very aware of which music I pick; which words I speak; which language I use. You have got to continually embrace difference. An Afrikaans guy has to understand what a Zulu guy is thinking.

'We see black and coloured kids at the [Sharks] stadium. We don't favour players because of their colour. They are the best. They tackle their hearts out. The best player in the world is Bryan Habana. Player 23 could be any one of 45 million people. We have moved so far beyond what we were.'

I had been hanging around Loftus for more than a year, on and off, before I made any attempt to see the big boss, CEO Barend van Graan. This was partly because I wanted to immerse myself in the nitty-gritty – the rugby and the culture – rather than the bureaucratic element, but also because I assumed it would be a chore. I assumed the head of the Bulls would be your traditional Afrikaner patriarch, but the first surprise came when Barend himself called me to change an appointment I'd made through his secretary. He apologised and negotiated a new date. The fact that he didn't hide behind a secretary and mess me around – as CEOs of other rugby unions had done – immediately endeared him to me.

Then I met him and found that, yet again, my preconceptions had been wrong. I've no doubt that he can be a brute – he wouldn't have achieved what he has otherwise – but in all my dealings with him, I can only describe him as delightful: irreverent, quick-witted, confiding.

He is a large man with a bald dome and glasses. Like Paul, he had started out as a teacher. Perhaps this early commitment to public service is an indication of character. In an attempt to get to know him a bit better, I ask him about his background and he tells me he was born in Tzaneen and educated at Pretoria's Hoërskool Tuine. He studied at the University of Pretoria and then went back to his old school to teach for seven years. He played rugby throughout but not with any great distinction: 'I was a weak prop, a slow loose forward and a short lock,' he says with a grin.

He's been a Bulls supporter practically since birth and has worked for them in various capacities for the past 20 years, so he has lived their recent history. Until the turn of the century, he says, my preconceptions about the Bulls would not have been far off the mark. The Bulls were rooted in the ruling institutions of the apartheid regime: 'We drew heavily on Tukkies, Correctional Services, the Army and the Police. If there were good rugby-playing policemen and soldiers in other provinces, the generals moved them here.'

Their style of rugby echoed this: there was a heavy reliance on brute force, with little sophistication in technique or rugby intelligence.

It showed in the results. Hard as it is to believe now, at the turn of the century, the Bulls came either last or second last in the then Super 12 log.

The city they were rooted in had been the command post of the apartheid government. Now it was run by black people from the ANC. Afrikaners had had to adjust from their lofty if precarious position as the rulers of the land to being ordinary citizens, one cultural group among many. This coincided with titanic changes in rugby from amateurism to globally competitive professional rugby. If the Bulls wanted to compete, things had to change.

'In 2000, we decided we wanted to be part of South Africa. Pretoria was a bastion of conservatism. If you look back to 2000, 90 per cent of our spectators were Afrikaans males. If you look at it now, there's a helluva change: it's still mostly Afrikaans, but there are lots of English-speakers and also lots of students – young, vibrant people, especially in the Super 14. Our challenge now is to take the Blue Bulls brand to black people.'

They also have to keep on winning and replenishing their ranks. 'We need to create six or seven Springboks a year. That is why players come to us for less and stay with us for less: because they have a better chance of becoming Springboks.'

Already, half their R140 million budget goes to players' and coaches' salaries.

The Bulls' difficulty with recruiting and retaining players of colour is that there are so few of them in their province, where black people mostly favour soccer. Many previously white schools, particularly those close to townships or on the route in to town, have become primarily black and the sport of choice is soccer.

Barend told me that he believed the Bulls had missed an opportunity in the early nineties when their historical recruiting grounds – the Police and the Army – turned from white to black. Instead of focusing on building rugby in the new Police and Army communities, they began to look elsewhere. Only now are the Bulls starting to work with Pretoria's white-turned-black schools, sending in coaches, supplying equipment. Slowly rugby is again taking over from soccer in some schools.

In the meantime, they have to fish in distant waters: bringing in black boys from the Eastern Cape and other provinces, and trying to make it work.

The decision the Bulls made at the turn of the century to engage wholeheartedly with the new South Africa went hand in hand with a rigorous shake-up in their rugby structures. This is when Heyneke Meyer was brought in and wrought his magic, but now Heyneke is gone and his successor, Frans Ludeke, is having a hard time of it.

The Bulls performed so abysmally in their first few Super 14 games since Heyneke left and Ludeke took over that, on 16 April 2008, Barend van Graan felt impelled to issue the following press release in an attempt to calm things down:

'1. Heyneke Meyer was not available to coach the Vodacom Bulls after the 2007 Super 14 Competition. Therefore another head coach had to be appointed.

2. The Bulls have previously been in this position, in the Super 12 Competition, and got through it.
3. A serious conversation was held between the coaching team and the players on Monday at which everyone accepted their own responsibility for their share in the dilemma.
4. The unanimous decision of the board of the Blue Bulls Company (Pty) Ltd and its shareholders, the Blue Bulls Rugby Union and SAIL, is that the situation will deteriorate if we change the coaching staff now. We must now allow our coaching staff to overcome the obstacles caused by the change in personnel and the new ELVs [Experimental Law Variations].'

Frans Ludeke is a different beast to Meyer. Slower, softer, heavy with patience and deliberation. I met him a few times and, on one occasion I bring along, without warning, two of my nephews, aged 12, both avid rugby fans. We rush into his office, late after being held up in the traffic from Joburg. He is gracious, asking them about their schools, and happily acquiescing to their sitting in on the interview. His office looks out onto the main playing field, the floor-to-ceiling glass windows interspersed with French windows, through which one can step out into the stands. It is an expansive, comfortable space, with couches and easy chairs as well as a large desk.

Frans Ludeke has a square, soft face with a bruised look under the eyes. Afrikaans is his first language. He speaks English rapidly and apparently with confidence but not particularly well. He comes from Polokwane, where he was taught by Victor Matfield's mother.

Super 14 is a tough competition, he says. When a team is not doing well and is being crucified in the media, as has recently been the case, it makes things doubly hard. 'You get players who feel they are useless and the newspaper guys are writing them off, telling them they don't deserve to be there.'

As a coach, Ludeke has experienced the full gamut of coaching, from youngsters to first team. Before becoming the Bulls coach, he was director of rugby at the Lions. 'I went to the Under 13 Craven Week. I knew all the players all over the country. I spoke to their mums: this is a really talented player. Which school is he going to? Paul Roos? Bishops?'

Here he looks at Matthew, a Bishops boy.

'Then you follow them because you have got scouts in the schools as well and you phone them up and say, "How's this guy going? Is he on track?" Sometimes it's a good idea to relocate him up here. You put him in a boarding school and then he is close. He is in your system. I invite them to clinics where they get individual skills training, unit skills training and back and defence skills training.

'At that stage, it's really exposing them and putting them under pressure to see how hungry they are. Do they really want it? You can't coach that. If you see a passion for the game, a hunger from the guys; if you can see they really want to go places – those are the guys you want. Once they are in the system, you can tell that easily.

'If you need to stand behind the guy with a whip, it's a problem. You can have one or two players like that, but not all of them. If you have to push them the whole time, they will fail. They will kill the system.

'We look at the Under 16 level because the earlier you spot talent, the better. Boys grow. Some fat guys get lean. They get more athletic. They go on diets. At Under 16, you can start telling if a guy's got speed. Is he very explosive? That's not going to change.

'You invite them to clinics – to skills sessions, mental sessions, gym sessions so that you can expose them to the Bulls way. You get them into your system. You put them under pressure and see which guys are fading. Then you tell them: this is how it works, and give them another test.

'By the age of 18, which is when you really want them in your system, you've already worked with them for three or four years. By then, you understand them, you know their personalities, their strengths and their weaknesses. That's when you give them a contract or a bursary to study, and then you pull them in.

'We at the Bulls are very lucky because Heyneke did a brilliant job. We have a lot of senior guys who are still out there so we don't really need to buy in older, experienced players from other unions. We've already achieved a lot: we've won the Currie Cup and the Super 14. Our challenge is really to get new youngsters in so that the youngsters are feeding the system by the time the experienced guys have come to the end of their game.'

I'm sitting on the couch with Matthew and Daniel on either side of me. Both, I know, are bursting to ask questions about their Bulls heroes – Matfield, Habana, Du Preez. 'Listen for now, guys,' I say to them. 'This is life as well as rugby Frans is talking about.'

Frans, on the couch opposite us, gives us his sweet, slightly sad smile.

As leader, he goes on, he has to decide where to put his energy. It tends to be channelled in two directions. The first is into his management team. 'Every day I sit with the specialists – the coaching staff: the kicking coach, the tackling coach, the manager, the medic and five or six senior players. We sit down and say: where do we want to take the system? I want to correct this; I want this vibe; this talk. If I'm not happy with particular behaviour, I'll put it on the table. I'll say: listen, this is not the Bulls. This is not the way we do things. The captain will then sort it out. So it's not always me speaking. If it comes from a player, they will accept it better.

'And the specialists: in the Monday meeting, we will sit

and say: listen, the scrums weren't good or the forwards didn't play well over the weekend. That's what I think. What do you think? Then the specialist will go and sort it out with the individuals.'

His other major focus is on maintaining the morale of the boys on the bench. 'The specialists look after the 15 guys who are playing. The 20 per cent or 30 per cent – the guys who are not making the squads; those who are sick; who are down; who have problems at home – I put my time into them because those are the ones who can bring negativity into the squad. I talk to them, try to sort them out because they are the ones who need the back-up. The guys who are playing: it's easy for them because they are motivated already. They are putting the jersey on on Saturday. They can move forward.

'You know, the Super 14 is tough. What makes a team perform or a team to fall away? If the guys feel they are useless and the newspapers are writing them off and telling them they don't deserve to be there, one guy might say: this is the truth, you can't ignore it. The other guy might say: just ignore it. It can't help us to improve.'

On occasions like this, says Ludeke, when, as a team you are down and being heavily criticised by media and fans, assaulted by a tide of negativity, you need to access that inner voice which should be attuned to the right airwaves after all the intensive mentoring the Bulls offer.

'It's almost like this voice in your mind that tells you: "Ag, why don't you quit, man? Why do it when you can go and sit on the beach? You don't need this." You need to ignore that voice. When life gets bad it may be that same voice – just in different clothing – telling you to take your life or take drugs. You have to ignore that voice and listen to the right voice. You've got to get your mind thinking positively; telling yourself: this is the right thing to do. It's a fighting spirit you need to create.'

Frans calls it 'the mental back-up'. In any team sport, he says, it is crucial to know that you can rely on the next guy. 'If, say, you are a centre and I am a prop, I might lose my battle at the scrum but you might still get a line break from broken play and we can still win the game. I therefore rely on you as well.'

That is what makes a team consistently strong and able to survive and triumph in tough competition. It's about resilience and determination. This must constantly and consistently be instilled in each and every individual.

The external pressure can be overwhelming. The media can be relentless: 'I never read the paper,' says Ludeke. 'I never watch rugby programmes on TV, because I think: "What is a negative message doing to me?" If you are having a bad time, it breaks you down even more.'

He acknowledges the power of the media but, like most of the players within rugby, also loathes and fears it. He puts it thus: 'I think they have got a role to play. They keep you honest. We need them to create perceptions with the public, whether negative or positive. However, when it is negative, it is bad for the coaches, because people recognise you and they point fingers at you and swear at you. This may happen when you are going to movies with your family. That's the thing about the media. They form South Africa's perception about you.'

Daniel can't keep quiet any longer. 'They swear at you at the movies! That's horrible!' Indeed it is.

The only way to deal with it, responds Frans, is to hunker down. Control the controllables. The media are a necessary evil. You can't control them. All you control is your response to them.

'You must know that theirs is only a perception. It's not the truth. It's just one guy's opinion.'

When he does need an outsider's opinion, Ludeke has a range of mentors of his own to call on: one for rugby, one for his financial affairs, one for his spiritual affairs and one for his marriage. If he has difficulties in any one of these areas, he will call up the relevant mentor, talk through the problem and listen to their advice.

'If they have criticism, I will listen to it, because I know them, I trust them. I know they don't have an angle on it. They don't want my job. That's why you need mentors – to help you to focus on what you want to achieve in life.'

This is Ludeke's first season with the Bulls and, according to his contract, he has two more to go. As soon as the Currie Cup is over and their Springboks have returned from the end-of-year tour, the off-season begins and that is when he plans to implement an intensive strategic session.

'I haven't had a lot of off-season at the Bulls and I can't wait for it because that is when you get everybody on the same page, from junior level to senior level. I want to see where we can take the game in the next three to four years. I want to see how we can take this whole system, the whole thought process, to another level.'

I ask him about religion, and he says he believes in submitting to a higher authority, a Christian authority. 'For myself, as a Christian, if you work hard, if you put in your hours, it's almost like farming. You prepare the ground, you put in the seed and then you must have faith that you will get results. Ninety per cent of the time you will get results because that is a Biblical principle. What you sow, you will reap. It's almost a promise you get and in my life I've learnt that is very true.

'Sometimes that 10 per cent makes the difference between winning trophies or not: that's what it's all about. Your strategies might be in place, as might your mental skills and conditioning, but games are lost by a forward pass or a dropped pass.'

About previous teams he has been involved in, he says: 'In the morning, somebody will say a prayer and somebody will say a few words about things in his personal life that may be important for them.

'Pretoria is an Afrikaans-speaking town. The English are more reserved. They don't really talk about things. They say those are church things. Let's leave it for church. I think the culture here is almost like let's live our lives and our lives must be a testament. It's not let's just do the church thing on Sunday and live like hooligans during the week. It's like: let our lives speak. That's why guys here tend to share when they have the opportunity. You know: always do the right thing. That's the only rule: you know what to do. Do it. Live it.

'The slogan here is: "Better people make better Bulls." You are not just a taker, but also a giver. You don't always ask what you can get out of a system, but what you can give to the system.'

I told him that what I'd seen of Paul Anthony's Under 19s had convinced me that not only is there a non-racist ethos, but also a conscious and consistent anti-racist ethos. Frans said it was a new thing – 'over the last five years'. The way the Bulls now deal with difference is to inculcate common values that transcend race and culture.

'Values are better because you can get a Zulu culture, an English culture and an Afrikaans culture, but what you must have is what is best for the Bulls. As a Zulu, as an Afrikaner, as a Xhosa, what values can we agree on so that we function best? Respect must be one of the main things. We respect each other. If you are Muslim, Hindu or Christian, I respect that. When you are at prayer meetings, I don't make a joke of it. I respect it.'

I feel a pang of guilt about my impatience with the Bros prayer meeting.

'We look at all the cultures and say: what do we want to take from them into the Bulls? Then we marry all that and it becomes the Bulls' way. This is what we agree on from

145

all the different cultures and it revolves around things like respect, honesty, discipline.

'Discipline is easy: it is punctuality, dress, foul play on and off the field. Without discipline, no-one can perform on the field. Never disrespect the jersey or the badge. You can stick to your own cultural things and you don't have to change your personality, but your behaviour must fit our value system.

'Honesty and accountability are important. You are accountable for your actions on and off the field. Family also comes in strongly here: remember the birthdays, the special occasions, make a big fuss when somebody achieves something. On the Monday morning, after a weekend game, there will be awards for the most tackles, the biggest hits and all that kind of stuff. You are rewarding players the whole time for the key areas in the game or the output that you want at the end of the day.

'You can be motivated by fear or rewards. You can say: there will be a consequence, be it positive or negative. What's important in our system, however, is positive rewards. We like to get guys looking at the positives, not the negatives because you can build on positives, even if it's just 10 per cent. You can keep improving every week on that 10 per cent. That's when you get momentum.'

Why does he think rugby is so important to South Africa? 'It's instinct. Men want to prove something. It is human to want to fight to survive. Any contact sport shows up your weaknesses.

'There are so many great things you can learn from it: to push yourself and not to quit, to finish what you started, and to work together in a team. To respect other guys and be loyal to your team mates. You hopefully take that through to your marriage, to your family, to your job. You are not a quitter. You don't just walk away from your responsibilities.

'That's what you learn from sport, especially team sport because a team is always above the individual and that's a good rule for life, isn't it?' he asks, smiling at the boys.

I made a point of sitting in the stands for the Super 14 semi-final at Loftus when the Bulls slaughtered the Crusaders from New Zealand on 23 May 2009, forgoing the comfort of the media box, where one is largely isolated from the Loftus faithful. I wanted the whole experience from the perspective of the punter. If one goes to Loftus as an accredited member of the media, you get special treatment: food and drink is laid on. You get to sit in a box and park in the stadium grounds.

Going as an ordinary fan is very different. The experience starts with the increasingly anxious search to find a space to leave your car. I eventually found parking a kilometre or two from Loftus, on Park Street, coaxed into a tiny parallel space by a persuasive black car guard. It was, as ever on the Highveld, a sunny, still autumn day, and white Pretoria was alight with anticipation. Their lads had now reached the semi-finals and the odds were on their making it through to the finals.

From the beginning, it feels like entering the territory of some foreign and arcane cult or tribe. Lining Park Street on the approach to Loftus was a series of braais, right there on the pavement, the tailgates of bakkies lowered to serve as tables. Little groups of two or three sat in deckchairs swigging beers or brandy around small, individual fires where mounds of wors and chops were being ritually burnt.

The phrase 'sacrificial lamb' came to mind. There was something Biblical about this sombre ingesting of a slaughtered beast. It struck me that there wasn't a salad in sight. This was undiluted red meat for red-blooded men about to go into battle, albeit vicariously. Sturdy people these, with unapologetically bulging bellies and beefy, red forearms.

Smoke scented with the fragrance of roasting meat curled into the air.

Park Street had mostly been surrendered to pedestrians and a sea of blue-clad people surged down it. I stuck behind a battering ram of three barefoot men in shorts and Blue Bulls T-shirts, all with identical hairy, boat-shaped calves. Brothers, presumably.

The only black people in the crowd were entrepreneurs: one young guy with a string of vuvuzelas around his neck kept pace with us, blowing one irritatingly all the way. Others sold ice cream and Blue Bulls flags.

I was supposed to meet Paul at Trademarx, but I arrived to find it packed to the rafters and charging R50 just to step over the threshold. A giant white beer tent covering the training grounds catered for the overflow. I felt briefly, irrationally, miffed. This was not the Loftus I had become used to. It had been taken over.

I gave up my search for Paul and headed into the stadium to find my seat. The stadium was awash with blue. In front of me was an English-speaking family: brothers, sisters, wives and small children strewn across laps. Beside me was a group of three teenage girls, giggly and flashing bare flesh. The atmosphere could best be described by that cliché, 'family-friendly'. I thoroughly enjoyed myself, swept up in the same nationalistic fervour as everyone else. How nice it felt to be celebrating my country's triumph with thousands of other white people, most of them Afrikaners. How unexpected.

EIGHT

By 2010, Heyneke Meyer was back at the Bulls. I met up with him over a period when his wife was away and he had primary care of his three young sons, so he was popping out to make sure they were fed and then disappeared for three days to take them out to his farm in the bush. It was a different side to this driven character and helped flesh out the sharp-edged, restless man I had encountered more than a year previously.

Being back with the Bulls clearly suited him. He seemed to carry more weight, both around his waistline and in his manner. He tells me he now has a permanent job, not the usual short-term contract offered to coaches. The deal when he came back, he says, was that he shouldn't threaten Frans, who would remain in sole charge of the senior team. Both Frans and Meyer report directly to Barend. All the other coaches, as well as the rugby vision and policies of the Bulls fall under Meyer, who also takes particular responsibility for development, which, he says, 'has slipped a bit' in his absence.

I had heard so much about Meyer's achievements – Fourie du Preez, for instance, credited him with the current excellence of South African rugby as a whole. Du Preez believes that the revolutionary development structures initiated by Meyer at the beginning of the century have been emulated by other unions and resulted in the current array of superlative Springbok talent.

Listening to Meyer in his rather poky office down the corridor from Frans Ludeke's much grander one, I began to understand how fundamental were the changes he instituted when he started at the Bulls in 2000. It was Year Zero: he erased everything that went before with an absolute ruthlessness. He had a clear vision of what was needed in its place, and the obsessive drive and confidence to see it through.

Meyer was the first professional Bulls coach: his predecessors had been either Army or Police officers or PhDs from Pretoria University. When he first arrived, there was a poor work ethic among the players and a huge sense of entitlement. Senior players expected fag-like obeisance from younger players. Gym was slipshod and amateurish, with wives and girlfriends frequently joining in, which tended to result in more preening than pruning. The ruling ethos was hierarchical and authoritarian, with strict rules. Fines were imposed for transgressions.

The first thing Meyer did was cull 11 of the 16 Springboks he inherited, and drastically cut the salaries of those who remained, such as Joost van der Westhuizen. The money that was saved went into a recruiting drive for coaches and young talent, and the average age of players dropped from 29 to 23.

I remark that one thing that always strikes me about the Bulls in relation to other unions is how many coaches they have. There is a whole raft of coaches at every level – Under 19s, Under 21s as well as the senior teams. This is exactly what he is talking about, he says, and it is the reason for the Bulls' dominance.

'I said: "Let's forget the players. Let's get in a very good management team and spend money on them, and they will develop players."'

When they recruit players, they look for character as much as talent. The man before the player.

I knew that Meyer, like Ludeke, was a practising Christian and this probably explains his use of parables. In demonstrating the kind of character they look for, for instance, he tells me a story about a bunch of people in hell sitting on either side of a long table covered with delicious food.

The people look pale and unhappy. The same scene is replicated in heaven, but the diners there are happy and laughing because each person is taking the choicest bit of food and feeding the person opposite before eating himself. In hell, each person has piled the tastiest morsels in front of himself, but if one looks closely at their hands, they have knives and forks attached which are too long to transfer the food to their mouths. It was all about themselves and, as a result, they starved.

'If you first try to help the guy opposite you at the table, the whole system benefits. For instance, we now have four Springbok locks, which is unheard of.'

I ask him about Christianity at the Bulls because I've encountered it so often and he hesitates before saying: 'That is a sensitive subject.'

Then he says: 'We are Christian-driven but there is no pressure to conform. We have Bible groups but there is no pressure to attend them. We respect difference. Before games, we pray. We pray that we play very well and to our full talents and thus let the Lord shine. We don't pray: "Let us win" because the other team might be praying for the same thing and then the Lord has to choose.

'If they pray, they go onto the field feeling good and feeling they are protected. Christianity also helps with the idea of caring for each other; of feeding the other guy first.'

In Year Zero, Meyer the Eraser eradicated fines and rules. 'I don't believe in the Kamp Staaldraad approach. Discipline must come from within or it doesn't work.

'If you get in the right people with the right sense of integrity, it works without rules. You need a guy who can think for himself because when he goes out onto the field, he is going to have to make split-second life-or-death decisions all by himself. We want guys who will speak their minds and challenge each other.'

Meyer believes that attitude is all, on and off the field:

10 per cent is what life throws at you and the rest is how you respond to it. Attitude trumps talent, skill, wealth, education, upbringing. In other words, you are the master of your fate.

Like all the Bulls coaches, Meyer does a lot of mentoring. 'Seventy per cent of the kids we recruit come from broken, dysfunctional families. Every player sometimes has problems at home and if they have problems at home, they can't play. For example, one kid's dad died when he was twelve. I sorted out his studies and his contract. If you help them out like that, they will die for you on the field. I've dealt with a boy whose parents are divorced and there is fighting and he hasn't spoken to his father for years. I advised him on how to sort it out. The guy is his father, after all.

'You can't just take a kid off the street and put him on the field. We can make a difference in regard to life skills. The rugby is always the last thing.'

I have always thought that one of the great gifts of Loftus was its size and physical cohesion: it is one of the privileges they have retained from the apartheid era. This huge space in the heart of the city, ringed by the great state schools – Pretoria Boys' High, Pretoria Girls' High, and Afrikaanse Hoër Seunskool – and the University of the Pretoria with its expansive campuses only a stone's throw way. The Loftus complex ranges from the stadium ringing the main pitch with two training fields to the side, flanked by that excellent café, Trademarx.

Senior management have a string of offices among the suites on the top level of the stadium while the more junior coaches and management each have their own office in the bowels. There is a large auditorium for press and player conferences and, since the FIFA-inspired refurbishment, a comfortable media centre.

For players in particular, Loftus works. They have a dedicated dining room where they are fed two perfectly nutritionally balanced meals a day; a state-of-the-art gym beside Trademarx, its floor-to-ceiling windows flanking the main training field. In the basement below the gym is a swimming pool. There is a lounge in the stadium where they can have a beer with management and their wives and girlfriends after a match. Twenty young players can be accommodated at the Bros, across from the training field and railway line, while the Academy is just over the road. Junior players train and practise alongside Springboks who are encouraged to develop relationships with them, ensuring a symbiotic transfer of values and skills from one generation to the next.

Meyer, however, thinks they are only halfway there. He has found a sponsor to fund another storey above the gym which will be a big players' room where they can relax throughout the day. It will contain beds and everything else they might need to feel at home. 'My dream is a one-stop shop: they eat here, they train here, they rest here. I want them to be here the whole day and enjoy it.'

He is also planning to get a second level built onto the Bros so that it can accommodate another 20 players.

As regards recruiting, he is digging even deeper: he has scouts in every province looking for promising players of 16 and under. If necessary, they will be moved to good rugby schools, and the Bulls will start their nurturing process: mentoring them emotionally and physically. Nutritional supplements will be provided. He is getting together a Blue Bulls Under 16 squad. The Bulls will train their coaches; the boys will be brought to Loftus for camps. 'We will teach them the Bulls way.'

A lot of this is about bringing in more boys of colour and ensuring they remain in the system. Increasingly, this means departing even further from the Bulls' traditional white Christian Afrikaner origins. Meyer says that for 2011, they have recruited two practising Muslim boys. If necessary, they will buy in halal meals for them.

At the lower levels, staff are selected for what they can add to the racial mix: the Under 19s doctor and masseur are black, as are the managers of both the Under 19 and Under 21 teams. This all helps to make the black boys more comfortable.

'People think the Bulls are an Afrikaans team,' he says. 'Probably 50 per cent of it is, but the rest are from all over. We make space for guys who are different. In the end, it's the culture and guys that can grow in that culture.'

In this respect, there is no compromise.

'The kind of player who wants to be a Springbok knows what it takes. He knows he can't stay out late and get drunk. We try to get the players to take responsibility for themselves. They know the system: if they don't follow it, the coach will call them in and talk straight. The senior players will call them in and tell them to get their act together. If none of that works, they won't play for the Bulls any more.'

It's all fantastically competitive: only 5 per cent of boys who come into the Bulls system get a senior contract there. Fudge Mabeta, the Blue Bulls lock, told me that only four of his Under 19s intake made it through to the seniors. 'The Under 21 year is very important because that is when you get to prove yourself. You want the coach to look at you and say: "there is the future." There is only one year in which to do it. Once you are 22, you have got to be a Currie Cup player, otherwise you will be in no-man's-land.'

Meyer is clear about the prerequisites for making a senior contract:

- Constant hard work on the field; make things happen.
- Come back after a mistake or coach's criticism.
- Never, never, never give up.

- Plan, evaluate and correct; encourage others.
- Take tips, ask questions, listen, admit errors.
- Perform in big games as well as less important ones.
- Maintain condition and improve skills.
- Stay motivated; come back and play well after setbacks.
- Adapt to stress.
- Stay cool and confident under pressure.

Meyer says that every team goes through certain phases, and understanding this and acting upon it is crucial to any union's ongoing success.

At the Under 19 level, the boys come in straight from school, where they have been heroes. Typically they have a strong work ethic, but are inexperienced and individualistic, and although they are talented and desperate to perform, they have a low success rate. Also, they have no sponsors.

In the second phase, they still have a strong work ethic and are gaining experience. If they function as a unit, they are successful and play better.

In the third phase, they have a strong work ethic, are highly experienced and feel part of a team. As part of a highly successful world-class team they attract more sponsorships.

In the final phase, they have no work ethic and act as individuals who regard themselves as bigger than the team; they earn big money, but have a low success rate.

Meyer's theory is that, at phase three, you have to start weeding out top players and feeding in young blood, otherwise you will end up with a team in phase four, which is what he inherited.

Shayne Richardson would be pleased to hear that he is very concerned about what happens to players who don't make it, or who do make it but have nothing else to fall back on once their rugby-playing years are over – at the advanced age of 30-odd.

There must be more focus on skills that will serve them after rugby. Jannie Putter's life skills course is very basic, he says, and he plans to introduce another level which will teach boys how to open bank accounts; gain computer skills; deal with agents and the media. He has arranged 40 bursaries at the University of Pretoria for student teachers. The boys initially aren't keen, he says, because of the low status and pay of teachers, but he tells them they can always aim for director of rugby or head of sports, positions more and more schools are implementing and which pay better than straight teaching. They must be forced to study, as in the Varsity Cup, where you have to be registered at a tertiary institution in order to qualify.

When I left Heyneke, I realised I had been with him for almost three hours without noticing it. He is so intense, so passionate about what he does – and what he wants – that it's hard not to be swept up in it.

NINE

What I find increasingly beguiling about the Bulls is their openness. I thought this transparency and willingness to communicate reflected well on the organisation as a whole: it spoke of confidence and good management. Barend told me that much of his time was spent on the phone with Bulls supporters, engaging personally with them, especially when the union was about to make some big new move. I suspect that, single-handedly, he has advanced the views of a great many otherwise recalcitrant white South Africans.

With his backing, most doors at the Bulls swing open for me, but the culture is such that many of them would have been ajar anyway.

On the eve of the Bulls' play-off with the Crusaders in the 2010 Super 14, I went up to his eyrie of an office. If the Bulls won, they would qualify for a home semi-final, which they would play at the Orlando Stadium in Soweto because Loftus would by then have been handed over to FIFA for the 2010 Football World Cup. He kept stressing that a home semi-final was not yet in the bag, yet they had had to start planning, just in case. 'It's complex, you know, moving 40 000 people to Soweto.' He's spent the past two days mastering the logistics of this great trek of the faithful from the Loftus citadel into the heart of the erstwhile enemy. The choice of Orlando Stadium was, he readily admits, a pragmatic one – 'otherwise we would have had to play overseas or at one of our rivals' stadiums'. Now that it's happening, the Blue Bulls are throwing themselves into it heart and soul.

They are organising trains and buses from Centurion and a park 'n' ride scheme from Nasrec, six kilometres away from Soccer City. Nasrec's parking area can take 10 000 cars; Orlando Stadium's only 450.

The Crusaders are training on the field below us and there is an endearing excitement in his voice as he identifies the players for me: 'Look,' he says, 'there's Dan Carter. And there's Richie McCaw.'

Over the past two days he's been taking Bulls people on tours of Soweto. 'You know, most of them had never been to Soweto before. They were surprised to see how normal it was: that there were people on the streets, and parks and chickens.'

Whenever I am with Barend, the phrase 'bull in a china shop' springs to mind, possibly because in his office, a jokey blue china bull takes pride of place, and he looks bull-like. The china would be absolutely safe with him, however: he is graceful and agile, in thought and in movement. There is significant brain power behind the Bulls. 'Six years ago, we wanted to be part of the new South Africa. That's why we wanted to bring soccer here. Now, in the week, you get a Sundowns father bringing his son here like you get a Bulls dad bringing his son on Saturday.'

He proudly shows me a BMI survey revealing that 2 per cent of Bulls supporters are Asians; 17 per cent brown; 36 per cent white and the rest are black. When I express scepticism, given that every Loftus crowd I've ever witnessed has been 99 per cent white, he explains that this is supporters, not spectators. A much higher proportion of white people than black people are rugby supporters, but because of the higher number of black people in the country, even a small proportion of black rugby supporters soon begin to outnumber whites.

He ascribes the low attendance of black people at Loftus to pricing – 'Our cheapest tickets are R50. Soccer tickets are R20.' There is an air of chagrin to this. He'd clearly be a lot happier if more of the white bums on Loftus seats during rugby matches could be replaced with black ones.

In the end, as we all know now, his planning paid off and the Bulls played – and beat – the Crusaders in Soweto. It was much more than just another successful game: Barend and his Bulls yoked the wagons behind them and carted them off to an entirely new world.

I was enchanted by the experience, as were large numbers of fellow South Africans.

I hitch a ride with the media bus which arrived in Soweto at the same time as a bus containing a batch of VIPs: Blue Bulls board members and sponsors. These are solemn-looking men in suits and ties with their wives equally formal and demure at their sides; two by two; mostly white but every now and again a darker face. Barend is here, there and everywhere, conducting operations.

I follow the sound of boeremusiek and come to a quite extraordinary sight: hundreds of men and women in blue shirts and blue wigs and blue hats flashing blue lights, milling around in the sunshine, quaffing golden beer from huge plastic glasses. Mountains of beer cans everywhere. A giant TV screen is replaying the last, triumphant Bulls-Crusaders match. Next to it is the source of the boeremusiek: a makeshift stage where two guys in blue cowboy hats are performing live. It's a hugely cheerful scene: in front of the stage, people are dancing sakkie-sakkie and lang-arm. Behind the stage runs a fence, outside which are several black men, jigging along to the music. Just beyond them is the road, and bus after bus from the Nasrec park 'n' ride pulls up, disgorging waves of more blue-hued Bulle, looking slightly bemused as they weave their way through the black bystanders, seeking out the narrow gate into the bull pen. Some stop to get their pictures taken with the locals, like tourists.

Up Mooki Street, the main drag fronting the stadium, several encampments of blue shirts can be seen spilling out from yards. I go inside the first: it is an ordinary house that has been turned into a shebeen. A young woman with a baby strapped to her back is serving customers from behind an iron grille. At the back of the room is a double-fronted fridge, rapidly emptying. There are only a few quarts of beer and some Smirnoffs left. The queue is long and very blue. They thrust 100-rand notes through the grille and walk away with armfuls of quarts, saying: keep the change.

I want a soft drink: they only have a warm 2-litre bottle of Sprite left, so I buy that. A little further along the road, an elderly woman surrounded by a cluster of children stops me and dispatches a child into the house. She returns with a clean glass, which she hands to me with a smile.

On the other side of the road is a stream of blue made up of Bulle who are walking from Nasrec rather than waiting for the park 'n' ride.

The only negativity I hear occurs as I am walking up the ramp to the fourth floor where the press suite is. A group of middle-aged white, English-speaking men are on their way to the suites on the third floor, and are loudly sneering: 'There's not a single rubbish bin in this whole fucking place. That's fucking Soweto for you. The whole place is a fucking rubbish dump.' This mean-spiritedness jars with the wonder and warmth I have just come from and, because they belong to the same tribe as me, I feel somehow implicated. I turn and glare at them, wanting to shout: 'Who the fuck's fault is that?', but wasn't quite brave enough.

The game kicks off at 17h00 promptly, dramatically, with a flypast and a drum roll from two black dread-locked drummers. The Bulls Babes do their flashing, dancing thing and our boys run on to an explosive roar. Then we belt out the national anthem and they get down to business.

The symbolic importance of this – the first time an important rugby match had been played in Soweto and the first time thousands of white Afrikaners had visited this iconic site of anti-apartheid resistance (an SMS subsequently did the rounds remarking that the last time there were so many Afrikaners in Soweto, they were in Casspirs) – is evident in the number of celebrities who turn out to witness it. Winnie Mandela, splendid in a long, shimmering, bling coat, followed by a phalanx of young men; Gauteng premier, Nomvula Makonyane, and Joburg mayor, Sam Masondo; the last white president, FW de Klerk; Springbok coach Peter de Villiers and football boss, Danny Jordaan.

The Bulls' songs bellow out across Soweto for the first time: Steve Hofmeyr's 'Blou Bulle'; 'Kaptein'; 'Loslappie'. It strikes me that, away from their power base, the Bulls faithful, all camped up in their blue wigs and horns, look quaint and folksy, not even vaguely menacing. Down near the front, a bunch of them join up with their black neighbours in singing, to the tune of 'We are marching to Pretoria': 'We are marching to Soweto, Soweto, Soweto …'

At the press conference afterwards, a victorious Victor Matfield says with a grin: 'It was so amazing coming here on the bus to be greeted by vuvuzelas – and boeremusiek! It is so great for SA to see how far we have come. It's a very special day for us.'

Even Richie McCaw, looking deflated, fiddling with a bandage on his thigh, manages to say: 'It was still great to be part of such an occasion.'

On the big TV screen in the beer pen, the Stormers' semifinal against the Waratahs is being screened. Hundreds of fans stay on to watch, beer in hand, clearly in no hurry to leave Soweto.

It is now in the middle of the 2010 season of the Currie Cup and just over two years since I first met Paul Anthony and his then Under 19s. Curious as to what has happened with the eight players I interviewed then, I meet up with Paul for a final Trademarx cappuccino. This would be a crucial time for them: they had had two years to prove themselves in professional rugby but, by now, their initial contracts would have run out. Which of the eight would make it through to one of the prized senior Bulls contracts? Who will be dumped? Gerhard van der Heever is clearly already a star of the senior team, but what about the others? Simpiwe Mtimkulu? Zane Botha? Cornell Hess? Oswin Mentoos? Tom Seabela? Morné Mellett?

Paul says Simphiwe and Tom are both in the Under 21 squad and Simphiwe will play in the next big game, against Western Province, that Saturday. Zane Botha has been badly injured again, his cruciate ligament this time, and he will be off for six months.

Oswin is still at the Bulls but not in the squad. Then he pronounces: neither Oswin nor Simphiwe nor Tom will be contracted next year. All, I remark, slightly shocked, are players of colour.

'They are too small,' says Paul. Maybe someone forgot to feed them, I thought bitterly, but I'm aware this must be hard for Paul too. He nurtured those boys.

'You can't keep them all,' Paul is saying. 'Their contracts come to an end after 21. Of the initial squad of forty, twelve to twenty won't be contracted by us. Of that initial forty, three will stop playing rugby. The rest will play for other provinces.'

That's not a bad thing, he argues. If they shine in the

second division, they will be snapped up by one of the big unions. Look at Björn Basson, recently bought from the Griquas by the Bulls. Victor went to the Valke after his initial stint with the Bulls. Bakkies went to SWD.

'If a guy has been at the Bulls for two years, he can play rugby. Ninety-three per cent will carry on playing rugby. That is a very high rate.'

His boy Chili is doing very well, though. He put in a cracking game in the Tri-Nations Test against Australia when John Smit let him take his place for a full 20 minutes. Finally, injury-free, it seems his time has come.

From my perch at Trademarx, I am watching Steve Plummer, stopwatch in hand, timing Fourie du Preez, who is running at slowly increasing speeds up and down the sun-baked training field.

After a while, Fourie heads for the gym and Steve comes and joins me. He is still living at the Bros, he says, as mentor for the Under 19s. He tells me he has been promoted from junior conditioning coach to the seniors. He worked hard for the position – with an initial human science degree at Tukkies, followed by honours in sports science and biokinetics. He did his internship at the Bulls and has been here for six years now.

What he is doing with Fourie is what is called end-phase rehab – bringing the players back onto the field after injury.

'When someone gets injured,' he explains, 'he first goes to the doctor who does the diagnosis.' After that comes any necessary surgery and the physiotherapy to treat inflammation and swelling, followed by the start of strengthening exercises in the area of injury.

'I will take over from the physio, working on the injured section until it is back to full strength.' Some of this takes place in the gym and some on the field.

'I will, say, put them through six phases of running which get progressively harder in order to get them fit and ready for the game again. It's like building a house.

'They want to get better so they take any help they can from me.'

After he has done his gym time and has had a shower, Fourie du Preez comes over for a chat. Trademarx is open to the public, which means he is likely to be constantly accosted by adoring fans, so we climb up the stairs to the second floor and find a quiet seat in a corner of the balcony. The problem here is that workmen are busy extending the deck below and we have to compete with jackhammers and drills but, after all, life is seldom perfect and I am so grateful for this rare opportunity that I will struggle through any amount of noise. Fourie du Preez is one of those Springboks who prefers to keep a low profile and I know that I'm lucky he has agreed to speak to me.

We order soft drinks and I ask how him how his rehab is coming on.

He has not played for three months, he says, and he is finding it hard.

'I've got a rotator cuff tear – I tore it in 2007. I've managed it the past three years, but there was never time to really fix it. The specialist said if you want to play in the World Cup, you've got to fix it now. I've had the op and now it is six months of rehab and I'm only in my fourth month. I'm starting to run again, and I'm doing strengthening exercises. It's the first time in my life I've been out for so long and its frustrating, but when I decided to do it [have the op], I sort of knew what was lying ahead for me and it was the right decision.

'I've never ever had a long-term injury. I can't even play golf; it's tough. You can never plan for an injury. You do what you can with conditioning to prevent injury, but accidents happen and it's part of rugby and you just have to have a positive attitude towards it. I've a lot more time at home now.

'I've been very fortunate. I was out with my hand for a month and my shoulder for a month but this shoulder injury has been bugging me since the 2007 World Cup and I've never had the opportunity to fix it. It's been getting worse and worse and it's a good time for me to do it now, 2011 being such a big year.'

Fourie du Preez comes from a traditional Afrikaans Pretoria family steeped in rugby. His dad played in Springbok trials and Fourie himself was educated at that mini-rugby academy, Afrikaanse Hoër Seunskool. He was recruited to the Bulls straight from matric, turning down an offer from the Lions to do so. He is also one of Heyneke Meyer's Year Zero creations.

'I was fortunate to come here exactly the year that Heyneke started and I believe the last ten years of success in South African rugby started here. As soon as I started playing under Heyneke, everything was about team culture; about the guys playing for each other. He was always talking about character; always looking for guys with character.

'He instilled a lot of belief in us and taught us the way to think about rugby and how to deal with critics. Especially in my first two years here, we were criticised quite a lot. We were criticised for being one-dimensional or only playing ten-man rugby, but eventually we won the Currie Cup and then the Super 14.

'We would rather be a successful rugby franchise than listen to the critics. Who knows what beautiful rugby is? We believe there are only two types of rugby – winning rugby and losing rugby, and we believe in winning rugby. A lot of our guys went on to play for the Springboks and I believe that we brought that winning rugby to the Springboks.

'Rugby-wise and character-wise, Heyneke imprinted his

winning way into us. He also emphasised the family thing, and we took that with us to the Springboks. You have to feel something for the guy next to you and then you will try harder, even if it is one or two per cent, and that makes a lot of difference. I think we've been able to create that over the past few years.'

Fourie is physically compact and contained, right down to sleek hair combed back neatly over a slowly balding skull. He comes across as a thoughtful, subtle man who thinks carefully about what he says before he says it. It's hard to imagine, sitting opposite him on this hot, noisy balcony, the passion and energy that will explode from this quiet man once he hits the rugby field.

'A lot of things can derail a team,' he goes on. 'In any team environment, there are different cultures; different languages; girlfriends come from all over; some have children. A lot of things can go wrong and there are a lot of egos around and we try to eliminate that and to create opportunities for the team to get together, for the guys to get closer, for wives to get together.

'At the Bulls we will have one or two beers together every third or fourth week after the Monday training session, or a braai, or an occasion when our wives and girlfriends can be together; just a nice, fun evening, an opportunity for us to mingle.

'I think where we are different from other unions is that a lot of guys just stay in the changing room after a game, but for us it is a great opportunity to have a nice time with our families without outside people or the media.

'Most of the guys are friends, so when we get off, some guys will take off for the bush or go to Sun City.

'I play golf once a week with Victor, Danie Rossouw and Pedrie Wannenburg; it's a standing foursome and there is some nice rivalry. Otherwise I relax by spending time with my family.'

Fourie's father is a chartered accountant who later went into mining, a wealthy man who is generous with his children, making millionaires of each of them when they turned 21. Fourie is married to his childhood sweetheart – they have been going out since he was in Standard Nine and are about to have their first child. His father-in-law is a dominee in the Dutch Reformed Church and both he and his wife have a strong Christian faith.

'Faith has been the biggest part of my rugby career and it has been easy practising it while at the Bulls because Heyneke introduced it, and Frans and Peter have continued with it. We believe we've been blessed here at the Bulls because we stand for something and what we achieve is for something higher and better.'

Does it help you play better? I ask. 'Yes, definitely. I feel there is someone out there whatever I do. Whenever I struggle with injuries and with issues off the field, I feel there is some higher power that has helped me.

'I feel I've been very blessed, especially with my career and in regard to injuries. That is why I don't stress too much about what I will do afterwards, because I know that there will be something bigger for me after rugby as well.'

I ask him whether he thinks the Springboks' Christian faith gives them an edge on the field. He thinks for a bit and then responds: 'I think every guy believes a little bit differently. You know you do better when you've got faith, but it is difficult to say we've got an edge, an advantage. It's not about results; it's more about the way you are on and off the field; the message you send out there. It's not about winning or losing. It's about the difference we can make.

'We pray: let's just go out there and do what we love and try to set an example.'

I ask him about the diversity issue: how can it be used to energise a team, rather than divide it? 'It's a matter of considering everyone, whatever decision is made; on or off the field. At the end of the day, you must do what is best for the team.'

What about language? 'It depends on the team – only two or three guys in the Bulls are English, so most of it is in Afrikaans, but a player can ask for English to be used at any time, and a lot more English is coming in.

'With the Boks, when the coach is English, everything is in English, but now with Peter de Villiers it is sometimes Afrikaans and sometimes English. Everyone is comfortable with that. If someone really doesn't understand, he says so, but most people understand English and Afrikaans.

'With the Boks, most of us started in 2004 when there was a new coach and he brought in a lot of youngsters. In the first year or two, it took a while for everyone to gel; to get to know each other; to get a family thing going.

'Now we have been together for six or seven years, so it's almost like at the Bulls where all the wives know each other. There is a very good atmosphere at the Boks at the moment because we've been together for so long. There is no provincialism or whatever. Sometimes you might see all the Bulls sitting together, but it is only because you want to be with your friends and we are such good friends here.'

I ask him about the Springboks' poor performance in the 2010 Tri-Nations and he replies: 'It is unfair to look at a two-month period and say we aren't doing well. You can't view it in isolation. It's better to spot the mistakes now and fix them. We've had a lot of injuries; we've had six or seven guys out this year and that makes a difference.

'I think things will get better again. It feels like when the Bulls worked up to 2007 when we won the Super 14. We took a bit of a dip in 2008 when Frans came in (and Fourie himself was captain) and Victor and Gary went away and we had a few younger players coming in.

'We struggled at first in the Super 14 but the main thing is that we all stuck together and the coaching team all stuck together and there weren't any heads rolling. After that we won every trophy we could have won. If we can keep the team together, we can get through this and get better again. You have to fix the problems; the leadership accepts that; but whatever happens, the players are sticking together. There are no knives in the back. We are still a tight unit. There is no bad feeling between the players.'

I suggest that one of the reasons the Springboks were struggling was because they were missing this particular scrum half, generally acknowledged not only as brilliant in his position but also as a generous and hugely motivational on-field presence. He looks down, smiling shyly, not to be drawn. The jackhammers are thudding away below us. The heat out here beyond the air-conditioning is stifling.

I ask him how he felt about playing in Soweto and he said that the knowledge that they might play there had made them even more determined to make the semi-finals. 'At the beginning of 2010, we knew we couldn't play the semi-finals at Loftus. When they said we might play in Soweto, we played towards that. I believe that we always had a great positive attitude towards it and that helped. After the semi-final a lot of the guys said that it was one of the best rugby experiences we have ever had – and we've had quite a few.

'Hopefully we will keep up the momentum we got then and not just leave it there. Perhaps we will go and play a big game there every year to keep it going.

'Just driving to the semi-final, it was unbelievable seeing what was happening. A lot of people say Pretoria people are conservative Afrikaners or whatever, but just driving to Soweto, you could see our country has come a long way. Everyone loves this country. Whatever is said out there, the average white South African loves this country and wants it to be a success. So, seeing what was happening out there in Soweto gave a lot of us hope for the future.

'We've got a very good chance of winning the World Cup again because of the talent we have in South Africa – to get two South African teams in the 2010 Super 14 finals just shows that.'

I ask him why he has chosen a life of relative reticence and he explains: 'I believe you don't have to be in the public eye if you don't want to. I stay out of it. I believe I am a rugby player. They can judge me on my rugby and leave my personal life alone. I will do one or two events a year and if I can help out, I will. I don't try to be on every second magazine cover or on TV, however. I'm not saying guys who do it are wrong, but you can make that decision for yourself.'

After the World Cup, he is going to Japan. 'My wife and I went there for the first time for a week three weeks ago. I really enjoy working with Eddie Jones.

'I always thought at some stage at the end of my career I would go overseas and do the adventure thing, and rugby gives you the opportunity to experience something else. I looked at a lot of options.

'To me, the English weather is absolutely horrible. In France, you have to play forty games a year. Japan is completely different to anything else I've experienced and I think it will be a great life experience for me. I'm going for about a year and a half. At that stage, my rugby will be finished; with this injury, I don't know if I will come back and play here.

'I love rugby and everyone says: "Do what you love." I always wanted to be a professional player but it's not something you can plan for. It's just something that happens.'

And after rugby? 'In my first two years, I studied financial management. In my second year, I got selected to play in the World Cup and that was during exams and I just couldn't get back into it. It's a problem in professional rugby with guys being selected so early. I see myself at some stage getting involved in coaching but I'm not sure when and it won't be my primary goal. I will probably get involved in the financial sector. First, you have to find something you really enjoy. I'm sure I will be fine.'

As I drive away from Loftus, I think about Fourie. Under the old order, he would have done as well at the Bulls as he has now. He comes from the right background, nurtured from birth with every material and cultural advantage. Unlike Bulls players from the Eastern Cape, he has not had to shift an inch from his comfort zone: city, church, girl-friend, language, culture. He arrived at the Bulls at exactly the right time, when their fortunes began to turn around.

Yet he has also had to face challenges and competition his father would never have known. That he has embraced these challenges and put his heart and soul into making the new team work, I thought, made him as much of a hero off the field as on it.

ELEVEN

Just before Western Province came to town to take on the Bulls for the second leg of the 2010 Currie Cup, Barend issued a press statement:

'The Blue Bulls Company would like to make the following very clear: All visitors, supporters and spectators – from all races – are welcome at Loftus Versfeld. The Blue Bulls Company will not tolerate any racist behaviour and would like to reiterate that anyone who does not agree with this principle is not welcome at Loftus Versveld. Should you be a victim of racism, victimisation, drunkenness or crude language, we urge you to contact the control room at the following numbers and kindly furnish us with your seat numbers.'

An official would immediately be sent down and, if appropriate, the police called for a formal charge to be laid.

This was more like it. If this injunction had been in force a couple of years earlier, I could have quietly SMS-ed the control room and got the racist sharing the stands with me at the Under 19s game dealt with.

I went to see Barend to find out what was behind this initiative and he told me that there had been 'incidents'. Apart from the attack on the photographer mentioned by Simnikiwe Xabanisa, there had been another, more recent, one: a white man told two black women spectators that he didn't want them sitting next to his family. The women immediately left but, unfortunately, said Barend, they only informed the Bulls about the incident the following day.

Yet again, I am impressed by the Bulls' muscular leadership; their capacity to face up to what is wrong within their ranks, tackle it effectively and decisively, and move on. The fact that they were publicly prepared to admit to recidivist racism seemed to me very brave. There is no mealy-mouthed denial or down-playing of it. Their commitment to its eradication shows in the risk they know they face: that some of their fans might stop coming to Loftus, with all the financial implications of reduced box-office revenue, and therefore less funding for their continued strength.

They remind me of young Germans, ever mindful of Nazism and the horrors committed in their name. It keeps them dynamic and forward-looking. They never rest on their moral laurels.

Are the Bulls representative of Afrikaners? I ask Barend. Yes, in the cities, he says. It is in some parts of the rural areas that you get the recidivists.

Yet it still seems to me that the Bulls can take credit for leading the way, because they reach parts no politician or dominee can hope to penetrate – the heart and the soul and the groin of the Afrikaner. If the Bulls say racism is not cool, it counts.

The Saturday that Western Province takes on the Bulls at Loftus is incredibly hot: around 33 degrees. The spring rains have not yet arrived and four months of winter drought means the air is sucked dry. For the curtain-raisers – the Under 19s and the Under 21s, I sit with Barend in his air-conditioned office overlooking the field. He tells me with a grin that they have already had one distressed SMS. 'This guy said there was a man behind him who kept farting and he couldn't stand the smell and could we please do something about it!'

Every now and again, the SMS number flashes up on the screen overlooking the field, leaving everyone in absolutely no doubt of the new regime. AfriForum pitch up with a banner trying to rally support for their boycott of ABSA after the bank called for more black players in the

Currie Cup. They are summarily evicted; their campaign looking increasingly doomed. It is the Bulls who represent Afrikanerdom now.

Would you call yourself an Afrikaner leader? I ask Barend.

He says: 'I think I've got the ability to redirect people's thinking, but not as an individual, rather as the leader of a team. I've been part of this set-up since 1983, through the good years and the bad years. I'm proud of where we are.'

Whenever I mention the words Afrikaner and Christian and Bulls in the same sentence, Barend does a bit of table-thumping. 'The Bulls are not an Afrikaner Christian organisation! We are a professional sporting organisation!'

We watch as the young bloods from this professional sporting organisation fall before the resurgent young pretenders from the south. Both Western Province Under 19s and Under 21s beat the Bulls.

The main game is about to begin. Barend invites me to watch the game from the President's box and I think, why not? A chance to view another layer of Bulls: the board and the rest of the hierarchy. He is tense now and needs to sneak off for a cigarette.

'We've got to win this game to stay in the play-offs. We need to be in the top four.'

The Bulls have struggled in this Currie Cup – beaten even by the bottom-of-the-league Pumas a few weeks before, demoralised by the arrest of one of their props, Bees Roux, for allegedly beating a black police officer to death. The Bulls' response to this was, I thought, exemplary. Bees was put on leave while his case went through the courts, and heartfelt condolences were despatched to the cop's family. Once again, they have been in a bad place and pulled through.

When I first met them, in 2008, they were in a trough. Having won the Super 14 in 2007, they came a miserable 10th in 2008. The following year, they won both the Super 14 and Currie Cup. In 2010, they again won the

Super 14 in that exhilarating all South African final against the Stormers in Soweto. I thought this was them all over: their capacity to reinvent themselves, to repeatedly mine an inner strength; to adapt to new challenges and come back even stronger. Darwin would have been proud.

I sit there in the President's box with the blue-shirted hierarchy and watch as they triumph yet again. The final score is 36–32. They have made it through to the semi-finals.

E N G A G E !

ONE

Increasingly I am in love with the game itself. It's something about its hidden complexity: the games within the game, the intricate choreography of the set pieces; the orgasmic whoosh of the crowd's delight as a player streaks towards the try line and the ecstatic roar as he flies over it. Then the trance-like stillness of the fly half, the world narrowed down to his boot, the ball and that distant rectangle through which he must kick it. For me, the most thrilling manoeuvre of all is the rolling maul, which just happens to be a speciality of Western Province/the Stormers. I love watching this straining, heaving mass of muscle and sinew inching its way forward, like some Trojan horse, the ball concealed within. It stirs an atavistic memory of war as a nobler, purer thing. This is a battle for territory fought man to man, not by remote, with long-range missiles and nuclear warheads.

As Anton van Zyl, the team's rugged and cerebral Currie Cup captain, tells me, it also represents the purest distillation of team spirit. 'If all eight guys are not pushing together, that maul will be obliterated. It can be very dangerous and you will lose.'

If executed correctly, the rolling maul is invincible, but it is all about the initial construction, which begins with the line-out. Anton explains how it works.

'The two guys who lifted the jumper become the pillars. Their responsibility is to keep the maul up so as to stop the opposition from sacking it. Then you've got the guy we call the ripper and he slowly works his way to the back of the maul. The next two guys go in as if they are scrumming and they bind onto each other. We call them the drivers. Then we have the rudder, which is what the ripper becomes once he has reached the back of the maul. There is also a spare forward. Once we are set – and being set means everyone getting into position perfectly – we are unstoppable. The challenge, however, is to get set properly without being disrupted or fractured.

'Once a maul is set, the opposition is not allowed to collapse it because it is considered dangerous play. Sometimes they do, illegally, and the ref lets them get away with it, but just imagine, if you've got eight guys who have formed a loose scrum or driving maul, how are you going to stop them? You can't tackle them. The ball is totally engulfed amongst bodies. The bottom line is: you can't stop them. The other side could form an oppositional driving maul, but if they do, they've got to pull in all eight forwards to make it a fair fight and as soon as they commit eight forwards, your man at the back can peel off because there is no one to stop him. The backs are too wide and if they were then to come in, you can let the ball go to your backs and therefore get space out wide.

'The driving maul is something we practise a helluva a lot and it's something we are very good at. It's become part of South African rugby culture. The All Blacks, for example, hate driving mauls. They believe there are much easier ways to get the ball over the line because the maul has got to be one of the most tiring exercises in rugby. A hell of a lot of energy gets used.

'The Cheetahs maul. So do the Bulls, but they don't maul to score. They use the maul further out to suck in your forwards so that they can have a better kicking game. There are all sorts of intricacies involved in the use of the maul as a tactical weapon.'

As with a scrum, any dissonance between players can be fatal. 'If you don't believe 100 per cent in your team mate or he doesn't believe in you, you are going to get found out. If I'm worried about someone – say a black guy who has been through his initiation and we don't feel comfortable with each other – we're going to be exposed on the field. The higher the level you play at, the smaller the room for error becomes, the smaller the crack the opposition is looking to exploit.

'As powerful as that maul is, if one opposition member can fracture it – which means he can get in between two of our guys – we're dead. The maul will collapse or stop because he is able to loosen it. The whole point of the maul is that it is this tight ball that's got no weakness; it's got no fissures. If, while the maul is moving, the opposition starts putting pressure on a particular part, it's so important that you've got that almost instinctive knowledge of each other to feel that and then respond accordingly. You'll often see a maul sliding off or sliding round and that's not a fluke either – we set up certain mauls so that we throw at the front. One of our guys will come and bind at a certain point and he will wait for the opposition to start hitting him. He will try to sweep them out the way so that the maul can move. It's all about split-second timing – a second too early and you're not going to move the opposition away; a second too late and they've already done too much damage. You don't have time to communicate. You're in an awkward position because you can't see anything. You've just got to go on feel, on instinct, and your understanding of each other.'

This image of the maul and the scrum as the litmus test of harmony within a team stays with me. Western Province and the Stormers are the most racially diverse of all the unions. The union is owned by 90 clubs spread throughout the Western Cape. Nearly two thirds are mainly coloured; 5 per cent are African; the rest white. Newlands is the only rugby stadium in the country where a substantial proportion of the crowd is not white.

Coloured people dominate demographically and, racially

mixed as they are, they combine between them the DNA of all of who live or have lived in South Africa: Khoisan, African, white and Asian.

It was in Cape Town that rugby was played in South Africa for the first time, namely at Bishops, the school for sons of the British rulers. Just as the British originally conceived of rugby as the perfect game to nurture 'the muscular Christian', equipped with the necessary moral and physical fibre to defend the Empire, so a similar cohort of rugby-playing 'muscular Muslims' evolved in the Bo-Kaap to defend their community. Rugby has always been the team game of choice throughout the coloured communities. Until the end of apartheid, most clubs remained racially defined, a situation that hasn't changed all that much. The upshot is that the Western Province and Stormers teams have a large, passionate and diverse rugby community to draw on.

For the first decade of this century, the success rate of Western Province/Stormers has roughly been inverse to that of the Bulls. Western Province won the Currie Cup in 2001, when the Bulls were at the bottom of every log. As the Bulls got steadily stronger, Western Province and the Stormers languished way down Currie Cup and Super Rugby league tables. In 2008, Rassie Erasmus was brought in from the Cheetahs in an attempt to turn things around. Like Heyneke Meyer, Erasmus understood that one needed to start at the bottom, identifying and developing young players.

The results have been dramatic. Although 2009 was not a good year, 2010 revealed a team on the edge of greatness. It was Rassie who recruited Allister Coetzee, a man who brings with him a breadth and depth peculiar to South African rugby.

I first interviewed Allister early one winter evening in 2010 at his home in a green and hilly part of Durbanville, just as Western Province was beginning its preparations for the Currie Cup. His wife, Diane, greeted me at the door and then went off to watch *Sewende Laan* in the TV room while I chatted to her husband in the lounge. Allister is a powerfully built man, though not tall. He has loved and played rugby all his life but, born in 1963, his playing years were blighted by the racist strictures on players of colour. He grew up in Grahamstown, and a powerful memory is watching white boys play the sport equipped with the best that money could buy at the posh Kingswood College across the road from his home. He had to walk to the much poorer coloured school down the road. Compounding the family's hardship was his father's death when Allister was still very young. His mother struggled to bring up four children on her own.

Like so many other prominent coaches, Coetzee started his working life as a teacher. For 18 years, he taught physical education at the Galvin Park Primary School in Port Elizabeth, all the while continuing to play rugby.

Until 1992, South African rugby was dominated by the whites-only South African Rugby Board. Players of colour fell under the non-racial South African Rugby Union. SARB and SARU operated in parallel universes, defined entirely by the colour of the players' skin, with the lion's share of resources going to the white-skinned teams. SARU teams could play each other but couldn't play white teams – nor could they travel abroad to play internationally.

Wallabies, the club for which Allister played, was top of the provincial SARU league. Top of the SARB league was the all-white Dispatch. They neither watched each other nor played against each other. In 1992, when this craziness came to an end and SARU and SARB were unified, Coetzee found himself the only player of colour in the Eastern Province side in the Currie Cup. Most of the rest were 'big Afrikaans chaps from the Dispatch team'. There were no issues, he says. 'There was a lot of respect for each other.' He retired from playing in 1995 at the age of 34 – 'Quite old for a scrum half!' Also too old to be able to compete at a time when his colour would, theoretically at least, no longer be used against him.

What's impressive about Allister is that there is no sense of bitterness or victim-hood although 'I do wonder how far I would have gone if I had had the chance to play in the new dispensation with all the opportunities. I'm not saying for a minute that I regret where I came from or blame others.'

After an intense hour and a half with him, I have the impression of a warm man, quick to see the humour in any situation. He comes across as low-key, reserved almost, but one senses the steel that must have built up during those years of struggle and frustration – and the strength it must have taken to put it all behind him and keep on fighting. Allister, in his unassuming way, has bashed his way to the top of South African rugby. In many instances, he was the first coach of colour to do so.

He was the first black assistant coach to the Springboks – the team which won the 2007 World Cup under Jake White. It was after the World Cup that Rassie Erasmus recruited him, first as assistant coach and then as head coach of Western Province. When Erasmus moved upstairs to become director of rugby, Allister took over the Stormers as well. In May 2010, he became the first black coach to take his team to the Super 14 finals – the historic Soweto final against the Bulls. What's more, it was the first time the Stormers had made it to a final in 11 years.

That is not enough. He is very pleased to have made it to a final, but now he wants to actually bring home a Cup. The 2010 Currie Cup would do very well.

From my exhilarating experience with the Ikey Tigers I've learnt that the only way to really understand a team is to stick closely with it through a tough campaign. I have resolved that this is what I will do with Western Province through the 2010 Currie Cup. I know that this won't be particularly easy as Western Province are nowhere near as open as the UCT team – or the Bulls, for that matter.

I think the fact that I am female helps. There will be no critical analysis of the team's and management's performance all over the newspapers and the airwaves week after week, unlike with daily and weekly journalists. Early on I publish a profile of Allister in *Business Day*, which proves that my focus is very different.

The next time I see Allister, it is in his office at the Western Province High Performance Centre. I'm delighted when he tells me, yes, he is happy for me to hang around there over the next few months, getting a sense of what it's like from the inside. I know this process of gaining trust – both from him and from the players – has only just begun, but it is a good start.

The High Performance Centre – more commonly known as the HPC – is the business end of Western Province/ Stormers. If Newlands is the stage where the players perform and engage with their audience, the HPC is where all the behind-the-scenes rehearsing is done.

It's in the gritty suburban sprawl of less-than-romantic Bellville, sandwiched between Voortrekker Road and the railway line. The long, sturdy blocks of Tygerberg Hospital dominate the view on one side and the Louis Leipoldt Medical Centre the other.

It's a stark, featureless place but, as the players remind me, not so long ago they had no real home at all and had to borrow school fields to train on. I think how much luckier the Bulls are, with their holistic, all-in-one training/competing/living space. When I remark on this to Allister – on the basis that it all seems a bit unfair – he says, well, that's why we have to win: the more finals you play at home and win at home, the more income you get, which means the more you have to spend on getting even better.

The HPC has two big practice fields, one on either side of an oblong, functional, two-storey building: one for the senior team and one for the Under 21s. In the parking lot, looming above the rows of modest sedans, are three big white double-cab bakkies, oozing machismo. They bear inscriptions: 'Toyota driven by Tiaan Liebenberg' and 'Anton van Zyl, proudly sponsored by Tata'. Another Toyota is devoted to Gio Aplon.

Allister has asked Greg Daniels, the team masseur, to show me around. Leading off to the left from the central lobby are a string of small offices for the team manager, Chippie Solomons, and the coaches: Allister, Rassie, Robbie Fleck, Matt Proudfoot, Jacques Nienaber. On the other side of the corridor are the medical staff's offices and treatment rooms. Right at the end is the gym which takes up the last chunk of the building. With its soaring double-height ceiling, it's a lovely room, with state-of-the-art equipment and a small swimming pool.

It's empty apart from Jean de Villiers, slowly flexing his right calf while gazing at one of the TV screens that dot the walls. He's on suspension from the Springboks for a dangerous tackle on All-Black wing, Rene Ranger, during the Tri-Nations and is using the time to train with his home boys. Close to the entrance is a spiral staircase that leads up to the changing rooms and, after checking there is no one in them, Greg leads me up into them. They, too, are generous rooms: two large tubs side by side, one for hot water and one for cold. Kit bags lie on the floor beside walls of lockers, with trainers and clothes spilling out of them. It looks very recently vacated. Opposite the rows of toilets is a counter with specimen bottles. This is for players to check their hydration levels, explains Greg. Dehydration is a big danger with all that sweat-inducing exercise. A chart on the wall gives them pointers: between 200 and 600: good: 300 millilitres for three hours. From 600 to 1 000 millilitres: warm: 500 millilitres for three hours. From 1 000 to 1 500 millilitres: dangerous: 500 millilitres for four hours.

The changing room leads to an all-purpose dining-cum-recreation room, also on the second floor and flanked by a narrow verandah. There are a few trestle tables and couches and, towards the end, a table-tennis table where Schalk Burger is playing one of the younger players. Others are sprawled across the couches. In the far corner is another door leading into the team room. It is lined with desks, each containing a laptop. At the end of the room is a whiteboard, then the computer room, where games are recorded, analysed and disseminated to the team.

As we leave, Schalk gives up on the table tennis and makes his way to one of the couches. Instantly, the players sitting there move to make way for him. It's easy to see who is the alpha male around here.

A bit later, they tumble down the stairs to the fields below. The Cape Town winter has done its unpredictable thing and given us some glorious days. It's sunny and still and the sky is a brilliant blue. The forwards are practising line-outs. I watch Schalk leaping into the air over and over again, fine blond hair flying.

He comes over to where I am sitting with Greg, picks up a roll of bandage and, lifting each leg onto the bench, one by one, carefully straps the bandage several times around each muscular thigh. It's precautionary, he says. He's feeling twinges. Then off he lopes, back into the fray.

Schalk and Jean are tourists today. They are on Springbok duty and won't be around for the big match the rest of the team are straining towards: their fifth Currie Cup game against the Griquas in Kimberley six days away. The Griquas are below them on the log (well, everyone is at this point) but the lads are not resting on their laurels. In their last two games against the Griquas in Kimberley, Western Province have lost – by one point. In 2008, they lost 20–21 and in 2009 it was 33–32. Even though they have easily won their first four games of the 2010 Currie Cup – 25–11 against the Cheetahs; 32–0 against the Lions; 42–23 against the Leopards; and 54–13 against the Pumas – they are not complacent.

'It's going to be tough,' says Allister. 'The Griquas have a huge kicking game and they know the conditions. The ball travels much further than it does here.'

Anton, who is captain until Schalk is released from Springbok duty at the semi-final stage, says: 'We've said it over the last few weeks: this is definitely a crucial phase of the competition. It's not only the last phase of the first round, but also the first phase of the second round.'

On the plus side, though, Province have got three of their Springboks back for the game: Francois Louw, Juan de Jongh and Gio Aplon.

Western Province is top of the log, very much hoping to stay there.

They go up to Kimberley and thrash the Griquas 50–3. It's barely a contest at all.

On the Monday, I ask Anton: 'How does it feel? Surely a touch of euphoria?'

He keeps it low key: 'Euphoria is a big word. You just feel it's a job well done. When you are so reliant on 14 guys and you get a score like that, it's a feeling of achievement as a collective. The team has performed well.'

You can never get too carried away, he says. 'If someone scores a try, you have to give a bit of a high five but you can't let yourself go. If you don't hit your straps at once, the other side might score a try and then you're back where you're started.'

I go down to Allister's office and find him slightly more

effusive: 'It was a great performance by the team. We kept them tryless. We scored 50 points. It's never been done.'

I'm learning that it's all about the long game. Triumphs are fleeting. Top of the log they might be, but they are very aware they could be toppled off it at any point. When I walked into his office, Allister – whom I discover is known within the team as 'Tuti' – was engrossed in a bound A4 document. It is 100 pages long and it is basically the Western Province Bible of the week. It contains a detailed analysis of the game against the Griquas, gleaned from various camera angles: SuperSport's and WP's own. Analysed electronically by a New Zealand-designed software programme called Fairplay, it breaks down each player's performance under headings such as: Tackles attempted, Tackles made, Tanker percentage, Attitude, Bad decision percentage, Aggression percentage. Robbie Fleck, the backs coach, Matt Proudfoot, in charge of the forwards, and Jacques Nienaber, the kicking coach, have all put in their reports. Every aspect of the game is meticulously assessed. It is very detailed, very methodical.

He flips over the pages, pointing out each category covered.

'Each coach has his own area of responsibility and has to draw up his reports. That goes for every game. You have the stats for the game and for each player. You get marked on everything.'

The thinking behind this document is that you must be properly assessed, both as a coach and as a player, so that you know where the mistakes are and what needs to be worked on. There is no guessing. 'Everyone sees how everyone else is doing – how many tackles you've missed. It's all colour-coded. Green for good; red for bad.' I was amused to see a line of pink for ineffectual play. That means girly then.

'What counts is each individual's and coach's work

ethic and this makes it all very transparent.' It also contains everything they need to know about the team they are to play the next week, as well as the idiosyncrasies of the referee and the physical conditions. 'So, for scrums, we will know what our plan is. When they get a certain line-out, they know what is coming. This book will tell me what the weather will be doing during the game. It tells me how many players have had how many physio sessions; how much rugby time each player has had during the year, and how many appointments with the masseur. It means I have a good understanding of who needs to be rested; who needs to be managed appropriately. There is the ref's report: an assessment of each ref and what decisions he has made and his strong and weaker points. It's a very good coaching tool. Perhaps it's a bit over the top, but it makes you feel so comfortable and prepared. Just a click of a computer and it's all there: everybody is empowered; everybody has the same info.'

He leans back in his chair, stretching his arms above his head, smiling tiredly at me. It's 16h00 and he can think about winding down for the day.

He says that he has been studying much of this since the day before, the Sunday. Planning for the next game begins the day after the last game.

'After a match, we want to get home as soon as possible. Sunday is one of the toughest days – it's when all the planning starts, and you've got to balance family time with that as well. In addition, you worry about calls from the doctor. By around 17h00, I have gone through the injury list with the doctor and assessed the extent of it. Some of those injuries have quite a serious impact on the next game. I have to make sure we have enough players on Monday.'

Also, he says with a grin, he has to deal with an interrogation from his 70-year-old mother who is already on top of the fact that Gio Aplon and Juan de Jongh have been recalled to the Springbok team for the Tri-Nations. 'She's still living in Grahamstown and playing rugby in her head. She phoned me yesterday and said: "What are you going to do now Gio and Juan have gone back to the Boks? How many injuries have you got?" I just put her onto Diane.

'Sunday, Monday and Tuesday are the toughest in terms of planning. It takes about six hours to go through everything on a Sunday, and on Monday you've got the same thing again – just to get the review done.'

Today, which is Monday, 2 August, they started at 10h00, rather than the usual 08h00. First off, the coaches met with the senior players. 'We look at the weaknesses that need to be fixed. We look at the plan. Are we seeing the same things or have they picked up something else? Then we draw up a plan which we call the Focus for the Week and they spread it to the others during the week. They know exactly what we want.

'We also look at things that bind the team together. We discuss rugby issues on and off the field with them, like emotional issues. The players are different and some handle pressure well, others have to learn to handle pressure, and some have personal issues. If a player has issues, that will affect the game. If he doesn't want to talk to me, we refer him to a specialist. The emotional side is a very crucial aspect of a player and will affect his performance as much as his play.'

On Monday afternoon, all the coaches and players meet. After a big win, like the one they've just had, they have 'a big blow-out session, either in the gym or on the field. After a brilliant win like that against the Griquas, it brings them down to earth again.'

They need to have their feet firmly on the ground for the next match: the Bulls are coming to town. After them come the Sharks, the Cheetahs and the Lions. It's going to be a challenging month.

As I leave the HPC, I glance at the juniors, training on their field on the other side of the HPC, and spot a familiar face: Dobbo has been recruited by Rassie to help out with the Under 21s and will be with them for the entire campaign.

It's unsettling, the Springboks being part of the team one week and then vanishing the next. It does result in a worrying weakness in the backline, especially with an epic battle in the offing. Gio and Juan have a higher calling, however: the training camp for the Tri-Nations game against the All Blacks the following Saturday. A third Springbok, Francois Louw, is still hovering between the Springboks and Province. Peter de Villiers has promised to let Allister know by Friday, the day before they take on the Bulls, whether he can have him back or not.

This loss, though, does mean opportunity for another of my old acquaintances from the UCT team, namely tall, curly-haired Tim Whitehead, who has been drafted in from the Under 21s to fill in for Juan de Jongh at outside centre. Tim has always trod a bit of a golden path: he played first team for Grey PE and, after registering for a business science degree at UCT, played with the UCT Under 20s under Dobbo for a few years and then progressed with him to the first team and the Varsity Cup.

'Then it got a bit hectic. I was offered a junior contract here, and all of a sudden I was playing for the Under 21 side. It had a snowball effect. I love the system here. I wasn't so keen on all the mindfulness and team functions in the Varsity Cup. I like to be by myself before a game: to think and to analyse.'

One casualty of the move to professionalism was his studies.

'I said to my parents: "Do I take this seriously and risk failing a few subjects, or do I drop the rugby and focus on study?" They said: "Take the rugby opportunity."'

'I got ten caps in the 2010 Super 14, mostly off the

bench. That was the greatest experience for me. I went on tour with them and I learnt so much from the Springboks. I stopped studying at UCT but was able to take a few credits across to Unisa, where I've registered for BCom Accounting. It's impossible to be at UCT for all the lectures – I'm too much out of the loop. At Unisa, it's much easier to keep up to date – there are only one or two exams a semester. I don't know if I want to be stuck behind a desk as an accountant after being outside playing, but I'm just trying to get my BCom. I want to start my own business and if you can get your foot in the door at rugby and forge good relationships, it's a step in the right direction for the future.'

We're chatting on the verandah overlooking the fields. Practice has ended and the other players are streaming past us to the changing room. Sweat gleams off densely muscled limbs. They look relaxed and cheerful, aglow with the well-being that follows intense exercise. Tim is telling me what he'd really like to get into. Because it's unexpected, I find it quite charming. It's coffee. 'I love coffee. I can only drink it at the beginning of a week because of its dehydrating effects, but that is what I'd like to focus on.' He and a friend have already made an exploratory trip into coffee-producing parts of our continent and want to try to interest local coffee shops in importing them. For now, though, there are other priorities: getting his degree. And beating the Bulls.

Like Province, the Bulls are victims of their own success, with eleven of their top players off on national duty. Unlike Province, the Bulls have got two of them back for Saturday's game: Zane Kirchner and Dewald Potgieter. Playing off the bench is one Bees Roux, whose life is about to take a dramatic turn for the worse. The Bulls pack have always been formidable, and played a large part in beating the

Stormers to the Super 14 trophy a few months back. The memory of that defeat is still fresh.

On the Friday morning before the game, I go to Newlands for the Captain's Run, the ritual which signifies the subtle yet important transition from coach to captain. The former has done all he can. Now he has to largely hand over to the man who will lead on the field. It is the captain who decides what needs to be practised one last time. I look over at Anton, leading an endless repetition of line-outs, graceful and faultless. At the other end of the field, Willem de Waal is getting the ball to soar over the goalposts from a variety of apparently impossible angles.

High up in the stands, I find Allister, poring over The Book. He reads out the temperature prediction to me, one of the numerous small facts faithfully recorded in it: 'At 17h05, when the game starts, the maximum temperature will be 16 degrees. The wind will be blowing at 17 kilometres an hour, from this direction towards the Railway Stand.'

Affable and charming as ever, he is nevertheless clearly tense.

'It's a big day tomorrow,' he says. 'The pressure is building.'

I leave him to continue reading and settle down to watch the lads. It's another gloriously sunny day, and everything seems peaceful and relaxed. By this time tomorrow, the stands, empty now apart from me and Allister, will be packed and pumping. Now all I can hear are the line-out calls, clear as a bell.

Along with Allister, Anton van Zyl has become an important touchstone for me because he is captain but mainly because he is a thoughtful man who exudes integrity. I know that whatever he tells me will be as close to the truth as it is possible to be. It will also be shorn of any self-aggrandisement. I initially get to know him over a coffee at Caveau, the restaurant close to the Newlands rugby stadium, just before the season starts. It is 14h00 and the place is still packed and noisy with the lunchtime crowd. I get there early and choose the quietest available seat: a couch detached from the busy tables, with a clear view into their pretty courtyard garden. Anton arrives and we introduce ourselves and, once again, I explain the themes of my book, now increasingly tuned to the rhythms of his team, my team.

A tall man, he folds himself into the couch. He talks slowly, with some hesitation, as if wanting to be absolutely sure of the veracity of everything he says. He tells me he is Cape Town born and bred. He went to Rondebosch Boys' High where his main sport was cricket, rather than rugby, and where he only made the second team. 'Rugby was only something to do while waiting for cricket to start. I also knew my chances of playing first team were not very good. I think of myself as a late bloomer.'

After school, he went to Stellenbosch where he did a BCom LLB and then spent another two years converting it to accounting because he'd decided to go the CA route. By 2003, he was captain of the Maties first rugby team.

From there, he won a rugby bursary to Oxford, where he completed a Master's degree in industrial economics and labour relations. I ask how he enjoyed Oxford, and he says: 'It was a revelation. It was the best year and a half of my life. There was such an amazing atmosphere of history and of learning. I got the chance to meet people from Europe. I got involved in AfroSoc and with the Rhodes Scholars and I met some phenomenal South Africans, New Zealanders and Aussies. A whole new world was opened up to me. The rugby side was wonderful – we went on two great tours and took on Cambridge at Twickenham, but mostly it was about mixing with people totally different but at the same time very similar to you. When I arrived there, nobody knew me from a bar of soap, so I started all over with a clean slate. One of the things that struck me within a month of being there was that you never know how South African you are until you leave the country. The UK is fantastic, but it's not South Africa. I always said I could happily live overseas as long as you told me it's not forever. Now I love being in South Africa. This is where I really want to be.'

When he returned from Oxford, he went to Johannesburg, where he started his CA articles at Deloittes. 'I was going to give up rugby but I missed it so much, so I joined Pirates to allow me to meet new people. One thing led to another and halfway through the next year I was in the Lions Currie Cup team. I was at the Lions for three years and then in June 2009, I moved down to Western Province.

'I resigned from Deloittes but now I'm back, trying to do my articles one day a week, but it's difficult because the rugby schedule changes at such short notice.'

I know his nickname within the team is 'Worms' and ask where it comes from. He smiles and says: 'I have a very healthy appetite. So healthy that my Stellenbosch residence mates thought I must have worms.' The name stuck.

He tells me that one of the things he appreciates about both the Western Province team and its supporters is the extent of the racial diversity. It's much more diverse than the Lions, he says, as well as being far more successful rugby-wise.

'The support we get from the Cape coloured community is unbelievable – it's both loyal and knowledgeable. Not so long ago, under Harry Viljoen, there were lots of cliques and divides but what's made a huge difference provincially and nationally is that you are getting leadership structures in place that are consciously harnessing all the diverse elements at each level. When everyone is pulling in the same direction, it makes us the best team in the world. It makes for a richer society. I generally find people here have a lot more passion than overseas because everything there is so uncomplicated, there is nothing to get excited about. Here, a lot of people have things they feel are worth fighting for; worth standing up for.'

This was when he first put forward this idea that a rugby scrum is the perfect example of diversity in action. I was intrigued and, by the time he'd finished, totally convinced.

'Rugby is a unique sport in that you get a lot closer to guys. At its core, it's a game of aggression and intimidation, some say violence – maybe it's controlled violence. Almost subconsciously, you are so dependent on your team-mate that you can't be worried about anything in each other's background. You've got to trust that guy to look after you and he's got to trust you. I did all the diversity workshops at Deloittes and facilitated them at Stellenbosch and it bugged me in a way. I thought: why can't it be as simple as it is in a rugby team?

'We don't have formal diversity workshops, but you get into that changing room and it's 15 men and you put on your boots and it doesn't matter who's got a degree or what your background is. You are in the same jersey and you run out there and you are each playing for each other, the same way they are playing for you.'

He's more relaxed now and talking freely, perhaps because he can see how engrossed I am. 'I find it very refreshing. I've also seen how those workshops happen almost on their own. Guys will be sitting on a bus from Bloemfontein to Kimberley and someone will ask a question which, if taken out of context, someone could say that's quite a crass, personal thing to say but it's just not that way at all. It's just the way we are with each other. It's an open environment where nothing should be taken personally and it's all meant in the best spirit.

'That's the way some guys express themselves: they come

across as hard and tough but they are not really like that. You have to trust each other. If, say, I have a lock partner who comes from the Cape Flats and I don't know anything about his background, it can bring a bit of distance between us, perhaps because of a fear of the unknown. Say for example he's carrying the ball, and I'm supposed to clean the ruck after he's tackled, it might make me stand off slightly. It shouldn't. I have to be totally hundred per cent behind him. That's the blood and guts of it.'

He pauses. 'Let me think of examples of teams that have failed: In Joburg in the late nineties, say, when you had personality clashes between the coach and some of the players, the Cats managed to get to the Super 12 semi-final and then lost to the Brumbies by 50 points, so something must have gone wrong in that team. When the Bulls beat the Chiefs 54–17 in 2009 – something doesn't fit right there.

'Perhaps it's also that the past just doesn't matter to us as rugby players: who your parents are or what they did; where you come from doesn't matter. All that counts is that I've been picked, you've been picked. We're going to pull together.

'Rugby is a game where it's second nature for guys to want to fit in. You don't feel as if you are compromising yourself by fitting in because you want to be part of the team. It works both ways. I don't think there is ever a situation where someone in the team wants to exclude you, and if there is, your team is going to get hammered. Guys really want to fit in and everybody else wants the guy next to them to fit in.'

I ask him about Christianity – is it as prevalent in Western Province as it is with the Bulls? And, if so, in what way does it impact on team spirit?

'We pray before every game because that is what we have always done. When Chris Jack was over here from New Zealand, he couldn't believe it. It was so foreign to him. Ja, that is something that is very South African. When I was at Oxford, we never prayed. We never did at Ronde-bosch. It might be an Afrikaans thing. We definitely prayed at Stellenbosch. The real issue could come in when you've got Muslim or Jewish guys. We have Yaya Hartzenburg in the Under 21s but generally, if it's only one guy, he's just going to go along with it because he doesn't want to make himself an imposition. We have a few guys at the Christian Revival Church and I'm a Catholic, but we're praying to the same God anyway.

'I think praying could be a way of helping guys deal with things – you're about to run out to put your body on the line – so it's just looking for some small sense of securi-ty, from wherever it might be. A mental edge – if it's one against one, it's whoever believes the most they are going to overcome the other who is going to win in the end. It's also another aspect of unity of the team – it says we are one. It's not me who is praying; it's we who are praying, even for guys who don't believe.'

In other ways, the culture is very different to the Bulls.

'Here the philosophy is: guys are encouraged to be them-selves, to do what they want to do how they want to do it. However, when you put on that jersey and step on that field, you've got to produce. I think that is great because from the little experience I've had of the real world – when I was doing my articles at Deloittes – that was exactly how it was. Deloittes doesn't care what you do after hours, but the minute you walk into that office in the morning, you need to look presentable and act appropriately with the clients because they are paying your salary.

'What I really admire about the Springboks at the Storm-ers is that guys like Jean and Schalk are best in the world in their position, but off the field they are so laid-back. They are always ready for a joke. They will give time to whoever wants it; nothing's a problem. When they're off the field, they don't want to talk about this move or that move, but the minute they step onto that field, they're still relaxed but they conduct themselves impeccably. That for me is the perfect balance; the best way to go about things.

'If we are playing in Durban, for example, you're not allowed to go out in any Stormers branded gear and you're not allowed to get caught in Teazers or some place like that. If you go and no one finds out, it's fine but it puts the team and union in a bad light if someone has a cellphone camera and snaps you, which may easily happen.'

As he says this, I notice how much the restaurant crowd has thinned out, which is a relief. I had felt a little too conspicuous sitting with Anton, who draws constant stares. This is the Newlands crowd and, for them, a Western Province star is a celebrity. He, though, seems oblivious to it, or perhaps he's just used to it. He goes on. 'At the Lions we socialised together a lot more. It was an unwritten though not enforced rule that after a game we are all going out to eat. It's a team culture thing. That was how we did it. Here it's much more relaxed; if you all want to go out together, you organise it and you all go. We will all generally go up to the players' suite where the wives and girlfriends are. Some of the guys who live in the northern suburbs will go to dinner together. Yesterday we had a team day when we all played action cricket. Perhaps in two or three weeks' time we will all go to dinner somewhere. When I talked about diversity workshops happening on their own, that's where it happens: you end up sitting next to someone you've never chatted to outside of rugby. You don't talk rugby. You talk about other things.

'Newlands is very much the spiritual home. It's always special to train there, but the HPC has been set up so well, so professionally, that it feels like you are going there to do a job. It's an outstanding facility: we've got a fully equipped gym; medical facilities; video facilities. We never had that at the Lions and it really bugged me. It helps so much with the levels of professionalism. The only two unions that have anything like that are the Bulls and the Sharks.'

He is now 30 and it is very important to him, he says, that he has another career available to him when rugby ends. 'What people don't understand is that there is only a handful of people who can do rugby in some form or other for the rest of their lives. Unfortunately, the rugby years coincide with the years when you should be finding out what it is you want to do and getting the necessary experience to make something of it. A lot of guys marry and have kids while they are still playing rugby and then they are suddenly out of a job and they have no work experience to fall back on.

'I will play rugby for as long as I'm enjoying it. A few more years would be great. If it's another two years, that's also fine. There are quite a number of guys who have a degree but there are not a lot of guys who have a career to fall back on, so I'm very lucky in that respect and very grateful for it.'

He is single. Surely there are girls crawling all over you? I ask. He says with a grin: 'If they do crawl all over you, they're not the ones you want to spend time with. The Springboks get a lot of attention but not the Currie Cup or Super 14 guys.' He's not in a hurry. 'When I'm lucky enough to meet the right one, I'll see.'

The game against the Bulls is every bit as bruising as expected. The bodies pile up from the word go. The Bulls come off worst: first their captain, Gary Botha, and then two of their Springboks, Zane Kirchner and Dewald Potgieter, limp from the field. Western Province win by 15–12, but the intensity of it takes its toll on them too. At the HPC on Monday, 16 August, Allister assembles his troops and assesses the damage: right wing Fabian Juries has torn a calf muscle, which will put him out of action for several weeks. Tighthead Brok Harris and number eight, Duane Vermeulen, have both damaged a shoulder. Anton and his lock partner, Adriaan Fondse, have bad colds.

Anton says: 'When you come off the field, you know you've been playing a Super 14 team. With the Bulls, it's a bit more so because of the rivalry. It was a massive event, and to run out in front of a full Newlands for a Currie Cup match is more than enough to get the goose bumps going. The game itself was a bit to and fro. The first half especially was frustrating because we didn't take advantage of all our attacking opportunities. The second half didn't go at all well – that could have been due to frustration and impatience creeping in from the first half, and not feeling rewarded for our efforts due to simple errors.'

After the review session, Allister gives the players the rest of the day off. They need to rest for the next game, which is going to be even tougher. It's their first game against the Sharks, who are now top of the log. Province is close and still unbeaten, however.

Two days later, the Bulls game is history and they are totally focused on the Sharks. Anton, still sounding slightly nasal, says: 'On a purely rugby basis, this is our biggest test so far. Together with the Bulls, the Sharks present the greatest challenge to us. They've built up a good momentum: the one bit of confidence they will have is that they have scored more tries than we have, but we have our systems, and our attack is improving. The Sharks have lost the fewest Springboks and they have got the most back. They've also got three okes bashing down the door to take each Springbok's place.'

They weren't doing much training this week, he said, because of the colds and the injuries. Nevertheless, they were well prepared.

They will be flying up on Friday so as to minimise 'hotel lethargy syndrome'.

'It will be very muggy and we are only playing at 7 pm on Saturday. Because there are no couches, you tend to lie on your bed to save energy.'

They are staying at the Elangeni Hotel. As a senior player, he gets to pick whom he shares with. 'It's your personal space so you need to share with someone you are comfortable with. I usually share with Francois Louw, but he's with the Springboks so I'm sharing with one of the young guys, Lionel Cronjé.'

There is, of course, another rather important match being played on Saturday, 21 August, which doesn't make things any easier: the Springboks' Tri-Nations Test against the All Blacks. John Smit will celebrate his 100th cap and it will be played at Soccer City in Soweto in front of 90 000 people. It will finish just before the start of the WP–Sharks game.

Allister is concerned: 'Just watching it will take energy from our players.'

He, too, looks as if he is having a tough week. Aside from the day job, he has parental duties to fulfil. His daughter is in the Under 16s hockey team at Stellenberg High School and he has promised to give a talk at the school tonight.

He tries it out on me: 'I'm going to talk to them about the importance of enjoying school sport, as opposed to the kind of professional sport I'm involved in. I will explain to them what we see the best players are made of, which is all about the mental approach. At school age, teachers are putting skills in place but the mental edge is what will determine if you are going to be professional one day. If you're going to survive, you've got to refuse to be defeated. The other is the error rate. If you carry an error rate around with you, you won't make it. If you understand these two things from a young age, you've got a better chance. However, school sport is mostly about understanding the ethos of teamwork and how to be as supportive as possible within a team context. Team sport teaches a lot of life lessons.'

I say: 'I'm sure they will be riveted.' His face creases into his big, warm grin. Then it's back to his more pressing preoccupation: how to beat the Sharks. Like Anton, he believes this will be their toughest game yet. 'They will challenge us mentally and physically; our attack and our kicking game. There is a perception that the Bulls are the ultimate challenge. They do bring a helluva physical challenge to the game but if you show more intensity, you can beat them. The Sharks are not a structured side, like the Bulls. They are very unpredictable and they have some players with the X factor: [Patrick] Lambie, [Lwazi] Mvovo and [Ryan] Kankowski. Their thing is to put pressure on the opposition with their attack.'

The Sharks also have home advantage. 'There is a very passionate crowd in KZN with massive support behind their team. The Sharks might have stuttered a bit initially but since then they are unbeaten. It's a proper top-of-the-charts clash. It will be our first night game and in berg wind conditions. It makes the challenge even bigger.'

If WP wins, it will give their confidence a massive boost. 'We are the only team playing without any of our Springboks. This team has shown tremendous growth. These guys have proved they can play Super 15 rugby. They must just keep trusting the system. It's going to be massive if we win this one.

'They've worked hard; they are well prepared. It's just the belief they need – the belief they can beat them.'

Unfortunately, they don't win. In fact, they are decisively beaten: at full-time the score is 27–16 to the Sharks.

Back at the HPC, I ask Anton: 'Was it because you were all still feeling battered from the Bulls game?'

He says: 'Rugby and excuses don't go together. This is our job and we are conditioned for it. If you look at the Springboks – they played the All Blacks on Saturday and are playing the Aussies this Saturday. We let a few things slip and in a team environment, it has a snowball effect you can't stop. Also, the Sharks produced a very solid performance.' Then he adds: 'Having said that, I can't wait for the return game.

'Rugby is a game of pressure and it's about handling the pressure. On Saturday, we found ourselves in a situation where we were constantly posing questions of the opposition: in other words, because you don't know their systems exactly, you try out different manoeuvres to find out where their weaknesses are. You've got to be able to think on your feet. The higher you go, the greater the physicality and the more thinking you've got to do. It is difficult to think in the 75th minute when you're dead tired. Concentration drops too: when you see a player dropping a ball, it's not because he's not good enough to catch it, it's because he's had a lapse in concentration. The senior players all feed me stuff but, at the end of the day, as captain, the call is mine.'

I feel a bit ghoulish, asking him to pick over his team's mistakes and to relive the failure. 'We can do this another time,' I say, but he is firm: 'No, no. It's fine.'

For the Sharks game, he says, their planning and training had been perfect. 'We didn't execute our plan the way we had intended and the few adjustments we made didn't come off. Our defence, usually our strong point, was found to have a few holes. We had planned for that and made contingencies, but they didn't work. If you lose your two flanks in the first half, as we did, it is a big disadvantage. Yet we had planned for it.'

You can't blame individuals. 'Not unless you're talking about a last kick in the dying minutes. When a team loses 27–16, then it's not through an individual. It's through a lot of individual errors. On the other hand, if you're going to lose a game, it's better to lose it sooner rather than later. If you're going to learn lessons, it's better to learn them early. After a loss, there is a massive sense of failure and disappointment. The talk in the changing room afterwards, though, is not about what has happened, but how to deal with it. It's not about falling off the horse. It's about getting on again. You don't have to say too much. Everybody is feeling terrible. Everybody is feeling cross and frustrated. You are also way more sore and bruised after such a game. The team that wins will have been more dominant so you will have had to tackle more.

'Because the next game is on a Friday, we have a day less to recover. That day makes a big difference. We believe in our systems and the way we do things, however, so we will just have to knuckle down and produce the goods.'

Later, I find a quiet minute to talk to Allister and get his take on what went wrong. He says he thinks their six consecutive wins had had an unfortunate effect. 'I think it's human nature to be floating a bit. We just weren't ready psychologically. I tried to take things back last week: the players understood how we felt when we lost the Super 14 final. They understood the physical intensity that comes with those top teams.'

Furthermore, the Sharks were ready for them. 'They had the luxury of having three Springboks released to them. As the home union, they could have asked for the game to be played on Friday because of the Tri-Nations Test on Saturday, but they knew that if they put the big screens up, the crowds would come on Saturday. They knew how their crowds would react.'

We're sitting in his office on the ground floor of the HPC. As ever, it strikes me how functional it is, how uninspiring. It is a small room with a small window. His desk faces the door. I think of the room to which his Bulls counterpart, Frans Ludeke, retreats for contemplation and planning – that generous, light-filled room with its floor-to-ceiling windows overlooking the pitch upon which his team will play – and think that Allister doesn't have a particularly good deal here. Not that he's complaining. His mind is on his team and how to manage them through this particular trough.

'We were bitterly disappointed in our second-half performance. It was just a matter of looking after our own ball. We've got a good kicking plan – they have got a good counter-attacking plan. They usually leave four or five guys at the back to field the kicks, so we slightly modified our plan: instead of kicking it back, we started to run it back. While we were attacking and not kicking, we couldn't hold onto the ball after we had gained possession. There was too much turnover so we had to tackle much more, and that makes it a very long day for you.

'To their credit, the Sharks did their homework well. Players like Beast [Mtawarira], Bismarck [du Plessis] and [Ryan] Kankowski had a huge influence in terms of ball-carrying momentum – which is their whole philosophy. They are momentum-driven and like keeping the ball in the air. To breach our defence, their plan was to form fewer rucks. If you keep the ball alive, it is difficult to shut them out completely.

'They played accurate rugby on the night and Western Province had their worst performance with regard to ball retention. Instead of playing against the Sharks, we played against ourselves, and that sums up what went wrong.'

He sighs, shaking his head. 'In the second half, there were just too many errors – you go into a downward spiral and you can't stop it and you can't get out of it. Towards the end, we showed a bit of character and fought back and scored a try [by 20-year-old ex-Bishops boy, Nick Koster]. I was pleased with that bit of fight towards the end.

'Immediately after the game, we had a chat and a late dinner, but the food didn't taste too good. Then you go off on your own to deal with it. You just go to your room. I give myself between six hours and twelve hours to mope. By the next morning, I'm over it. I've got to start making plans, fixing it. To mope for too long is energy sapping. It's a waste of time.

'Sunday is a tough day. You've got to start your review process – look at the game over and over again; do your cuts for the video session; plan what you are going to say to your senior players and the coaches, not to mention the media – that is always quite challenging.

'As coach, it's tough when they lose. You've got to make sure you hit the right buttons. You have to identify what went wrong technically and also assess the emotional state of the team. I talk to the captain and get the feeling from him. We meet with the senior players and coaches. As coaches we are very harsh and open with the senior players and they will give their input and say if we are over-reacting or unfair. Once we have dealt with issues, there is a collective plan we go to the team with.

'The senior players – Anton, Conrad Jantjes, Duane Vermeulen, Frikkie Walsh, Tiaan Liebenberg and Dewaldt Duvenhage – have as much responsibility as we coaches have because we trust them. We want them to spread the message to the team. They are the gauge. If things go wrong on the field, they must also take responsibility. When we leave here, there is a strong feeling of what needs to be rectified and how to rectify it.

'It's ongoing – with the Super 14, at least you get a week's break from rugby. With the Currie Cup, once it's started, it's week after week and it's intense. You've got to come up with plans every day; you've got to manage a whole team; you've got to make sure things are working; you've got to piss some players off and make unpopular decisions at times too.'

On the positive side: the Stellenberg High School talk went well, and two of the Springboks – Gio Aplon and Francois Louw – are on their way back to Cape Town.

As if the Currie Cup weren't intense enough with a game every single weekend – seven on the trot now – the next game is on Friday, which gives barely any time at all to recover from the Sharks game and prepare for the next game, against the Cheetahs. They are Currie Cup specialists and the only senior player they have lost to the national side is Juan Smith.

On the Monday, I'm back in Allister's office, sitting across the small desk from him. 'Tell me how it's going.' What has been preoccupying him since the previous day is the body count: 'Who is injured? Who is coming back from injury? Who is next in line? How many players can train and will be available; and who can't train but will be available? You have to start thinking about replacements because today you've got to select your team. You've got to tell a player on an individual basis that he's been dropped and explain why. They must never read about it in the paper. It's very important, and the most difficult part of my job. It's like firing a worker. You must make a decision and it's a gut feel: even if the guy hasn't done a thing wrong, this is the player you need. I'm open and frank with them. I don't bullshit them. They don't wander around here wondering where they fit in: they know where they fit into the plan. Every one of us needs to know that: where we fit in. Are you appreciated? Can you make a contribution? Rugby players are no different.

'I have a selection policy and guidelines. I speak to Robbie about backs and to Matt about forwards. We discuss and debate and we go back to our criteria: is he the perfect player – what is his attitude? Is he a team player? Does he fit into a certain combination better than another? Is he a youngster or experienced? You have to weigh that up: which do you need? You also have to weigh up his potential – is he just a stopgap or is he potentially a Super 15 player or a Springbok?

'You tend to become emotionally involved with certain players. You develop a soft spot for them, but if you have a selection policy, it cuts out all emotion and it makes it dispassionate. It is very difficult to love all your children the same way but you have to. That's what the players want.'

Today, 23 August, they started a bit later than usual and did the review but didn't do a blow-out session. 'Because it's so physically taxing – they've been playing the Bulls and the Sharks and it's a short week – logic says don't do a blow-out. Their bodies are starting to tire. At this stage of the competition, it's important to have fresh players for each game. Their bodies recover completely by Thursday and on Friday they take a battering again.

'On Monday, we normally have one session; on Tuesday, two sessions, split into backs and forwards. We have to give them a day off, which is Thursday, so that only leaves three days instead of four to prepare. A win this weekend would fix everything.'

FOUR

Another week, another game. Another chance for the team to redeem itself. Anton muses: 'It's a microcosm of life. If you look at companies and boards of directors, they will review their performance regularly and have a big review at the end of the year, but even when they do, they don't really know how well they are doing. It all gets put into context and blown up. Whereas in rugby, every week you run out there, you do what you do and, straight after that, you have won or you have lost. You can see that this went well and that went badly. Then you've got to start again and you've got to get better. You've got to fix the things that weren't good and improve on the things that were and just produce a better performance.

'You are never allowed to become too good or too important because once you have won a game, that counts for nothing as far as the next game is concerned. Once you've won a Cup, that counts for nothing as far as the next season is concerned. Your opponents are coming at you even harder. You don't get any special rights. Actually, when you lose, that's all that keeps you going: the fact that you've got a chance to rectify things.'

At the Captain's Run at Newlands on the Thursday before the Cheetahs game, Allister is looking much better than he had earlier in the week. He has finally had a good night's sleep, he said. Tim Whitehead has injured his hamstring but at least Gio and Juan are back in the team. After practice, the coaches and team are off to the Vineyard for lunch. The next day, they will meet there again for lunch at 15h30, four hours before kick-off. After lunch, they will repair to their day rooms at the Vineyard for an hour and a half before meeting again for the coach's talk.

Unlike the Springboks and the Ikey Tigers, there is no ceremonial handing out of jerseys by someone inspirational. 'I'm more focused on the team,' explains Anton. 'I think it's a great tradition to have but, as far as I'm concerned, it's something the Springboks do.'

Coincidentally, at that very moment, I spot Dobbo, there with his Under 21s. He needs to decide whether to go back to UCT for another run at the Varsity Cup or whether he should throw in his lot with Western Province. He invites me up to the Newlands boardroom, where he has been trying to inject a little Ikey Tiger-style team spirit into his Western Province charges. I can see why the choice between UCT and WP is not easy. After the comradeship and purity of the amateur game, free of individual ego and the subtle corruption of sponsorship, this can seem a bit soulless. These boys are only after a senior contract: it's each for himself.

Dobbo has divided them up into groups of four and five. Each has to act out a scene from a play. Some are more convincing than others, but they all seem to enjoy it hugely. It ends with Nic Groom, one of the bigger hearts to come out of the Ikey Tigers, shouting: 'I love black men!' Everyone roars with laughter. Afterwards, there are chocolate bars for those who performed best.

Dobbo gets up and says: 'Okay, that was just to get you out of your comfort zone.' Then he gets them all to sing their new team song. It's called 'Superheroes', an adaptation from a song by American group Five for Fighting.

The Under 21s could use a little magic, as they also lost to the Sharks last Saturday. Like the senior team, they take on the Cheetahs tomorrow, kicking off at 17h15.

Friday, 27 August, 17h15: The Under 21s win – by one point. There is a 15-minute break, and then drums roll for the big game. The crowd roars out a welcome as Western

Province emerge from the tunnel, as if newly born for the new day's battle. The crowd is stilled for a moment's silence in memory of the ten Cape Town children killed earlier in the week when their taxi hit a train. Then the field explodes into action. Within minutes, Gio Aplon flies over the tryline. Disappointingly, the try is disallowed. Throughout the game he is a force of nature, whipping in and out of the smallest gaps between opposing players with magical speed and guile. At half-time, the score is 12–3 against us, however. Matters don't improve much in the second half. What stands out for me are a couple of magnificent Western Province rolling mauls: player after player locking into this jigsaw puzzle of shoulders and thighs and arms. Anton at the centre of it, powerful legs driving into the ground, inching forward. Young Nick Koster runs maniacally at the ball at every opportunity.

It's not enough. It ends in another loss. At full-time, the score is 29–24 to the Cheetahs.

At the press conference afterwards, Allister looks dejected. Anton looks distraught, his head in his hands, as if this is the last place he wants to be, gazing into cameras, tape recorders shoved in front of him, his loss picked over. As usual, he does the brave soldier number, taking it on the chin. 'We were bitterly disappointed in ourselves ...'

There is more bad news the next day. Hooker Tiaan Liebenberg has torn a ligament in his ankle and will be out for the rest of the season. Flank Pieter Louw is out with a rib injury. Tim Whitehead is still touch and go. He doesn't train with the others. Sitting on the bench with me, watching the others train, he says: 'All the seasoned campaigners tell you to look after your soft tissue. The coaches might get irritated on the day if you aren't training but they would be more so if you tear your hamstring and can't play for weeks. Basically, you see the doc and the physio and they tell you what they think and then it's your choice.'

For the next game – against the Lions in Joburg – Allister has 17 fewer players to choose from, lost either to injury or to the Springboks. He is going to have to dig deeper and deeper into his reserves of youngsters. This is good news for two Ikey Tigers, namely wild man Yaya Hartzenberg, and Marcel Brache, Man of the Match in my very first UCT game. Each gets a seat on the bench. I've been watching Marcel training with the squad over the past few weeks, thrilled to be with them.

He's also been hit by injury. He was concussed during a recent UCT league game, and was then out for another two weeks with an ankle injury. He's fine now. Tiaan Liebenberg has been replaced by Deon Fourie. Prop Wicus Blaauw, also injured, is getting a rest on the subs' bench. JD Möller will start in his place. Gio Aplon has been summonsed back to the Springboks for the game against the Wallabies in Bloemfontein, so he will be replaced by yet another youngster, JJ Engelbrecht.

Lionel Cronjé is going back to the Under 21s, however. Allister explains that Lionel needs the experience of playing a full 80 minutes, rather than the brief forays onto the field he has had from the bench up to now. It is a temporary measure.

As if all this weren't enough, Allister is coming under pressure from the president of Western Province. 'He's saying: "What can I do to help? Is there a crisis? The suite-holders are saying there is no commitment." We won six games in a row and they said nothing. Now we lose two and there is a crisis! Absolute rubbish! I'm not making excuses, but both the Cheetahs and the Lions are fielding Super 14 sides. We have lost our Boks and we have had so many injuries. It is difficult to get a team going with players in and out all the time. We are still second on the log! We are four points ahead of the third-placed team.'

Anton says: 'We haven't done very well over the last two games. Our priority is to get back on track. Now we're going to Joburg and we want four log points at least. Our young players are fearless. They will always have a go. They aren't afraid of making mistakes.'

It turns out to be yet another defeat. A crushing 46–28 to the Lions. Our youngsters do well, with both JJ Engelbrecht and Maties star Conrad Hoffman scoring tries. The hero of the night is that golden young Lion, Elton Jantjies, who seems to be everywhere at once, and staggeringly accurate. Not only does he score a try, but he kicks the ball through the goalposts ten times: four conversions and six penalties.

Back at the HPC, Anton talks it through: 'Of the last three games, the Sharks game was the only one during which we were outplayed. The Cheetahs and Lions picked up on our mistakes. It's the bounce of the ball. It's credit to the opposition to have the system to capitalise on those errors. You can't blame injuries. Everyone gets them.

'After the Cheetahs game, I said to the guys: "We're being tested." You don't test the strength of a team when you've won five times in a row. You test a team's character and that of individuals when you haven't done well.

'For us, it's about getting back on the horse. It's not easy. If winning becomes a habit, so does losing. We need to get the winning habit.

'Losing is tiring; if things are going well, it's easy. That's why all sport is an analogy for life. When one thing goes well, everything goes well.'

What is going to make his own life much easier now, though, is the return of more Springboks.

'As captain, it's just really helpful to have so many good, strong players in the squad. Sometimes something happens on the field and you will turn round and look at the younger guys and they won't know what's going on. If you look at one of the senior guys, on the other hand, they are calm and collected and they know exactly what's going on. It's something you have to learn through experience. It just makes your job as captain so much easier. That's the challenge when you have a younger team.

'With sport, you get a chance to start again every week, and you try to make sure it's in your hands. If you win one game and you think you're great, you're going to get cut down.'

At the weekly press conference at the HPC on Wednesday, 12 September, Allister reveals that the Lions game has claimed another two casualties: Fabian Juries and Frikkie Walsh. The good news, though, is that Jean de Villiers is back. This means, says Allister, an entirely new backline. It is one glittering with Springboks: Gio and Juan are also back. He's retrieving Lionel Cronjé from the Under 21s: with the Boks back, Lionel has lots of experience around him.

'Peter Grant [who is playing in Japan] and Willem de Waal will not be around forever, so we need to look at someone new. Lionel is therefore coming in at number 10. I always intended to give Lionel a run at this stage. We gave him a run at fullback for the Western Province Under 21 team last week just to get him up to speed with his decision-making. The good thing for Lionel this week is that he has someone like Jean de Villiers on his outside, and he also has the support of other great backs in Gio and Juan.'

Afterwards, he says to me: 'I had to get that in about Lionel at the presser.' Over the week there has been much media criticism, taken up on the various rugby blogs, of his decision to put Lionel Cronjé back in the Under 21s for the Lions game. 'I told them last week that I was doing it to give him a full 80 minutes' game time. He got that.

Now he's back. Having worked with a top team for so long, it has opened my eyes to the fact that you've got to have patience – you've got to realise that a guy might have a 26-year-old body but may otherwise still be a 19-year-old. You've got to take a step back. It's not about results. It's about growth. That is my ambition – to grow the youth. I've given young players like Marcel Brache an opportunity. He has just played his first big match and he's learnt some hard lessons, like Tim Whitehead. They have still got things to learn, but they are good players. You must pay attention to their development. Next year they might be our front-rank players and that is how I'm looking at things. If you just invest in short-term goals, there is no future.

'The Under 21s and Under 19s are doing really well and that is our future. Giving these guys top match rugby experience is crucial. The Currie Cup is the breeding ground for young players. We can't just say that and not do it. There is no crisis.'

The criticism stings, however. 'What is written in the papers has a massive influence on how people perceive teams. With Lionel Cronjé, I knew I needed to give him game time. I don't discuss strengths and weaknesses in the paper, but you can't blood players in hostile environments.'

This has been a difficult week all round for Allister, media-wise. Not only has he had to deal with the Cronjé issue, but Jake White has been punting himself as emergency replacement for Peter de Villiers, once again subjected to media flagellation for a poor Tri-Nations campaign. Either he or Allister could do the job, Jake has been saying, or Allister could be his side-kick. Allister is irritated.

'When Jake talks his rubbish, I try to put a lid on it. I'm focusing on getting Western Province rugby back on track.'

At least this week, there has been a slight easing of pressure and he was able to give the team Monday off. For the first time there is an eight-day turnaround: the Lions game was on Friday. The next game is on Saturday. It is at New-lands and against bottom-of-the-log Leopards.

'On Monday, I thought I needed to give them a rest. We are sitting with tired bodies – especially our forwards. An-ton and Duane have played all the Super 14 and Currie Cup games. Then there are the injuries. If you have three or four guys who can't practise because of niggles it's a waste of time, so I give them time to recover. It's also just a mental break after another disappointing performance. It's good to get them away from the HPC. Let them have a long weekend and a break from this place. At this stage of the competition, less is more. It's not about fitness. It's about making sure they are fresh for this Saturday. That will help for the next week when it's a shorter week again.

'At this stage of the game it's just about maintenance, and I try to keep them as fresh as possible. It's like Super 14. You have a lot of tired bodies out there. You get a peak of injuries, so you have to individually rest and manage players better.

'Last week, we relied on a lot of the young guys because of the injuries – not just blooding them but relying on them. So, although we really hate losing, there was never a lack of effort from these players. There were critical mistakes; critical penalties we conceded that cost us. Hopefully this weekend, players will take that responsibility. The most important thing is ball in hand.'

It's the end of another long day in what is probably the most stressful week of the campaign yet. It's the relentlessness of weekly games, each with very high stakes, nine on the trot. There's the challenge of keeping up standards in the team with lots of injuries and the missing Springboks; and then all the outside pressure on top. Allister is in philosophical mood.

'Ah Lizzie!' he says with a sigh and a rueful smile. 'You've got to accept as the coach that you have to be selfless. It's not about you; an ego is the killer of man. Give other people the credit.' Nelson Mandela has always been his role model, he says. 'To live what Mandela stood for is a difficult thing. It's a fundamental Christian principle to serve others. It's not about what you can get out of something; it's how much you can contribute and make others successful. Indirectly, you will receive abundantly – you do get back in life.

'Mandela's example of forgiveness has had a big influence on my life. It helps when you have to prove yourself as a person of colour and when you have to be ten times better in order to be taken seriously, although it was not for me ever to say that I am better. It helped in my playing days, when I was on the bench because the coach didn't trust me. Just after unification, the coach could play me but he didn't because he trusted the white guy more.

'I was the backline coach in the Springbok team. Then I got an opportunity to be head coach of the Stormers. I was still the same guy, however, so it took some time for my ability to be accepted.

'That has been the challenge. People don't really understand or recognise my past. That is the difference between the established guys and us. They don't know we played rugby and we were talented. There is no forum to try to explain their perceptions and ours. That is why you have got to keep pushing and prove yourself. My only gauge is the people I work with in the team – the players and the other coaches – and the mutual respect we have for one another. There are still eruptions out there, but it is very different to what it was like three years ago.'

I ask him about quotas and whether he thinks they were useful.

'As the only player of colour in the Eastern Province side in the early nineties, when there was no quota system, I'd proved myself at club level. You had to prove yourself. I would never ever have wanted to be in any team or in management because of my colour. I think quotas had their relevance at one stage but it wasn't managed properly. A player like Habana would never have had the opportunity without the quota system. The majority of coaches were white and wouldn't have had that trust in a black player.

'I don't know how you make that shift as a white coach. You suddenly have to trust this oke now. There is always a bit of doubt. Then players like Bryan and Ricky came along. It was a slow process, but guys started to earn respect because of the way they performed. There wasn't enough discussion about the quota system. It could have been managed much better than just putting numbers to it. Eventually it became a numbers game and it had an influence on team dynamics.'

It's after five when we part. The field below us is empty and the players are making their way in ones and twos out of the changing room and up the long drive to the car park. Through the open doors of the gym, I see Anton and Buhle Mxunyelwa, lifting weights. I wave goodbye. They look as if they will be there for a while yet.

FIVE

Eleven September is a date that has become synonymous with disaster on the international calendar. At Newlands this fine Saturday, it spells disaster only for the Leopards. The Newlands crowd obviously didn't expect them to put up much of a fight, and only around 12 000 of them pitch up. Still, that's enough to produce a resounding roar when Western Province runs on. Lionel Cronjé, after all the fuss, misses his first penalty and the crowd boos. It all feels a bit jumpy at first, not helped by a sudden sharp explosion from the stands. It sounds like a gunshot and the game stops for a minute. When it becomes clear it is nothing serious, play resumes and the lads find their rhythm. As the game progresses, they start flying over the tryline with monotonous regularity: Francois Louw, Brok Harris, Anton, Deon Fourie, Dewaldt Duvenhage, Juan de Jongh and Yaya Hartzenberg score tries, nine in all. Cronjé finds his feet and converts four of them. In the second half, Willem de Waal converts another three. The final score is 59–17.

The Under 21s won their game 59–11. It has been a good day for Province.

At the press conference afterwards, we learn that the bang in the first half was caused by the explosion of a soft-drink bottle packed with dry ice. There were no casualties except for the Leopards, whose coach, Chaka Willemse, looks very downcast. His contract expires at the end of the Currie Cup and he does not yet know whether it will be renewed. Their problem is that other unions keep poaching their best players, he complains. Both Willem de Waal and Brok Harris, for example.

Then Anton and Allister come in, beaming, heads held high, the polar opposite to the despair they evinced two weeks before in the very same seats.

Asked how the players felt about the explosion from the stands, Anton says: 'It was a helluva bang and it gave me a fright. First I checked all the players to make sure it wasn't a sniper. Then I looked to see if it was a prank by Jean de Villiers.'

It was 'absolutely massive to win again', he says. 'With this competition, you can never taking winning for granted.'

Allister says: 'Winning was very important to get our confidence back. It was a very forwards-oriented game. You think that because you have got your Springboks back, it will all be plain sailing, but the pack lays the foundation.'

He says, with some satisfaction: 'There were six Under 21 players in the team. That is what the Currie Cup is all about.' And winning, of course. At the end of week 10, we are still second on the log, with 33 points but the Sharks have 41 and the Cheetahs are very close behind at 32. The Bulls have slid down to fifth place, behind the Lions.

In Week 11, Province does even better. They play the Pumas in Nelspruit and score eight tries. There's another great driving maul, powerful and impenetrable with its seamless interlocking of bodies. The backline have found each other again and are beginning to match the brilliance of the forwards. Jean de Villiers, the golden veteran, and Juan de Jongh bond in a perfect pairing. The final score is 62–10. Back at the HPC, I test Anton again on the euphoria-barometer. He says: 'Euphoria is what you feel when you win the Currie Cup. You should beat the Leopards and the Pumas.'

He is, nevertheless, very pleased. Tired, but pleased. 'Last week [against the Pumas] was our most complete performance so far. Every week, there is a plan on how we are going to play. It differs only slightly week to week. The first game against the Lions, we didn't get the bonus point but what we set out to achieve, we executed down to the wire. That was why we won and it was probably the most enjoyable game for the players.'

Then he has to leave to give a talk at Somerset College. Performance on the field is only part of it for rugby leaders like him. He is constantly being asked to talk about what he does. He doesn't begrudge it. 'The people of the Cape own Western Province. That's what makes playing here special.'

Talking at these events does mean meeting new people … 'but then all they want to talk about is rugby!' he says with a laugh.

The attrition wrought on the team by injuries increases his load: 'Every game we lost, we lost two guys. Tiaan won't be back this year. Neither will Tim Whitehead. On the plus side, from my point of view, it is fantastic having Gio and Jean and Juan back.'

There's a day off now and he is supposed to relax. 'Switching off is not something I'm good at. I'm trying to furnish my house. I cook. I read. I watch movies. I eat to keep my energy levels up.' Then he's off, because Somerset College is waiting.

I find Allister, who is also looking tired, but less stressed. He says: 'It's week eleven for us and it goes on and on. That gets to you a bit. If you don't work hard every week, you can lose a game and put yourself under pressure. Those three weeks of losses were quite testing – testing the character of the side; testing the belief in the systems. It's not about just winning because no side wins all the time.'

It's very important to get out of that downward spiral and get the team's confidence back. That is why the win against the Leopards here was important. However, then you go away from home and that is a test again. You're playing on a field you've never played on before. They beat the Bulls the week before, so it was a pretty impressive performance to go there and put 60 points on them.

'It's very important for a coach to gauge the confidence of a side. Now that confidence is back, it shouldn't spill over into complacency. The players must realise that putting on their Province jersey entails responsibility.

'There should be anxiety but there should also be enjoyment and that is the balance I'd like to put right. I have to find the balance between their sense of responsibility and over-confidence. They mustn't get over-confident because of last week's win because then they will lose. They must realise they have a responsibility to the team, the supporters and province at large.

'It's not just about the technical stuff. It's about emotion; it's the friendship within the team. You are in a better position in tough times when you care about the people you are playing with. In defence, if you miss a tackle, I'll make up for you because you are my mate. It cuts out the ego thing. I will give the ball to the player in the better position. It's our try. It's our line we've got to defend.

'These things are really in the subconscious and once under pressure they come out automatically because we are good mates and enjoy each others' company. It's a relaxed environment. I enjoy being with my team. The fun gauge is up. You see that in their play as well.

'Being coach of a Super 14 or Currie Cup side looks glamorous, but it is really tough and you've got to have the right management members around you or it becomes a lonely job. If you feel you're alone and you start wondering what others are thinking, it's not a nice place to be. Up till now, as a group we've been very open with management and with the players, and I enjoy the relationships that have been built here. Every relationship is about trust. As regards team selection, the player understands that if he does get an opportunity he won't be out again unless he plays poorly. I keep the opportunity going. I manage the player. All these processes are clear to the players. They understand what I'm thinking and why I'm doing it.

'I think it's crucial to be ruthlessly honest with yourself and the people around you. Sometimes you've got to make unpopular decisions, but when everything is done in the interests of the side, you know you've done the right thing.'

Week 12 is upon us and the Griquas are coming to Newlands for their return match. It is the last game in September. The Currie Cup began at the beginning of July: three full months of weekly matches.

Anton tells me: 'Our bodies are beginning to feel a bit tired and at the same time this is the bit we get excited about because these are the games that really matter. The stadiums are full and there is a great buzz. Semi-final places are up for grabs. Every game is played at a higher intensity. For me the big thing is: if we win the next three games, we win the Currie Cup. In last year's Currie Cup, we lost the last league game and that had a big effect on the final. When it gets to the knock-outs, it's all about momentum and it's all about the confidence that comes from within yourself. It's a very raw, basic situation – winners will keep winning.

'The biggest mistake you can make is getting too far ahead and worrying about the semi-final. The only important game is this week's against the Griquas.

'There are only five weeks to go, and then rugby for 2010 is over. That's what I keep focusing on. I love it. It's such a privilege to be here.'

One thing that has struck me over the almost three years I have been immersed in the rugby world is how nice these men are. Almost without exception (and at every level) I have found them unfailingly polite, friendly and unassuming. This impression is reaffirmed as I sit on a bench after practice at the HPC one morning chatting to Gio Aplon. Here is a man who is one of the country's heroes, a new star in its firmament, and yet he has no airs and graces, and is almost bashful.

It might be something to do with the almost superhuman struggle he has had to endure to get where he is now. He comes from Hawston, which he describes as 'a small fishermen's town where the general living is from the sea. The basic living is through fishing and crayfish quotas. Like all small towns, you have the influence of alcohol and drugs.'

In apartheid times Hawston was the coloured dormitory town to the adjacent wealthy white Hermanus, and as a result, much of Hawston supports the All Blacks.

'That's because of what happened in our country. A lot of people are supporting the Springboks now. I don't want to say it is because of me, but maybe it is. A lot of them have made promises that after this World Cup, they will support the Springboks.'

He is deeply loyal to his home town. 'They are fantastic people. There are not a lot of rich people. The support I get makes me so humble. Not just my parents and my family support me, but all the people of Hawston. It's so nice for me to go back to Hawston for the people who really support me for who I am and where I come from.' One of these supporters from Hawston is his long-time girlfriend, now a student at the University of the Western Cape.

Both Gio's parents are primary school teachers and all his schooling was in Hawston, not at one of the more privileged rugby schools. Already, he had missed out on the conventional route to professional rugby. He started playing in primary school but was considered too small, a lifelong cross he's had to bear. He didn't play initially at high school, he said, because he had braces, but started again in Grade 9. By matric, he was in the first team. 'I went to trials while still at school – it was always: "Maybe good enough, but too small." I hope they don't make the same mistake with other guys. I hope they give them a chance.'

Sitting beside him, I can report that he might be small, but he is clearly very strong. Nor did he miss out in the looks department with his long, slanting cheekbones and clear green eyes.

After school, Gio did a year at Wits, experiencing their bridging year to ready kids from previously disadvantaged schools for university. He then registered for accounting at Stellenbosch. 'I didn't make Craven Week or any of those Weeks because of the weight thing, so the only option I saw was studying. I wanted to get an education.'

At Stellenbosch, he initially played 'koshuis' football 'because it wasn't so hectic on the studies'. Later he went to trials for third, fourth and fifth team rugby. 'I didn't go for the first or second team trials because the issue of being too small was still there, and I didn't want to fight that battle while doing a tough course. They moved me up to the second team, but I only played one week on, one week off because of my studies.'

By his third year, he was playing for Maties first team. By 2005, he was in the Western Province squad after a brief début in the national club championships. Then Western Province contracted him, first for the Currie Cup and then for the Stormers. He made his Springbok début in Wales against Wales. He is determined to finish his degree, however. 'I have learnt a lot from guys who played back in the day and didn't look to past rugby. Every day, it's a matter of enjoying the moment and giving it my best but also thinking about my future.' He is still finishing his CA – he has only three subjects to go. 'Until 2009, I did one subject a year, but with the Springboks and away legs, it's a bit tough.'

It's always been tough for Gio and possibly this is one of the reasons he has acquired a very strong faith. He grew up in a mainstream Christian household: his parents are Anglicans. In 2004, he was 'born again' and now belongs to His People, a charismatic congregation. 'The Bible says you must get born again to go to heaven and that doesn't happen in the Anglican Church because of the tradition and stuff.' He believes it was being born again which enabled him to finally start achieving in rugby. 'From where I came from to where I am now: it is all God who is making it possible. You get born into a new life. Every day I realise how privileged I am to be here. Every day, I wake up thinking of the blessing the Lord gave me. It takes hard work and discipline, but the main factor for me is God.

'My room-mate at the university residence was born again way before me. One day he told me he had had a dream and the Lord had spoken to him in his dream. He saw me in all the newspapers. I was only playing soccer then. My future was to become an accountant.'

His faith has given him the huge courage he needs to compensate for his size. 'The mentality of being smaller is that you will always have to fight against the odds. You have lots to prove. No one but your parents and family are going to stand up for you, so you must front up, whatever challenge comes your way. People say I'm too small. I can't make tackles. Sometimes, when I make tackles, I don't know where they came from. I don't know how I did it, so I must thank the Lord for that. If you think about where I come from and the way I am built, it flies against the standards of modern rugby, so there must be a greater force allowing me to do this.

'I believe it must come from somewhere. I also believe you must use it for good. The reason God gave me talent was to use it: to help other people and to help yourself become a better person. It's wonderful to be a joy to people on the field. You are also confronted with a lot of people asking for autographs and stuff. When I was a youngster, and I went up to someone like Robbie Fleck, my only wish was that they would be nice to me. I wanted to experience a special moment. Now I try to do that. None of this would be so big without the supporters. They pay our salaries through their support.'

His faith, he believes, also protects him from physical harm. 'The only injury I've had is a torn posterior cruciate ligament in my knee during the Sevens World Cup. I was off for eight weeks, the longest I've been off. If you take all that into account, I have been blessed. Something must be protecting me. A lot of bigger guys get injured and are off for six months.'

The fact that the team prays together helps unite them. 'You look at each other on the field and you know we are all looking at the same source to give us help.'

I'm curious to know where Gio Aplon comes from: his accession to national glory has been so different and so much harder than for many of his team-mates.

I ask him if I can go out to Hawston to see his parents and he readily agrees, setting up an interview for me. Hawston itself is a surprise: knowing its history of race-driven deprivation and its ongoing high levels of unemployment, I had expected it to be much more run-down and obviously poor. However, it looks like a middle-class suburb with its solid, detached brick houses, many with speedboats in the driveway. The setting is gorgeous: lapping the ocean, with a front-row view in season of the passing parade of whales and dolphins.

Cedric and Nellie Aplon live in a large house slightly back from the sea, but on a small hill so that they still have a good view. They are warm and welcoming and feed me tea and biscuits, only too happy to talk about their superstar son. I discover that Gio's heritage is a rich one. Cedric was politically active from a young age. He was studying teaching at Hewat Teachers' Training College in Cape Town in

1976 when the uprisings that had begun in Soweto spread south. Hewat was a centre of resistance and although Cedric was involved in the education boycotts that followed, he managed to finish his studies and then moved to Hawston where he got a job at the local school. Cedric says he has always felt an affiliation with the French. Gio's name, he says, was inspired by the Italian name, Giovanni. It strikes me again how interesting is coloured identity, how fluid and diverse. Gio looks more like Nellie, who comes from the Karoo, the heartland of South Africa's original people, the Khoisan. Her features still show traces of their bony beauty.

I assume it was the outsider status forced on coloured people by apartheid's racist hierarchy that bred their rebellious allegiance to the Springboks' chief rivals, and the fact that far more of the All Blacks looked like them than did the Springboks. As Cedric points out, it is not a rational affiliation.

'Lots of people here still support the All Blacks. I say to them: "The All Blacks didn't support the struggle. They sent teams here to play the Springboks in 1970 and in 1976." Peter de Villiers' argument is that if you support the All Blacks, you are saying you are not good enough for the Boks, and yet you won't get picked by the All Blacks either.'

Cedric is infuriated by this stubborn allegiance, particularly as it manifests within his own family. Their son-in-law supports the Kiwis. 'If we are building a new South Africa, we must all pull together. If Mandela could pull on a number six jersey in 1995, so can we. If I want my grandson to play for the Boks in 15 years' time, he must support the Boks now. He must support his uncle.'

Nellie confides: 'He's three. We take him to Newlands when Gio is playing and we always put a Springbok jersey on him.'

They brought Gio up on rugby. 'We took him to Loftus when he was a little boy. He learnt to count by remembering the numbers and names of the Blue Bulls.'

Hawston has always been rugby-mad. 'Gio just wanted to play all the time, with the guys around here.' The entire community comes out to support the Hawston team and they hire buses so that the locals can support them in away league games. 'It's very good for the youngsters. Very good for bonding the community.' It helps to keep them close. 'Youngsters don't want to leave Hawston. They were born here and want to die here. Their girlfriends come from here and start families while still very young. We had one guy who played for Border Bulldogs and one who played for the Lions Under 21s. They came back home, however. They didn't want to live away from here.'

As Gio says, most Hawston residents make a living from the sea. Much of it is legal, some not. 'The biggest problem is poaching-related,' says Cedric. 'If you deliver abalone, I will provide you with tik.' It's pretty well crime-free, though. We haven't had a murder in seven years. There was a rape last year, but it was the first in five years. There's not even much house-breaking. People look out for each other.'

Knowing what a struggle Gio had to reach the big time, compared to some of his team-mates, I ask Cedric what it was like for them, trying to give him every opportunity, against the odds. 'I think because Schalk and Jean's parents were better off and because of the community they came from, it was easier to get into the right schools and get the right coaches. We had to do the best we could for the kids. We didn't have the same role models. The Hawston community has delivered three or four lawyers in its history.'

The Aplons feel Gio owes much of his success to Peter de Villiers. 'Peter was willing to give him a chance. It wasn't about colour. It was about who was the best player. It's all about opportunity. In the past, guys of colour just weren't given a chance. White guys were picked even if they messed up. For players of colour, the self-confidence just wasn't there because you were picked one weekend and dropped the next.'

They are very protective of De Villiers. 'He is in the hot seat,' says Cedric. 'He isn't alone in his responsibility for selecting the team. If the team isn't performing well, he gets the blame. That is not fair. If he made his own selection, you could blame him.'

Another person who staunchly defends Peter de Villiers is that titan of the South African political landscape, the Minister of National Planning, Trevor Manuel. Shortly after the 2009 British and Irish Lions Tour, when public criticism of De Villiers was at its most vociferous, Manuel wrote a letter to *Business Day*, calmly pointing out Peter de Villiers' impressive record as Springbok coach. Surely, he asked, it was only on a man's results that he should be judged?

The letter had an instant effect. Subsequent references to De Villiers were more respectful. The lampooning that had accompanied most references to him died away.

This was the second time Manuel had made a dramatic public intervention in perceptions of South African rugby. His first was in 1996, the year after then President Nelson Mandela and Springbok captain, François Pienaar, had theoretically healed the wounds of rugby's racist past with their joint hoisting of the Webb Ellis Trophy. Manuel was caught up in a frenzy of media fury over his assertion during a Test match against the All Blacks that he supported the New Zealanders rather than the Springboks. Mandela had recently appointed Manuel to his Cabinet as Minister of Finance, the first black man ever to hold this crucial post. Within a few years, Manuel was to achieve god-like status amongst the business community and South Africa's middle classes in general. In 1996, however, this same strata of South African society – which encompassed the rugby fraternity – regarded him with intense distrust.

Over a drink at the Vineyard Hotel, a few kilometres from the Newlands stadium, where the drama began, he recalled it for me.

'There was an unbelievable hoo-haa about the fact that I said I would support the All Blacks. Actually, it was a particular set of circumstances. It was the beginning of Rugby Union as a professional sport. The turning point was the 1995 World Cup. This was the first full season of professionalism. In that particular Test, a guy called Tromp was on the Springbok bench. He was an incredibly strong chap – a hooker – and they decided to bring him into the team.'

Tromp had been convicted of manslaughter after beating one of his black farm workers so badly that the man died of his injuries. The racial and power dynamics of such a death in the context of the country's history made this crime particularly revolting.

'There was a huge row in our box. I happened to be in the Old Mutual box, and the row was actually about Tromp. The argument put forward by some who were there – who happened to be white – was that winning was the most important thing.

'I had a different take on this issue. National teams must engender national pride, and it can't be about winning at all costs. Hopefully my sons, who were very young at the time, would aspire to wear the jersey and you can't demean everything for the sake of winning. That was the debate and that was why I took this strong stand.

'It was clear was that this didn't matter to people. It wasn't an issue. It didn't matter to the chattering classes that this guy had beaten one of his black workers to death. If he could help win the game for us, that was neither here nor there.

'All this happened within a year of winning the World Cup, which in many respects was a great turning point for nation-building. In respect of rugby itself it was also a turning point because, at the time of the 1995 World Cup, the only black player was Chester Williams. This was not regarded as an issue, and we were just going to continue in the same vein. There was great recalcitrance on the part of the rugby administration when it came to effecting change.

'Of course there were howls of derision when I took my stand, because if it's only about winning, then you support the team that plays the most attractive rugby. It's not about anything else, regardless of what happened at the World Cup.

'I suppose people who hold Cabinet posts need to be very measured and can't wear their hearts on their sleeve, but I actually think that there was a voice that needed to be heard and a missed opportunity for debate. I include myself in that. I considered whether South Africa would have the appetite for its Minister of Finance to be involved in debates around sport, and I stepped aside.'

Of course, Manuel was right. The battle to rid rugby – and, by extension, its supporters – of racism was in its early days.

Rian Oberholzer, then CEO of the South African Rugby Football Union, said of its selection of Tromp: 'Sarfu is fully aware of the history of Henry Tromp, but the player has been selected for the squad and deserves his chance.'

That Oberholzer and the coach, André Markgraaff, should have even considered fielding such an individual to represent the newly minted rainbow nation was extraordinary.

The following year, Markgraaff was forced to resign after being secretly tape-recorded referring to black administrators as 'fucking kaffirs'. The year after that, Oberholzer's father-in-law, Louis Luyt, took Nelson Mandela's government to court in an attempt to halt a commission of inquiry into rugby to investigate allegations of racism and financial mismanagement. Andy Colquhoun, now the Springboks' strategic communications manager, wrote: 'The fact that Mandela was forced to take to the witness box so outraged black sports administrators that they threatened to return rugby to international isolation. Luyt won the court case – although the result was later overturned on appeal – but lost the war. He was forced to resign, and quit rugby completely two years later ... Luyt's departure heralded a new era.'

Trevor Manuel says that during this 'dark period' of rugby's history, he distanced himself. 'I'd go to games, primarily at Newlands. It's always a bit difficult. You don't want to be thumped by one of these chaps who has had too much Klipdrift and Coke. At the same time, you want to avoid the strictures that come from sitting in the box of a huge corporate. I was fortunate in that I had friends from small corporates and for a while, a few of them shared a box and I could always slip in there. You were amongst mates and it didn't matter who said what.'

A waiter comes up. He has recognised Manuel and wants to greet him. Manuel responds with warmth, smiling and shaking the man's hand.

The waiter leaves and Manuel continues. His three sons, he says, were growing up rugby mad. Govan, his eldest, persuaded his dad to take him to Paris for the 2007 World Cup. They watched a couple of semi-finals but Govan had to return to university and Manuel went on to a meeting in the US and so they missed South Africa's triumph in the final. 'We had lunch with the team, however, and a good rapport was built up.'

At the same time, his second son, Pallo, was playing in the Western Province Under 18 team at Academy Week in Polokwane. Afterwards, Western Province offered him a bursary to their Academy in Stellenbosch and he spent a year there.

Soon after this, Manuel said, he came across Peter de Villiers for the second time, having known him 'tangentially' in the eighties when Manuel was leading the mobilisation of the Western Cape against the apartheid government. De Villiers was 'not a big activist – he was a teacher in the area'.

Now Govan was playing in the Under 21s for Schotsche Kloof and De Villiers was coaching him. It was already clear that De Villiers was an outstanding coach.

'Govan said to me: "I have never met a coach like this. Technically he understands every position and he understands the player in that position. He plays to the strengths of the players. You can trust him. But, Dad, just don't ask this guy to make a speech."'

When De Villiers was made Springbok coach, Manuel made a point of tracking down his phone number and phoning him to congratulate him. He has watched De Villiers' career with great interest.

He also watched the merciless pillorying of De Villiers and decided to make the intervention that halted the prevailing narrative and sparked a new one. 'I had the very strong sense that in the minds of the rugby writers, Peter de Villiers could do nothing right.'

This was during the 2009 Test series against the British and Irish Lions. 'I was at Loftus when the Test series was clinched,' recalled Manuel. 'At the end of the game, Oregan [Hoskins] said: "Come with me. Let's go down to the dressing room and say thanks to these guys." As you come in at the tunnel there is a corridor, with the South African changing room on the right, the Lions on the left. We greeted various players as they came through, including the Lions team. Then we sort of hung around because the captains were doing some post-match TV stuff. We had to wait for John Smit to come through.

'They said: "Don't come into the changing room just yet. Just allow the players and management to do their thing – there is the prayer and all of that stuff." So we hung around and then we went to meet the players. Now, Peter De Villiers says his opposite number didn't come up to him and congratulate him on winning the series that day. This could have happened anywhere. I was with Oregan Hoskins, right there. I saw the coaches come through together and they may have done it on the field. They didn't do it in the tunnel; they didn't do it at the point where they separated to go to their separate dressing rooms. It didn't happen. I was there. But then South African journalists wrote – because the British media were saying it – that they all saw the handshake.

'I don't know why Peter mentioned it [the failure of the British and Irish Lions coach to shake his hand and congratulate him]. The upshot was that the media said they saw it happening and made Peter out to be this scoundrel, this liar, this poor communicator. Everybody just piled into the guy, and this continued up until the start of the Tri-Nations. At that point I did this crazy thing, responding to [*Business Day* editor] Peter Bruce's "Thick Edge of the Wedge". I said he was completely out of order.

'What matters most in sport is the end result. Measure Peter de Villiers by the same instrument that you would measure other coaches, and you would find that he has actually done better than others.'

There is another brief interruption as the manager arrives to greet Manuel. Once he has left, Manuel leans back in his chair, contemplative now. 'I suppose it's not well advised for ministers – unless you are the Minister of Sport – to get involved in this stuff, but I did.'

Shortly afterwards, before the first Tri-Nations match

against the All Blacks in Bloemfontein, the Springboks asked Manuel to hand out the jerseys.

'I'd heard that, for the Durban test against the Lions, Johann Rupert had been asked to do this, and he thought it was very important. The gist of Johann's talk to them was: "I'm sure that if I asked what any of you know about me, you'd probably say I'm a very wealthy man. You'd probably be right. Yet no amount of money can buy me this jersey. You've earned it and you've got to wear this thing with pride."

'The message that I gave the players was: if you go back to that day in June of 1995, there is that one image of François and Madiba with the Web Ellis Trophy, but the more important image was probably of black people dancing in the streets and claiming it as their victory. The ability of rugby to be more than just what happens on the field is phenomenal. I said the challenge in 1995 had been to bring into the rugby fold the black people who had been excluded. The challenge that we face now before this test against the All Blacks is to bring in the white people who feel they no longer own rugby. As you walk onto the field, bear that in mind.'

On 24 September, we play Griquas in a chilly wind. Before half-time, Province has scored five tries. The forwards are formidable. I watch Anton in the line-out, with bared teeth made more menacing by the blue gum guard and a white scrum cap that looks like a gladiator's helmet. He looks like a wild man, very different from the measured gentleman who will later sit beside me on a couch at the HPC, mulling it all over.

Late in the second half, he and Jean de Villiers leave the field for the first time in this competition. The game is well won and they need to conserve their energy for the big games that lie ahead. The final score is 48–32. At the press conference afterwards, the Griquas coach bemoans the fact that they have had five crucial injuries, one of whom is a former Ikeys Tiger, Matt Rosslee. The Griquas also have financial difficulties. 'We need a million rand and fewer injuries,' he says. A tall order.

Then Allister and Anton come on. They've also incurred a costly injury: Wicus Blaauw. Allister says he's happy with the team's performance. Anton says: 'It's about momentum. Who is in control. It's about making the right decision at the right time.'

The 14th game is the return match against the Bulls. At Loftus.

Anton says: 'The Bulls as a team pride themselves on executing a game plan that they have had for years. Against the Bulls, you know what type of game you face. That is, the challenges of encountering it, not as in working out what you are up against. There will be a lot of up and unders. The Bulls are going to kick the ball. There is no doubt.

You know it's coming, but the challenge is in catching that kick, handling the ruck and then clearing the ball.'

The next day I go to Pretoria to spend a few days with the Bulls. I watch the game from the President's box at Loftus. The Bulls win the game 36–32.

Western Province started well and at half-time were winning but then progressively lost it. The Bulls not only had home-ground advantage but they were also desperate to hoist themselves out of fifth place and secure a place in the semi-finals. Jean de Villiers got a yellow card for a high tackle, a big loss. At the end of the day, however, we are still second on the log, way behind the Sharks but two points ahead of the Cheetahs.

Back at the HPC the following week, Anton says that in fact the build-up to the game had gone very well. 'The game went very well for forty minutes, but in the second forty minutes it couldn't have gone worse. That's not lekker when you're captain because you take it personally. You feel responsible.'

Allister is equally downcast. 'I'm tired. A coach's exhaustion is caused by the fact that he has to put up a positive front at all times because the team feeds off it. No matter what is thrown at you, you have to put up a front. You have to be in control, no matter if it is burning inside or how little confidence you have. You have to make them believe things are okay. It was tough going to Loftus and knowing we had a great opportunity to beat the Bulls. We started off well but lost concentration a few minutes before half-time. It was 16–3 to us at that point. We had worked all week to handle the high ball. We caught eight, but dropped the ninth, and that was the one they capitalised on. Then Jean de Villiers got a yellow card and it was very hard to come back. The Bulls were having to fight for their lives to make a semi-final and we had to come back with 14 men – it was too little, too late.'

The pressure now is to beat the Sharks and secure a home semi-final. 'A home semi-final is very important to keep the coffers full. An away semi-final brings you nothing. The Bulls have always had home semis and home finals and that is why they are so powerful.'

I've become increasingly fond of Allister over the past few months. I find him unfailingly honest and down to earth. He is mature and magnanimous. He has a sense of humour. Above all, I'm grateful for his ongoing warmth and openness.

He tells me that, compounding the pressure of the past week is what appears to be treachery from within his own ranks. Members of the Western Province board have been saying publicly that there are not enough players of colour on the side. 'It really messes you up when you talk to your own officials about racial selection and then they go and criticise you in the press.' What he is saying is that it is particularly wounding to be publicly accused of perpetuating racial discrimination, given his own experience of it.

I wander outside to watch the forwards practise their line-outs for the Sharks game. As ever, it appears effortless, graceful. I hesitate to use the ballerina analogy because it might not go down too well but that is what it always reminds me of. As they come off the field, I waylay Anton and he sits down beside me on the bench. I put my ballerina theory to him and he says with a smile that the more graceful it looks, the more effective it probably is.

'Think about the height you have to achieve, and the timing. You have to have eight forwards who are on exactly the same page, who know the required movement for each specific call. That is the key to it. A lot of people give the locks the credit for the line-out, but the truth is that you need two supporters who know exactly what the jumper is going to do, and a thrower whose throw is exact in regard to weight and timing. It's a collective effort. When you make a call, there can't be any doubt or hesitation about what that call is, or the line-out will probably be a failure.'

How do you decide on your codes? I ask. 'Some guys just use numbers. Some just use letters, or language. If you use English or Afrikaans, it's usually a sign of something. There isn't a perfect system. When you've got a good system, you develop it by playing with the same individuals. It's constantly evolving. Sometimes you just change because opponents have picked up a trend. Contesting first phase is such an important part of the game, so you spend time analysing your opponent. It's virtually impossible to crack an opponent's code but you may pick up a trend

'It's all about the dummies, in other words the guys who don't jump but look as if they might, or who support another jumper. The two locks, together with one or perhaps two loose forwards are the main jumpers. You need four jumpers – that will give you more than enough options. The whole idea is to jump into space – where there isn't anyone else. To create that space, you need to make your opponents believe that you are going to jump somewhere else or half a second earlier or half a second later.'

The field before us is empty now. He tells me he needs to head off soon for a team meeting upstairs. I check the time for him on my cell phone. There are still a few minutes to go.

'Rugby is about winning the small battles to win the war. As such, each player needs to be a specialist in his position. I'm involved in the line-out. I don't always know exactly what move the backs will make from that lineout. Even as captain, I know the backs' moves generally but I won't know the details of their moves. The opposite applies to the backs when it comes to line-outs: they just see the ball being won! There's the irony, though: despite our different areas of speciality, we are so dependent on each other. If any one individual underperforms, it could lead to the demise of the whole team.

'The higher the level you get to, the more emphasis there is on the mental side of each aspect of the game. It's not always only about who is stronger and faster. It's who can do the right thing at the right time – precision decision-making. It's about thinking on your feet.'

He has told me before that the guys he has played with on this field are as sharp as anyone he has met at Oxford or Deloitte. My experience bears this out. I've yet to interview a rugby player who is unintelligent.

It's time and he's off, loping up the stairs two at a time.

I miss Trademarx. There is nowhere at the HPC to hang out over a cappuccino and still get a bird's-eye view of the action. When it's chilly, as now, I find a warm refuge in the office of Chippie Solomons, the team manager.

There is a lot of traffic: players come and go, asking for tickets for friends and family for the Sharks game. They get four each, the rest they have to pay for. There is a box for wives and girlfriends. One player asks if there is space for his mom as well as his wife. Chippie grumbles: it only takes 24, but he will find room.

Don Armand, the Ikey Tigers lock, comes in. He's training with the squad, hoping to get a contract next year. 'It's much more serious here than at UCT,' he says. 'For half the guys in the Varsity Cup, that was as far as they wanted to go. Only half wanted to play professionally.' He's finished his first degree – a social science degree in psychology – and has only one more subject to complete to get a postgraduate degree in sports management.

Buhle Mxunyelwa, who played for the Maties against the Ikey Tigers in the Varsity Cup, teases him: 'The first game was close, hey. You were all over us.'

All the Springboks are now back. They have been on a month-long conditioning course and then two days of tests at the Sports Science Institute in Newlands. This is most inconvenient for Allister, as it is scheduled to last all of the Monday and Tuesday before the Sharks game. As a consequence, he gave the team the day off on Monday. On Tuesday they practised without the Boks. Only on the Wednesday were they finally able to train together.

The newly returned Boks do represent serious reinforcements: Schalk Burger, who takes over as captain, Bryan Habana, Jaque Fourie and Ricky Januarie.

At the press conference on 7 October, Allister says: 'The family is together again.' He now has an embarrassment of riches: three world-class centres, namely Jaque Fourie, Jean de Villiers and Juan de Jongh. How does he distribute them? He decides to put Jean de Villiers on the wing, which inevitably attracts flak. Jean played wing for the Springboks earlier and it wasn't a hugely successful experiment. 'That was at a different level and we had to make a decision that was good for the team,' responds Allister. 'This is really looking at the weekend only.'

Gio is at fullback: 'The Sharks play with the ball in hand and they don't kick as much as the other teams. We've got to match pace with pace. We've got to make sure we're covered.'

Later, I corner Schalk for a chat. He sits beside me on the couch in the rec room, turned towards me, big bare knee pulled up. He is a hugely physical presence, radiating an almost tangible energy. Everything about him is large and generous. The only delicate part is his mouth, which is surprisingly beautiful with its wide, undulating curves. It makes sense to me when he says how difficult the last month of conditioning has been for him. He just wants to get out there and play. 'Rugby comes naturally to me. I have always understood it. I love everything about it: the camaraderie; the changing rooms, drinking beer after.'

He tells me he was born in Port Elizabeth in 1983. His family later moved to Wellington and began farming. He went to primary school in Wellington and then to the noted rugby school, Paarl Gimnasium. After school, he registered for a BA LLB at Stellenbosch University. 'I tried to study but didn't really and in my second year, I became a Springbok.' He has now bought himself a smallholding near the family farm in Wellington. 'That is where I want to live. I'd like to be involved in the farm but also to start my own business – maybe in TV.' He is also about to marry the girl he has been going out with since school.

That's in the future, however. All he is thinking about now is winning the semi-final. 'This is my fourth semi-final, but I haven't played in a final. We really want to make it to the final this time. The more you get into a leadership role, the more decisions you've got to make about how you want to play; what's going to work that weekend. You go in with a game plan but if that doesn't work, you have to change it at half-time and then it's not easy. The games that haven't gone according to plan are the ones we haven't been able to turn around.'

I ask him about his experience of melding different cultures and races into a coherent team. His answers reveal the same mental agility he shows on the field. This is a clever man. 'When you're getting the on-field stuff right, it's easier to get the rest right. Getting a tight-knit group off the field is more difficult, but once you do get it right, it makes rugby completely unique because it is so team-driven, even though an individual may shine every now and then.

'The off-field aspect is the major difficulty. I've been in teams where it has come spontaneously. Some I've been in have had clashes of personalities and egos. With the Springboks and Western Province, we have got a nice group of guys and we all come from the same background, rugby-wise. At the moment, we've got a very good thing going. In the past, I've been in teams where it hasn't worked and we have lost games by seven or nine points and I often thought that if the guys had cared more about each other, we might have turned things around.

'When I started playing, there might have been a bit more of an issue – more Afrikaans versus English or north versus south, but now there is none of that. I think teams have grown past that point. We now accommodate everything. Earlier, things were more sensitive, more difficult to handle. Now it is still sensitive but a lot less than it used to be. It's a bit more complex being a South African than being a New Zealander or an Australian. If you get it right, it makes for a much stronger bond than in countries where you don't get those issues. If you don't get it right, it doesn't work at all.'

I ask him about the language issue and, again, his answer is thoughtful.

'As an Afrikaans guy, I was probably more comfortable being surrounded by Afrikaans blokes but that has all changed for me. A lot of my friends are English. When you are younger and your English is not so good, it becomes a bit of a confidence issue.

'With Afrikaners, there is more respect. It's a matter of knowing your place. The English are more upfront. My girl-friend went to the English school in Paarl and her home language is English although we speak Afrikaans to each other.' In fact, his English is fluent. He seems completely at home in the language, in its formal as well as its idiomatic guise.

'I've always been in sides that are representative and, for me, it's never been an issue. In Cape Town, it's no issue whatsoever and I'm glad because it's a very sensitive issue and we as South Africans can't talk freely about it yet.'

I ask him what advice he'd like to pass on to kids and he says: 'The most important thing is to enjoy it and play as much sport as you can. Play all types – cricket, rugby – whatever you enjoy. It changes as you go up through the age group levels and you get a contract and more respon-sibility. I was lucky with my timing. If I'd come through three or four years earlier, I wouldn't have played 50 caps because there were so many good players coming through. When you do get an opportunity, you must make the most of it.'

He's mad about South Africa, he says. 'I've travelled all over the world with the Boks and there is no other place I'd like to live. Living in Australia is like living in a zoo. Living in South Africa is like living in a game park.'

Forty-five thousand people pack Newlands for the Sharks game. It's a biggie for us, given the humiliation of the defeat in Durban. 'I can't wait for the return game,' Anton had said at the time. Now I can see why. The forwards are superb, setting up flawless opportunities for the backs. I think of something else he once told me, about an idealised game of rugby: 'Heads-up rugby. Everybody is intuitively on the same page, so when the fly half looks up, he sees what's in front of him and he immediately identifies the space over there. There are no real positions. It's just free play.' Maybe it was just the elation of beating the Sharks, but this game seemed to me to be approaching that level of fluency. There's Gio Aplon, streaking down the touchline like a bullet, his head sheathed in its protective white cap. There's Jean de Villiers, outpacing the Shark prodigies Patrick Lambie and Lwazi Mvovo, to score another brilliant try.

There's Anton at one point calming down an inflamed Deon Fourie. There are Schalk and Anton on either of Jean de Villiers, giving him a hand up after he was tackled to the ground. A team united, a team in full flight.

After 79 minutes and 50 seconds, the crowd starts the countdown: 9, 8, 7, 6, 5, 4, 3, 2, 1! We've beaten the Sharks 33–21 and have earned a home semi-final.

———

SEVEN

Next door to the players' changing room at Newlands there is a fairly large room with high, stretcher-type beds. This is the first aid room, where the players don their armour before a game, otherwise known as strapping. It looks like a dressing station in a casualty ward and is as much a part of preparation for a game as donning their jerseys or intoning the team prayer.

In the run-up to the semi-final, I prop myself up on one of the beds with my laptop and watch. I've been around such a lot by now that they are used to me and don't seem to mind my presence at what is really quite an intimate ritual. The atmosphere is jokey and relaxed. They lounge around on the beds in shorts and T-shirts, passive now.

They are waiting for Lize van Schalkwyk, the quietly efficient physiotherapist, to get round to them with her bundles of tape and bandages and scissors. The team doctor helps out. Some players get impatient and seize a roll of tape for the initial binding, at least. They all want the expert touch for the rounding off, however. Lize says there is a therapeutic basis to it: 'Once a joint has been injured, it loses its sense of where it is. This pressing down on it helps it to recreate its sense of where it is.'

It looks like something less scientific, more primal or psychological: like medieval soldiers sheathing themselves in coats of chain mail before braving hand-to-hand combat, or Zulu warriors of old coating themselves in muti to render themselves impervious to enemy spears.

I've generally found that players at every level are reluctant to talk about injuries. The attitude seems to be that it is part of the deal: accept it and move on. This room is all about injury, however: injury faced up to and girded against.

Big Tiaan Liebenberg is there, more for the company than anything else, it appears. Injury has sidelined him from the action for a long time. He tore the ligament between his tibia and fibula in the first Bulls game. For the next six weeks, he has to keep his weight off the leg to give it a chance to heal. While he's out of the game anyway, he has had an operation on a shoulder injury that has been troubling him for the past year. I know that the team are sorely missing his strength and experience, and his enforced absence is equally painful for him.

'It's easier if you are at home and out of the vibe, but as soon as I come in here, I just want to strap and inject and play. The moment I do start playing again, I'm going to strap everything.'

Each player has his own vulnerable area. For Anton, it is his ankles 'because I've had big injuries to both and I don't think we were made to be thrown up in the air and dropped'. He straps on the first layer himself, then Lize winds a long bandage round and round, until each ankle is bound in a tight white sheath. 'Injuries are part of the game,' he says. 'You do your best. There is new research being done every year on injury prevention, and a lot of what we do in the gym is to prevent injuries, but there is only so much you can do. I tore the ligament that holds tibia and fibula together, so I had a screw there for a while. That was quite a long one – nine months off. I damaged my right ankle while I was at Oxford – that was four or five months off. Then I tore my right calf quite badly in 2008 – that was four months off. You never completely recover. I'm pain-free, but after a day on my feet, my calf still gets quite stiff every now and then.'

Lize straps Gio Aplon's knee next, then Francois Louw's ankle. He explains that it rolled over in a game against Australia, tearing all the ligaments and chipping a bone in his foot. He was out for 15 weeks and has a big scar up the front of the foot from where the surgeons opened it up to repair the damage. Now he straps it before every game and practice. Last year, Juan de Jongh broke a bone in his left foot and was in a cast for four weeks. Now he has both feet strapped – 'for balance'.

They all tell me that one thing you cannot do is run out onto the field fearing injury. What they don't attempt to deny are the scars, both physical and psychological.

Take Conrad Jantjes. He was injured here at Newlands during the 2009 Super 14, in a game against the Chiefs. 'I was up against a flanker who had about 15 kilograms on me, so I didn't want to dive on the ball because he would have wrapped me up. I saw Schalk on the inside and he put his hand up so I tried to slide in towards the ball and kick it to Schalk, but the flanker came in at the same angle. We were both at full pace and his knee connected with mine.

'I heard my leg snap. It was like a gunshot. Then it was all a blur. I was aware of what was going on around me but your world slows down. I was sitting on the field and I looked down at my leg and it was at a weird angle. The game was going on three or four metres away from me and I started panicking because I thought they would come back towards me. That was when I started screaming.

'I heard the ref say: "Too much pain. We're stopping the game." I heard the whistle go. The game stopped for 25 minutes. They had to straighten my leg on the field because there were so many nerve endings, and the adrenaline was still pumping, so it was better to do it then. I've never experienced such pain.

'It was a seven 'o clock game so I was lying there, looking up at the night sky. It just got smaller and smaller. I was blacking out. I remember the doc saying: "Connie, you've got to stay with me." I was bleeding from my lip from the same collision, so they were checking to see if I was concussed.

'Then they brought me in here and gave me morphine and I started tripping. When they tried to take my boot off, I thought they were pulling my leg off and I screamed at them to stop.

'Just like that, everything is gone. Your life changes.'

In subsequent operations, pins and screws were inserted into his leg and the long, painful process of rehabilitation began. 'I was in bed for six weeks. Then they removed the bottom screws and I had a bit more movement in my ankle. I had to teach myself to walk again. There were times when I had to crawl around my house. It took eleven weeks before I could drive.

'I've still got a pin and two screws in, but physically I'm good to go. I still need to get that image out of my head – of my leg lying skewed on the field. I've seen a sports psychologist, but that is still my biggest challenge.'

He looks so shaken after having dredged up all these dreadful memories that I feel bad about having been the catalyst for it. What does impress me is that he does it in front of his team mates, clearly feeling totally comfortable about expressing this quite acute vulnerability in their presence. They are silent. No one teases him or expresses any discomfort. That kind of empathy from your team must help with the healing process.

I had encountered the same kind of solidarity a few years before in a very different rugby context. It was in a cramped but well-kept lounge in Rosettenville, a lower-middle-class suburb in southern Johannesburg.

I had come to visit Jzuan Dreyer who is sitting in a corner of the room in his wheelchair. He is over 1,95 metres tall and still appears to loom over everyone else, even folded double as he is. There is a dissonance between the immobility conveyed by his paralysis and the ceaseless activity of his right thumb and forefinger hunched over his cell phone, in constant contact with a world of friends out there while he pretends to take part in a conversation I am having about him with the rest of his family.

A terrible thing happened to Jzuan Dreyer on 15 March 2006, just a week after his 17th birthday. He was playing wing for the first team of President High School against a rival school, Brandwag Hoër from Benoni, when he was tackled by two Brandwag players at the same time, one from the front, one from the back.

'I was on the ground. I tried to get up but couldn't. I felt numb all over.'

His cell phone pings and he goes back to texting. After a minute, his mother, Dowlene Halim, takes up the story. 'They continued the game. It was only a few minutes later that they realised he was badly hurt.' Unlike her son, she is a small, neat woman with a soft voice.

An ambulance was called and he was taken to Union Hospital in Alberton where he was in the ICU for 12 days. An MRI scan revealed that his neck was broken. The C5 vertebra had snapped and been pushed back into his spinal chord. He was permanently paralysed from the chest down.

One could have forgiven Jzuan and his family for lapsing into an orgy of bitterness and blame at this point; at the boys who launched the fateful tackle ('they sent me flowers the next day,' he comments, with only a trace of wryness); at the ref who kept the game going; at the school that organised the game. One might have expected talk of lawsuits and claims for damages.

But no. They just seemed to accept that they had arbitrarily been dealt a dreadful blow and would have to get on with it. It helped that they were very religious.

'The Almighty is testing us,' said Dowlene. 'It was the will of the Lord. It was meant to be.'

This family represented one of those fascinating cross-cultural, cross-racial mixes that has bloomed since the end of apartheid. Jzuan was the product of Dowlene's first husband, a white Afrikaner, as she is. She has subsequently married Naeem Halim, a brown Muslim and, between them, they have produced a daughter, Jzuan's mixed-race half-sister.

Dowlene says that when Jzuan was paralysed, she said to her husband: 'It is going to be very hard. He is not your son. If you are going to go, go now.'

Naeem was going nowhere.

It *was* hard. 'In the beginning, we cried every night,' says Dowlene. 'I didn't sleep for the first three weeks. The worst thing was to see him lying there. It was just heart-breaking. I had to go away and cry. It was as if someone had put their hand into my chest and pulled my heart out.'

His injury hasn't put Jzuan off rugby. It was what got him through the first five months of rehab. He just watched rugby on TV – any rugby. He doesn't admire the Springboks, he says, because of the racial quotas. He prefers the All Blacks. His hero is Jonah Lomu, who played with the same number on his back as he does. I can't help pointing out the contradictions in this statement: that the places allocated to black players put him off his national team but his hero is a black man, his stepfather is Indian and his own sister of mixed race.

Dowlene interrupts: 'His little sister does not see race. Perhaps it will take another generation.'

She talks about the extraordinary support and warmth this accident has evoked. 'The whole school was at the hospital, filling up the corridors. They organised themselves into rotas: two minutes with him, and then the next was sent in. His teacher brought us a bowl of food every single night.'

Even now, two years on, his friends – and the school –

cannot do enough for him. His classroom is on the third floor and there is no wheelchair access so his friends carry him up and down the stairs. The girls in his class take him to the girls' loo at break and make sure no one else goes while he empties his catheter.

On a Friday and Saturday night, his mates arrive in a car and take him out to pubs and clubs. They lift him and his wheelchair in and out of the car. It's a mission, says Dowlene, yet they do it. At the pub, they know they have to put the glass in his hand and then fold his fingers around it. He has only limited use of his right hand and no feeling at all in his left. He can't move any of his fingers. The incessant texting I see is apparently the dogged thudding of a rigid thumb.

The ultimate hero of this story is probably Naeem, the faithful stepfather. It is short, stocky Naeem who lifts this damaged boy-man into his van every morning and evening to take him to school and back; who cleans up after him when he messes himself. Once, says Dowlene, his shit spilt all over the car. Now they always spread black bin liners over the seats. It is, she says matter-of-factly, very hard to deal with adult shit.

I'm struck by how openly they talk about all this. What happened to their son was catastrophic, but they face up to it and deal with it. He is left in absolutely no doubt about their love for him.

In 2008, the year I met Jzuan Dreyer, rugby claimed its first female victim, a 25-year-old from Butterworth who died from a head injury. Two more boys became quadriplegics: an 18-year-old from Pretoria Boys High and a 22-year-old from the University of Johannesburg.

The following year was a particularly bad one, with five deaths and three new quadriplegics. A 17-year-old from Linden High School became concussed during a game, didn't tell anyone and went back onto the field. He was hit again and died in his sleep. The second was a 24-year-old from the Eastern Cape who fractured his neck and died 48 hours later. The third was a 17-year-old from Bloemfontein who collapsed and died while running. It was discovered that he had a congenital heart defect. The last two were also heart-related: a 35-year-old and a 25-year-old.

In 2010, there were two rugby deaths: a 21-year-old from Masiphumelelo who tore a membrane in his brain during a collision in a game in nearby Noordhoek. The other was a man from Piketberg who broke his neck, suffered a severed spine, and died on the field. Two of the 15 players who suffered catastrophic injuries while playing rugby in 2010 have irreversible spinal damage.

Appalled by the extent and intensity of injury in South African rugby, Morné du Plessis started Boksmart, a campaign to manage risk on the field. Gail Ross runs the programme from her office in the Sports Science Institute, next to Newlands.

'Now we analyse and research serious injuries,' she tells me. They try to educate coaches, refs and administrators on areas of risk and how to manage them. If there is a serious injury, Gail will be contacted. 'They can phone in and we can arrange an ambulance to anywhere in the country and take them to the most suitable place. We are trying to avoid hospital hopping. If you are in a little dorp, it is no good going to the day hospital because they won't have the right equipment and expertise. We can check for the nearest place where there is an MRI scan, an x-ray machine and an orthopaedic surgeon.'

This works in urban areas, she says, but rural areas are more of a challenge. 'Not all clubs are registered. The fields are not ideal. The coaches are enthusiastic parents.'

Boksmart runs prevention programmes, for example advocating the use of gum guards to protect teeth and jawbone, another frequent casualty. It also emphasises warming up properly prior to the game to prevent soft-tissue injuries like ligament and muscle tears.

Gail is also involved with the Chris Burger/Petro Jackson Players' Fund which provides moral and financial help for the catastrophically injured and paid for extensive renovations to Jzuan Dreyer's house to make it more wheelchair-friendly.

He is doing well, she tells me. He has got his matric and is working in a call centre run by one of the banks. But he will be in that wheelchair for the rest of his life.

EIGHT

There are two very tense games on simultaneously before Western Province takes on the Cheetahs in the semi-final on 16 October. One is the other semi-final between the Sharks and the Bulls at Kings Park, which is being screened on TVs all over Newlands. The other is the game being played on the field below us between the Western Province Under 21s and their Cheetah adversaries. Both are cliff-hangers. The result of the Sharks–Bulls game is crucial to us because it determines whether we get a home final against the Bulls – much the preferred option – or an away final against the Sharks. The game is characterised by bizarre onslaughts from nature: a stubborn swarm of bees on the field that delays the start, and then a drenching downpour of rain. In the end, after a massive, hugely physical battle, the Bulls go down 16–12.

Meanwhile, at Newlands, our Under 21s are neck and neck with the Cheetahs, which shouldn't be happening. After 80 minutes, the score is equal and they have to go into extra time. In the end the score is 49–49, but we are ahead on points and have made it through to the final.

Newlands is now packed to capacity, engulfing the Western Province team in a roar of delight as they run on. The chant: 'WP jou lekker ding!' starts softly and becomes louder and louder. As the game progresses and Western Province clearly has the upper hand, the cheering becomes a wall of sound, lining this lovely amphitheatre. It's a balmy, windless evening, the sun slowly dropping behind Table Mountain, looming over us.

Behind me is a row of glamorous coloured women, vocal and engaged. When Ricky Januarie comes chugging past, one shouts: 'Ag Januarie! Dis nie Desember nie!' They all pack up with laughter at their own wit, clearly finding themselves wonderfully entertaining.

When Jean de Villiers gets close, they croon lasciviously: 'Kom, Jean, kom na mamma toe!' once again, accompanied by shrieks of raucous laughter. They are hugely enjoying themselves, totally owning the game.

We win by a very comfortable 31–7.

Willem de Waal's metronomic boot contributed 16 points, which makes him the Currie Cup's leading points scorer. Two of the kicks were from inside our own half. At the post-game presser, an ebullient Schalk says: 'I just look at Willem and if he nods ... I mean you can't argue against 1 400 Currie Cup points. He obviously knows how far he can kick the ball.'

The Bulls defeat means that we have to go to Durban in two weeks' time, as do our Under 21s and Under 19s. They will each take on a Bulls team, second on the log, before the senior team squares up to the Sharks.

Back at the HPC the following week, Willem de Waal is practising his kicking for the final. When he has finished, I ask him: how does he manage that intense concentration, particularly when they are playing away and he has to perform in front of a big, hostile crowd, like at Loftus?

'I clear my mind,' he explains. 'I focus purely on the ball in front of me. I screen everything else out. I don't focus on the posts. Once it has left my boot, it is out of my hands. The backdrop is the training here. The hard yards. If I know I have trained properly during the week, I feel confident.' In fact, Loftus is easier to deal with than a smaller, less crowded stadium. 'At least sustained booing is a low, constant sound. One voice shouting out is more potentially distracting, so I prefer the Bulls at Loftus to, say, the Griquas.'

Jean de Villiers is always a heartening presence around the HPC. He has a light touch, always ready with a joke. Like the others, he is utterly unassuming. The combination of his long experience – both at Western Province and the Springboks – and the fact that he is an intelligent man, means he is also interesting to talk to. In the run-up to the final, we settle down on the couch and I ask him to describe his route into rugby.

'Rugby has always been part of my life,' he tells me. 'My dad played for Province as well; I got contracted straight out of school. What I've noticed the most since then is how rugby keeps on progressing. It's only been professional for a short time – since 1996. It still hasn't gone the full cycle. It's still not as professional as it needs to be. For instance, I don't think we've seen how being a professional rugby player for ten years will affect you. We still don't know what the effect on the body will be in the case of guys who have played since leaving school until they are 30 or 35. There is still a lot to be learnt. If we look at football, the whole package is more professional. It's no longer just training Monday and Tuesday and playing on Saturday. It's what you do off the field as well, for example your responsibilities when you are approached by fans and kids. I see how the culture has grown. They accept responsibility off the field as well.'

One of the reasons he enjoys playing for Province, he says, echoing the others, is the diversity: 'There are players from different schools and different ethnic backgrounds, but everyone gets treated the same. It keeps what the Irish call the 'craic' – the vibe in the team – alive all the time. You will still chirp the Bishops guys or the Rondebosch guys about the game we played against them for Paarl Gim in 1996, or the Stellenbosch guys for their game against UCT. At the Boks, it would be Western Province versus the Bulls guys.

'In the past, this could have disrupted the team, but it has evolved into something that is healthy and makes it fun. You just learn so much, being a rugby player. You could share a room with a guy who grew up in Langa. I grew up in Paarl and had a very decent life and went to a very good school but we are in the same team, sharing the same goals. Despite that, we are so different.

'What's important is the willingness to learn from those guys and learn from each other. We can each add value to the other. It's the willingness to take all that in.'

I like this about Jean: his openness and empathy. It's an intriguing contrast to his aggression on the field, as are his fine-featured good looks. He goes on: 'I'm 29 and I was never really part of the apartheid era, yet I can't imagine things being very different from what they are now. When I watch movies about those times, or people tell you stories, it is scary and I realise how privileged I am and how bad it was back then. So sport can teach you a lot.

'When I started, Gert Smal and Du Plessis were the coaches and they were fantastic. Western Province has always been a strong team because we have all these good schools in the province, as well as strong university teams. I think what Rassie Erasmus has done is put structures in place for the union to take our rugby forward, and that is why next week is so important for us – not only to be in the final, but also to win because we are ready for it now. Credit to Rassie and also to the coaching staff who have taken over. We have fantastic coaches now who have put their personal touches to the structures he put in place.

'I started off as a 21-year-old in the Straueli era. Since I can remember it had been my dream to represent my country. Then came the disappointment of playing the one game and getting injured within seven minutes and having to go off with a crocked knee. I was out for nine months. I came back into the 2003 World Cup squad, played twenty minutes of the last warm-up game before we left for Australia and got injured again. That was Kamp Staaldraad time and the World Cup that didn't go so well. South African rugby was in a pretty bad state at that time so maybe it was good to not be part of it.

'Jake White took over in 2004. He had put structures in place at the Under 21 level, and he did the same at senior level. He got a core group together and you could see how that core group kept on getting stronger and believing in each other and how they worked as a team. Luckily I was part of that from the first day. Peter took over two years ago and he saw what was in place there. He saw it was a settled team with guys who had won the World Cup and didn't need much coaching. He didn't come in and try to change everything. He just put in his personal touches in regard to his management team and just grew the team that had performed so well. This year wasn't that great, but last year was pretty special.

'I could see a much bigger shift in the team, in the team psyche, in the happiness of the team. When I started off with the Boks, there was a lot of provincialism, with a lot of guys staying with the players from their unions. Now I'm friends with a Bulls guy, a Cheetah, a Shark – whatever.'

He stops and grins at me. 'What else?'

'What else can you tell me?' I say.

'Well, rugby is a job, but first of all I do it because I really do love it and I enjoy it. The opportunities that you get to travel the world and to make friends are as important as anything else for me. Last year, in Ireland, when I was with Munster, I played with different nationalities, which was a fantastic opportunity. A rugby career is short, so it's important to take what you can from it as a person and grow as a person and learn skills to take into your next job. I made fantastic friends there. We had Irish nationals, Aussies, a Frenchmen, New Zealanders. I think it was easier for me because I had played with guys from different backgrounds here, so it was very similar at Munster. It was very good fun.'

Jean returned from Munster earlier in the year after one season because Peter de Villiers had said South Africans playing outside the country would not be considered for selection for the 2011 World Cup.

'I was injured before the 2003 World Cup and got injured again in 2007. I tore my biceps in the first game, so I missed out on the campaign. I chatted to my dad and family and we all felt that a World Cup is a pretty special thing to be part of, and playing for the Boks is pretty special as well. If I didn't try to make the team and give the World Cup another go, I would probably regret it when I look back in 20 years' time, so I came back, played for Province and will try to experience a full World Cup. Hopefully we'll win the thing! If I don't make it, then so be it, I will just move on.'

He shows me his operation scars: criss-crosses on his knee, his arm, his shoulder. This man has paid a price. 'When I'm 40, 45 years old, I don't know what my body will be like. I've had four knee ops, more ops on my biceps, and one to repair my shoulder. It is tough to get back into the national team when you have been out for nine months. You know who your friends are at those times, and you learn a lot about yourself. That is where the hard work comes in. It is easy to train out there when all the cameras are out and they are interviewing you and you're in the limelight. It is difficult when you are going through the hard times. Then you are training all alone, doing the rehab, sweating and experiencing massive pain to get the joints right and the muscle supple again. That is where you really build character and where some guys make it and some guys don't. It's tough – people see the good stuff about being a rugby player but if I get injured today, another guy will take my place and the crowd will shout just as hard for him and they won't give a rat's ass about what happened to me. They forget about you like that. It can be cruel like that, but it comes with the job and that is the job I chose. The good times outweigh the bad times, even though the bad times can be pretty bad!'

Do you do a lot of strapping now? I ask. He laughs.

'Strapping before the game takes half an hour. I strap both my ankles as a precaution, both my shoulders, both my wrists; all the joints basically. I do strap a lot! It feels protective and maybe it's just a mental thing, but I think it definitely helps. It doesn't look that good and I get the odd chirp from the guys, but it works for me.'

Are you not afraid of injury after all that damage and pain? 'You can't be. You can't worry about it. You can't go into a game thinking you are going to be injured again because that's usually when it happens. You have to give 100 per cent to the cause, and what happens happens. A lot of my injuries were freak injuries. You fall the wrong way or another guy falls on top of you and your shoulder pops out. That's part of the game. You have to know that at some stage of your career you will have an injury. Some guys go through a whole career without having surgery, but those are the lucky ones.

And after rugby?

'I've got a 30 per cent share with my brother and my dad in a short-term insurance brokerage business and we are building that.

'I'm getting to a stage in my career when I need to start looking at life after rugby and that is something I have been worrying about for a few years. The fact is that I could get injured at training tomorrow. My rugby career could be finished, and I don't have any qualifications. I only studied for a year at Stellenbosch. Unfortunately, in South Africa, there are a lot of guys who are not studying and don't have anything to fall back on so I'm putting a lot into that at the moment.' It's hard to imagine this graceful man doing anything as prosaic as selling insurance. But I suppose the bills will have to be paid.

'Hopefully the move from rugby to the next job will be easy. I hope it will still be some years away. Stefan Terblanche is 35. I don't know if my body will hold up, but as long as I enjoy it, I will keep on doing it. I'm just hoping to be part of the World Cup. It's such a big part of South Africa. Only a privileged few get the opportunity to play for their country. Also, it is quite special going into the World Cup as the defending champions. There is obviously an added responsibility there. It's such a special occasion that you don't want to miss out. Hopefully we will be the first team to defend the title successfully. I think it's very possible. It will take hard work.'

I say that, as the best in his position in the world, I can't imagine him not being in the World Cup team. He laughs again: 'Put that in your book!'

'The one thing about rugby since I can remember is the camaraderie between the guys. You come to practice and it's a job but it's something that you love and you are having a good time doing it.'

Jean has a strong Christian faith. 'I grew up in a Dutch Reformed house. I went to church every Sunday, and to all the classes. It's always been part of my life, and it's a big thing for me. With the injuries, there have been three things that got me through: my faith, my family and my friends – and probably in that order. I believe we are put on earth for a purpose. If you do lose a game, there is a bigger plan for you and that is why, tough as it is to lose, you keep on going and just work harder.

'If you've been given the talent and you can learn from your mistakes – then, like the Bible says, there won't be anything put in your path that's too big for you to handle.

So get over that and learn from it. It's not how many times you fall down, it's how many times you stand up again. It's when you stay down that you are beaten. It's not always easy, but that is the challenge we have.'

Then there are the temptations of the female attention a Springbok attracts. 'From a Christian point of view, it can be a tough environment. A lot of guys fall into the celebrity trap. I got married two months ago and it can put strain on a relationship. It's tough on the partner, so it's about having a strong relationship and working from that.'

He says he's been thinking about South African football and how it could match the success of rugby. As in rugby, it needs to start with schools. 'Something we've done right in South Africa is to identify guys at a young age and put them in good schools, like Paarl Gim, my school, where you can learn the skills on the field and how to behave off the field as well. That would probably be how soccer could improve. Guys could go to traditional soccer schools where they get good coaching from a young age, then enjoy a good tertiary education and join a club. Some guys would fall out and some would be added on the way, but you do get a jump start if you go that route.'

Another thing, he says: rugby could do with a few sports psychologists.

'I think there is a great need for a mental coach because that is such a big part of becoming successful. Some guys have got all the talent. Physically they're perfect, but mentally they're just not strong enough. We don't have any [mental coaches] here. You can have all the talent in the world and be the best team, but if you're mentally not up for it ... Sometimes you just need someone to talk to if something's bothering you. If you keep it in, it may start affecting you on the field.'

Ultimately, all you can control is your response to what

is thrown at you. 'If you come from a bad background, for example, your attitude can be that the world owes you something, or this is an opportunity to escape. In the end, it's how you respond to circumstances.' The same applies to everything else: 'How you respond to negative media. How you respond to positive media. Like anything in life, everything depends on the decisions that you make. If you're not doing well and people write about it, you feel bad. Ninety per cent of the time they're writing the truth, but you still don't like to read in the paper that you did this wrong or you're not the best in your position any more. It can either drive you or it can make you quit. It's up to you how you respond. It's bad when it's a personal attack from people who don't know you. Again, you have the choice of reading it or staying away from it, so there is a way to get round that. It's mainly good at the moment because we're winning,' he says with a hearty laugh. 'I think it's the right time for us!'

I say: 'It would be very good for my book if you won the Currie Cup. He laughs again and says: 'Okay! Then we will!'

Unfortunately, of course, it doesn't turn out that way. Cheered on by a 52 000-strong home crowd, the Sharks are sharply focused. Hope flares briefly for us at the start when Willem de Waal successfully kicks a penalty, awarded after Stefan Terblanche is penalised for a dangerous tackle. The score is 3–0. Then De Waal misses two kicks at goal. Within thirteen minutes, the Sharks are up 17–3. Then Schalk scores a try from a rolling maul. De Waal converts it and the half-time score is 23–10. By now, Province have lost both Juan de Jongh and Ricky Januarie to injury. Schalk cracks a rib but soldiers on.

In the second half, Province frequently have possession and dominate territory but they cannot score. The full-time score is 30–10 to the Sharks. And 25 of them have been scored by Pat Lambie, who is Man of the Match.

When I meet up with Anton for a final post-mortem, I am ready with a host of excuses. What sort of bad luck causes Juan de Jongh to fracture his ankle in the warm-up? Before the game has even started! The bounce of the ball! Never mind the incandescence of young Lambie, with everything to prove.

As ever, he won't have it. 'Rugby and excuses don't go together.' The Sharks were just better on the day.

The performance of our own young guys, the future, attracted little notice. Dobbo's lads won the Under 21 Currie Cup, beating the Bulls by 43–32. The Western Province Under 19s also won the cup in their age group, beating Paul Anthony's Under 19s by 26–20. Western Province youth are looking hugely promising. The senior team has made it to a final for the second time in a year. Already they have begun training for the Super 15 which will present the next challenge and another opportunity for redemption. This time they will bring home the Cup.

I'm stuck with that image of the rolling maul, brown and white bodies linked, moving inexorably forward.

AFTERWORD

*'Anyone who has seen that great rugby, the fury and
fire of the attack, with the ball flashing from hand to
hand, and everywhere caressed by great sculptors of
motion ... The great player is a sort of priest or poet ...
and he should always parade his excellence.'*

Roy Campbell, *Broken Record*

April 2011

It is now more than a third of the way through the Super
15. The Stormers have won six of the seven games they
have played. Schalk Burger is again captaining the team,
after a month off for a knee injury, during which time Jean
de Villiers took the helm. The UCT Ikey Tigers have shaken
off the ghost of their 2010 loss to the Maties to take home
the 2011 Varsity Cup. In their third final in the four years
of the Varsity Cup's existence, they finally emerged as the
champions in a fast-paced 26–16 final against the University of Pretoria. Dobbo, their founding coach, has gone
professional as head coach of the Western Province Vodacom Cup and Under 21 teams. Therlow Pietersen, recover-
ing from his grief over his stepfather's death, has embarked
on a new career: Stormers backline coach, Robbie Fleck, is
mentoring him in his quest to become a coach. Fourie du
Preez is back from rehab, once more igniting the Bulls.

And the World Cup looms. I am making plans to go.

It is more than three and a half years since I began my
journey through South African rugby and I am hooked.
It's a journey I took almost by chance. I was brought up
in a rugby family but, like most women, didn't take much
interest in it beyond big occasions such as the World Cup.
Then, in the heady aftermath of our 2007 win, my pub-

lisher Jonathan Ball suggested I write a book on rugby. A woman, he surmised, might produce a fresh take.

I started my research tentatively. Ignorant and not a little prejudiced, I began by circling the periphery of rugby: interviewing past greats such as Naas Botha and Joel Stransky and acute observers like Hugh Bladen, Tim Noakes and Paul Dobson. Feeling more confident and increasingly intrigued, I came to the conclusion that, in order to really understand rugby, I had to get closer to its centre. I realised that I needed to get into the minds and hearts of the players that count, on the field and off it.

This involved months of persistent effort: to gain access and to build up trust. I spent many nights in B&Bs around Loftus and many, many hours hanging around the edges of fields all over the country, waiting to speak to players and coaches. I must have interviewed more than 100 people, only some of whom made it into this book. I followed my nose: if a certain direction looked particularly enticing, I followed it. Some led to a dead end. Others took me off on fascinating tangents. I learnt a great deal about our country and about our capacity for change.

It seems to me that South African rugby has come a long way since the World Cup of 1995. One example of this is the difference between the way the rugby fraternity handled the Tromp incident, as described by Trevor Manuel, and the way they dealt with Bees Roux. Both involved prominent white rugby players and the violent deaths of black men. Bees Roux has been charged with murdering a black police officer but his innocence or guilt has yet to be tested in court. At the time of writing, we don't yet know the circumstances surrounding the death. With Tromp, it was unambiguous. Tromp was convicted of manslaughter for beating one of his black workers so severely that he died of his injuries. Yet SA Rugby did not hesitate to include him in the Springbok team. When Bees Roux was arrested, the Blue Bulls instantly put him on leave and sent heartfelt condolences to the dead man's family. This sums up for me the new spirit of integrity and sensitivity within the ranks of rugby.

From schoolboy rugby to the Springboks, I found intelligence, humility, decency. Particularly on the professional level – at the Bulls and Western Province – I found a conscious anti-racist ethic. I admired the values that were inculcated: of taking responsibility for one's mistakes; of giving as well as taking; of surrendering individual ego to the greater good. Contrary to the stereotypes of brutish rugby players, I found them highly emotional and frequently sensitive. The deep bonds they develop with each other seem to augur well for their capacity for rich emotional relationships in other areas of their lives. I thought rugby provided a space in which they could be openly and intensely vulnerable. No one who has seen the devastation after a defeat could say that South African men are not in touch with their emotions. I admire their courage: in professional rugby, every time you go to work, you could go home with a career-ending injury. Many of them have suffered dreadful injuries yet they go back into the fray as soon as they can put themselves back together again. They master their pain and their fear and they do not hold back.

Another stereotype that was shattered for me was that rugby players are brawn without brain. Particularly at the higher level, you have to be quick-witted and intelligent because you have to make split-second decisions on the field. Rugby's rules are in constant flux and you have to be bright enough to absorb and adapt. Engagement with the media – particularly in South Africa – requires a political intelligence and fluency in English as well as whatever your home language might be.

I thought that, in a country where fewer than half of

our children live with their fathers, rugby provides some excellent male role models. I met many exceptional men who were inculcating decent values into their schoolboy charges on the field and off. At the professional level, the physically punitive nature of rugby means new talent is constantly being brought up through the ranks and the older players are required to nurture the newcomers. At Newlands the other day, I watched lanky veteran Andries Bekker take a moment in the middle of the game to stoop down to embrace 20-year-old hooker, Siyabonga Ntubeni, as the latter came off the bench to play his first Super 15 game. I saw many such moments over the years and was always moved by the contrast between this tenderness and the aggression that erupts a moment later.

But, above all, what impressed me was rugby's creative capacity. I came to the conclusion that it was something to do with what happened on the field – some alchemy spun by the game itself. Much of this comes down to the fact that it is the ultimate team sport: there can be flashes of individual brilliance but the team wins or loses as a unit. There has to be absolute trust between them. They have to care about each other.

This means transcending the wounds and divisions of the past; and differences of culture and race. And it has to be real. As Anton van Zyl told me: if you don't have absolute trust in the guy next to you, the scrum will collapse. You will get hurt and you will lose. There is no room for doubt here. Technical excellence is one thing. Winning is another. It requires something intangible. It's often called the mental edge. The other description I've heard is 'playing out of your skin'. For me, it brings to mind Roy Campbell's description of great rugby players as 'poets and priests'.

Several of the Springboks spoke of playing for something higher and greater than the actual game: whether for God or country. I thought this was what gave us our edge. We are not a homogenous team from an ancient established society. Whether black or white, today's Springboks are having to reinvent themselves in ways their fathers never did. They are uniting across race, class and cultural barriers like no team before them. This calls for a depth of imagination and self-awareness required of players from few other countries. And a dynamism and a capacity to adapt. They are not just playing for their country: they are playing to unite and inspire their country.

From what I've seen, it's enough motivation to keep us winning for a long time to come.

ACKNOWLEDGEMENTS

I'm grateful to Jonathan Ball for his inspired idea that I embark on this book, setting me off on a thoroughly enjoyable and revelatory three-year journey. To Jeremy Boraine, Jonathan Ball's publishing director, who guided and supported me throughout those three years, this book owes a lot to his excellent judgement and always spot-on suggestions at tricky junctures. Thanks too to Francine Blum, Anika Ebrahim and the rest of the highly professional Jonathan Ball team. Thanks to Jan Schaafsma for his meticulous editing of the book.

Over the years, many people have helped me in a variety of ways: with their rugby knowledge and contacts; offering me places to stay on research trips and quiet places to write; or their love and support in times of stress. I'm immensely grateful to them all and list some of them in no particular order: Peter Bruce; Andy Colquhoun; Grant Nupen; Paul Dobson; Archie Henderson; Bryan Maclean; Hugh Bladen; Vata Ngobeni; Howard Khan; André Odendaal; Albert Grundlingh; Neil Macdonald; Caroline Nicholls; Gcina Malindi; Andrew, Matthew, Guy and Bronwyn McGregor; Coco Cachalia; Jaqui Goldin; Sister Francis; JJ Harmse; André Watson; Imtiaz Patel; Naas Botha; Joel Stransky; David Bush; Vernon Boulle; Paula Ensor; Margaret Hoffman.

REFERENCES

www.keo.co.za
www.rugby365.com
www.sport24.com
Independent online
Cape Argus
Cape Times
Albert Grundlingh, André Odendaal and Burridge Spies,
    Beyond the Tryline: *Rugby and South African Society*
Abdurahman Booley, *Forgotten Heroes: History of Black
    Rugby 1882–1992*